"In the great Black American tradition of the remix and doing what you can with what you got, my friend Bryant Terry goes hard at vegetables with a Hip Hop eye and a Southern grandmama's nature. To paraphrase Maya Angelou, Bryant wants us to know that once we know vegetables better, we will cook vegetables better. He ain't lyin'."

W. KAMAU BELL, comedian, author, and host of the Emmy Award-winning series *United Shades of America*

"*Vegetable Kingdom* is an artful and inspiring volume that is not only a collection of innovative plant-based recipes, it's also a multifaceted celebration of culture, family, ecology, and health. Bryant Terry's true artistry is in his ability to celebrate and remix global foodways in vegan creations that are full of vitality and beauty. This gorgeous book gives everyone access to Bryant's amazing creative vision: it's a joyous collection of Afro-Asian recipes that delight the eye as well as the palate."

THELMA GOLDEN, director and chief curator of The Studio Museum in Harlem, New York

"*Vegetable Kingdom* is an altar to our Diasporic ancestors, a legacy offering to our children, and a shrine to the plant friends who nourish us. As a parent, I felt inspired by the ingenious ways that Bryant 'Blackifies' uncommon vegetables and makes them kid-friendly. As a Haitian, I felt particularly jubilant as I prepared spicy Pikliz to the steamy Creole love ballad 'Ou Fe'm' that Bryant paired with the recipe. As an overworked, time-scarce person, I appreciated the tips for advanced prep on the weekends and inclusion of efficient meals."

LEAH PENNIMAN, co-director of Soul Fire Farm and author of *Farming While Black*

"Bryant Terry wrote *Vegetable Kingdom* for his daughters and we're so lucky we get to have it on our shelves, too. Whether or not you're vegan, it's full of recipes we all want to make in our kitchens. From crunchy slaws to creamy soups and vegetable po'boys, Bryant has created an inspiring collection of dishes that channel so many influences."

JULIA TURSHEN, author of *Small Victories*, host of *Keep Calm & Cook On*, and founder of Equity at the Table

Vegetable Kingdom

bryant terry

photographs by Ed Anderson

Vegetable Kingdom

the abundant
world of
vegan recipes

TEN SPEED PRESS
California | New York

to mila and zenzi

introduction
fennel for zenzi

Vegetable Kingdom is inspired by my daughters, Mila and Zenzi. They have blessed this book like my ancestors blessed meals, by humbling me to that which is greater than myself. When Mila pulls a gloriously resonant hum out of her cello and when Zenzi dances in energetic spins and wild flourishes, they are turning the love and effort I pour into them into a vitality and power that they will carry far beyond what I could ever know. I wrote this book to make a diversity of foods of the plant kingdom irresistible to them, to inspire their curiosity, and to show them the pleasure of a lifelong adventure with good, nourishing food. That mission drives this book.

Vegetable Kingdom reflects the essence of how my wife, Jidan, and I root and raise our children. Mila and Zenzi have been rooted in the garden with farm-fresh ingredients and raised on a diversity of dishes, springing from the deep well of Black and Asian foodways. We help shape their multicultural identity organically by creating and consuming Afro-Asian food and the spectrum of flavors they engage, often in the same meal. While I emphasize ingredients, cooking techniques, and classic dishes of the African Diaspora, Jidan does the same with Asian food—Chinese, Japanese, and Vietnamese. So this book features a number of ingredients and flavors from East and Southeast Asia, sub-Saharan Africa, the Caribbean, and the American South.

With such an expanse of cultural ground to cover, it is serendipitous that it was the Mediterranean—a region at the crossroads of Africa, Asia, and Europe—and one of its hardiest vegetables, fennel, that acted as a catalyst for unifying the dynamic spirit and energy that permeates this book.

A few years ago, I was at the farmers' market checking out the late summer/early fall bounty: flavorful Seascape strawberries, fresh cranberry shelling beans, vibrant Red Burgundy okra, and plump pomegranates, to name a few. That morning, fennel was all over the place. The bulbs glowed bright white. The stalks and fronds were moist and fresh, and their aniselike aroma was strong. One stand offered samples of crunchy sweet slices with fresh lemon juice squeezed over them. I had never really bought fennel unless a recipe required it, but that day the fennel was calling me! Ya boy bought four bunches on the strength of that smorgasbord for the senses. Driving home, I decided I would use every part of the fennel. I envisioned the feathery fronds as a garnish, flashing back to Instagram posts by some of my favorite chefs (like JJ Johnson, Rob McDaniel, and Jeremy Fox), creatively balancing color and making dishes pop by arranging fresh herbs, microgreens, and citrus zest on top of them. I figured I would put the fennel stems into the freezer, along with other vegetable scraps reserved for stocks. I had no idea how I would cook the bulb that day, even though it's the only part I really used in the past.

Regardless of how I prepared the fennel, I was a little nervous that Zenzi, my five-year-old, would not be into it. Mila, my eight-year-old, has always had an adventurous palate; she loves to try different cuisines and takes pride in eating unfamiliar dishes. Zenzi, on the other hand, would be happy if she had pasta, bread, and crackers at every meal.

My other goal was to create a dish through the lens of the African Diaspora. Inspired by visual artists Romare Bearden, Jean-Michel Basquiat, Deborah Roberts, and Derrick Adams, as well as some of my favorite hip hop producers like Prince Paul, The Bomb Squad, DJ Premier, RZA, Organized Noise, and Madlib, I have approached recipe development as a collagist—curating, cutting, pasting, and remixing staple ingredients, cooking techniques, and traditional Black dishes popular throughout the world to make my own signature recipes. But this approach is bigger than creating cookbooks.

Many people build altars, visit gravesites, and reminisce with photos to engage with loved ones who have passed. For me, recipe creation is a praxis where I honor and bring to life the teachings, traditional knowledge, and hospitality of my blood and spiritual ancestors by making food. While it may not be obvious, most recipes that I develop stand on the shoulders of relatives, mentors, historical heroes and heroines, and those who inhabited the land on which I live and work. Educating my girls about and introducing them to foods and flavors of the African Diaspora allows me to teach history and share memories with them; it helps them learn about and take pride in the contributions of their ancestors, culinary and otherwise; and it celebrates foods of the African Diaspora in a world where European cuisine is at the center and Black food is often at the margins.

So how did I Blackify fennel, use the entire vegetable, *and* create a recipe that even the most finicky eaters would enjoy? In my first pass, I pan-seared it in olive oil, then basted it in a tangy citrus and garlic-herb sauce inspired by mojo, a condiment/marinade popular in Cuban cooking. It was solid, but something was missing. To bring more complexity and balance while building on the Afro-Caribbean

theme, I thinly sliced some of the fennel stalks and added them to the sauce while simmering and basting the fennel. I also pulverized savory plantain chips in a spice grinder and sprinkled the powder on top before serving. The fennel was fire! It even passed muster with my girls: As I nervously looked on during dinner, they were all smiles, and they couldn't get enough of the plantain powder. Turned out, freestyling an African Diaspora-inspired vegetable dish (that kids enjoyed) was easier than I thought.

Our girls tasted and approved most of the recipes in this book, so even if dishes don't appear to be "kid-friendly," they are. In fact, I want real food to be seen as kid-friendly. It incenses me when we eat at nice restaurants and the kids' menu is limited to hot dogs, fries, and chicken fingers, when it could flourish with Millet, Red Lentil, and Potato Cakes (page 175), Pan-Seared Summer Squash Sandwiches (page 121), and Jerk Tofu Wrapped in Collard Leaves (page 143). We serve our girls whole-food meals at home, but the idea that kids can't enjoy what adults eat is horribly reinforced when those menus bearing heavily processed crap and edible food-like substances are plopped in front of them as soon as they sit down. At home I will often take the most obscure vegetables and prepare them in familiar ways so that Mila and Zenzi raise their food IQ and expand their palates. Throughout writing *Vegetable Kingdom*, I realized that this educational approach would apply to anyone. You may not have tried (or heard of) kohlrabi, but I promise you'll be hooked once you simply coal-roast it and serve it with a west African-inspired peanut sauce, garnished with peanuts, Fresno chiles, and lemon zest.

Even the structure of *Vegetable Kingdom* was inspired by my daughters. I initially planned to organize the book around the four seasons, as I mostly build meals with an eye on the beautiful, seasonal produce growing in our home garden or piled on tables in farmers' markets throughout Northern California. But after Mila mentioned that her gardening class at school classifies vegetables according to which part of the plant is eaten, I decided to follow that structure for this book: Seeds, Bulbs, Stems, Flowers, Fruits, Leaves, Fungi, Tubers, and Roots. For vegetables that fall into multiple categories, I strive to use all parts of the plant. For example, beets offer their commonly used roots, as well as their delicious, edible leaves, which are too often discarded.

The literal vegetable kingdom is vast; this is just my snapshot. In *Vegetable Kingdom,* you'll find more than 175 recipes (including subrecipes and pantry items) that bring out the best in more than thirty vegetables. I also share my favorite tools, tips, and ideas for cooking vegetables and building creative meals on your own. You can find most ingredients at a farmers' market or quality supermarket, but you might need to visit specialty grocery stores or order some ingredients online. It's worth it to get the full flavor of the recipe and to fall in love with vegetables, grains, or legumes you've never had before. My sincere hope is that this book effects real change in your world by inspiring your journey into the vast and verdant pleasures of botanical bounty. If this book moves you to try new vegetables, and to think more critically and creatively about how and what you eat, I'll have fulfilled the calling to create this homage to health as learning and pleasure. Now, go forth, and explore *Vegetable Kingdom.*

homie, you should compost

As my mentee, DJ Cavem Moetavation, reminds us in his song "Breakground," "Homie, you should compost." In recipes throughout this book I call for "discarding" peels, seeds, and the like, but what I really mean is you should compost them. While more cities are providing green bins for yard waste and food scraps—which the city turns into compost—transforming organic material into rich soil amendment at home is pretty easy. In fact, creating a home composting system is a great way to catalyze your gardening efforts. One of the most obvious advantages of home composting is that the amendment feeds soil with a diversity of nutrients and microorganisms that benefit edible plants, flowers, and shrubs. Composting also helps reduce greenhouse gases since organic waste in landfills breaks down to create methane gas, which is highly toxic to the environment. Find master gardeners in your community (or watch some YouTube videos) to learn the basics of composting and make a positive contribution to your local food systems and to our planet.

how to use this book

I've had dozens of people tell me how much they love my last book, *Afro-Vegan*, and that they look at the pictures, read the headnotes, play the suggested songs, and show their friends and family the book, but seldom cook from it (these people usually admit that they rarely cook from *any* of their cookbooks). I get that. I have hundreds of cookbooks, and many of them function more as thoughtful, unique, and beautiful coffee-table books. But I want you to cook from *Vegetable Kingdom*!

I imagine these recipes helping you become a better cook, and improving your culinary skills takes practice. The first dish in each section is a simple skills-building recipe, teaching you things like how to fry tempura, how to make flavorful purees using fresh veggies, how to make pickles, and the like. These are typically quick dishes that are easily prepared on weeknights. Many of these recipes also serve as building blocks or supplemental components to other dishes. For example, the Creamy Cauliflower (page 102) can be eaten as a simple side during a meal, but it is also prepared with a thicker texture and used as a topping for the spicy lentils in the Grilled Spring Onions with Lemon-Thyme Oil (page 60) and thinned out to serve as a base for pureed fresh green peas in Smashed Peas and Creamy Cauliflower (page 28).

Many of the salads, soups, and sides that follow can be made in less than 30 minutes, so they make practical components of weeknight meals. I encourage you to use weekends for making more involved main dishes. I also see this as a time for doing two other things: 1) making meals in bulk that can be eaten throughout the week, and 2) connecting with family and friends to collectively shop, prep, and cook while building community. My family will often take Saturday to meal plan, shop, and prep ingredients. Then on Sundays we make stocks, soups, stews, grains, sautéed vegetables, and healthy snacks so food prep throughout the week is a bit easier.

I encourage you to stick closely to the recipe as it's written when making a dish for the first time. This will allow you to enjoy the dish as I imagined it and provide a basis from which you can freestyle and make the recipe your own from there. That being said, don't be obsessive about making recipes exactly as written. See them as a guide that can be modified using local ingredients, favorite spices, and other flourishes to make the recipe uniquely yours. I always use the example of putting together a dish that requires collard greens to illustrate this point. If you are growing Swiss chard at home, don't go out to buy collards. Substituting the chard you have on hand should work just fine.

Another important step in the process of making a recipe is reading it all the way through—maybe twice, for good measure—before you get started. Then prep all your ingredients before you start cooking. You don't want to get to the third step in the procedure and realize that you need to make a cream, spice blend, or roasted pepper in order to keep the recipe moving. Making subrecipes beforehand, sometimes a day in advance, can expedite the process and make meal prep and cooking more manageable, especially during the week. So stagger or spread out cooking projects over the course of a day or two, and make things like Umami Powder (page 239), vegetable stock (page 230), and Creamy Cilantro Sauce (page 235) in batches that can be refrigerated or frozen for later use.

Another tip for smoothly making recipes is setting up your *mise en place* (French for "everything in its place"). This simply means gathering all your cooking tools ahead of time, as well as slicing, dicing, and preparing all your vegetables, measuring out spices, and mincing your herbs so everything is on hand and ready to go when you need it. I know it seems like you're preparing for a cooking segment on a TV show, but you will feel like a pro once you start making a recipe and all you have to do is dump ingredients into your pan and keep it moving.

In my recipes you'll prepare lots of things from scratch that you might normally buy. For example, where you might have purchased heavy cream or something similar, I teach you to make Sunchoke Cream (page 191). I simply want to give you the tools for making from-scratch condiments, spice blends, and stocks devoid of additives and preservatives. But I have also become less finicky about using store-bought prepared items such as plant-based mayonnaises, cheeses, and the like, since the quality of many of those items has dramatically improved over the past few years.

tools

While I certainly don't expect you to do a complete kitchen makeover to prepare the dishes in this book, there are some key tools that will make cooking these recipes (and others) a little easier. This is a great opportunity to gradually replace older items and get your hands on equipment that you've long coveted to upgrade your home kitchen.

good knives

Good knives are one of the most important gifts you can give yourself. You want a sharp chef's knife that feels good in your hand—not too light, not too heavy. I also encourage you to get a serrated knife as well. They are perfect for cutting tomatoes and slicing your loaf of country bread. A paring knife is useful but not necessary. They are great for tasks that require more precision, like cutting segments from citrus fruits. Whatever knives you have, it is important to keep them sharp. The first thing I learned in cooking school was that you're more likely to get cut using a dull knife than a sharp one. Purchase a good-quality knife sharpener or find a sharpening service in your area and drop them off regularly.

cutting boards

Wooden cutting boards are the best. While marble and glass cutting boards might look fancy, they will ruin your knives. Wooden boards can handle the intensity of good knives. Clean your wooden boards well after using, let them dry adequately, and oil them so they don't dry out.

mortar and pestle

This is one of the most important tools in my kitchen. In fact, given their ubiquity in cultures around the globe, it's safe to say they are one of the most important kitchen tools in history. I use them to pound spices, crumble nuts, and make pastes.

spice grinder

There is nothing like freshly ground toasted spices to add life to your dishes. If you are in a rush and want to skip the mortar and pestle, a spice grinder will cover you. If you have a coffee grinder, it could double as a spice grinder, but I recommend getting a separate one to avoid corrupting your spice blends with coffee flavor. Buy one with a removable bowl to make it easier to clean.

high-powered blender

A really good blender will help you make the silky-smooth sauces, soups, and creams in this book. But they are also great for making fruit smoothies, blended veggie drinks, and the like. If you have been thinking about springing for a Vitamix, this might be a good opportunity to do so. While Vitamix may be the Bentley of high-powered blenders, there are a number of brands on the market these days at a lower price point that work just as well.

immersion blender

You may not see a need for an immersion blender (also called a stick blender) when you have a classic standing one, but immersion blenders can streamline recipes that require pureeing, especially when liquids are hot.

food processor

I know, some of you have an expensive blender that purees soups, makes nut butters, and even grinds grains into flours, so why do you need a food processor? They can perform similar functions, but there are some items that need to be chopped coarsely without being pulverized, and a food processor will make it easier to do so.

dutch oven

If I had to choose one pot to cook in for the rest of my life, it would be a Dutch oven. These babies are great for deep frying, sautéing, and simmering. Plus, they look pretty.

cast-iron skillet

If I had to choose one skillet to cook in for the rest of my life, it would be a cast-iron skillet. They last a lifetime, and they are often passed down from generation to generation. Read up on how to care for them to ensure that yours becomes a family heirloom.

rimmed baking sheets

These are great for the obvious things like baking cookies, roasting vegetables, and toasting nuts, but they also are useful for keeping prepared ingredients and tools organized when you're working on a recipe.

charcoal grill

A number of recipes in this book require grilling. Invest in a good grill. We have both a gas grill and one that uses chunk/lump charcoal so that I can make things like Ash-Roasted Sweet Potatoes (page 185). Avoid charcoal briquettes, as they typically contain chemicals that you don't want near your food.

metal spider

I use these long-handled spoons with a fine-mesh basket for pulling vegetables from boiling water when blanching, lifting food from fat when deep-frying, and scooping up hot, cooked pasta. I like the old-school kind with bamboo handles.

mandoline

These might seem like an unnecessary fancy tool, but trust me—they make cutting vegetables paper-thin a cinch. I use mine often for making dishes like Shaved Asparagus Salad (page 71), but get one for the Barbecue Sunchoke Chips (page 186), if for no other reason. They will change your life.

pickling/canning/fermentation supplies

I mostly quick pickle in this book, but it is worth having a supply of canning jars and lids in various sizes, fermentation weights for ensuring that food is submerged in brine, and fermentation crocks when you want to take your game to the next level.

playlist

If you've seen my other cookbooks, you know that I include a "soundtrack" with my recipes. That's because music is in my blood and my family culture, and it's also in the recipes I create. Throughout the process of researching and developing dishes, I listen to a lot of tunes. As a result, the music that moves me and the recipes I create are inextricably linked. My earliest memories include my maternal grandmother singing in her kitchen and in the choir at her COGIC church, mom crooning while making dinner, and my aunts and uncles harmonizing at family gatherings. My maternal grandfather was the lead singer of Eddie Bryant and the Four Stars of Harmony, a sanctified vocal quartet formed in Memphis during the late 1930s. They traveled throughout the South and were the first Black gospel group to broadcast on Memphis radio (WMPS). Most of his children were brilliant singers, and my uncles formed the Five Bryant Brothers. My uncle Don Bryant was a member of two other groups, the Quails and the Four Canes (later renamed the Four Kings) before launching his solo career under the mentorship of Willie Mitchell at Hi Records. He later became the staff songwriter for the label and penned some of his wife Ann Peebles' biggest hits.

Growing up around such gifted musicians I gained a lot of musicality and creativity through osmosis. I also took piano lessons while in elementary school and briefly played trombone in high school. But I really fell in love with music in third grade when I discovered rap. Thanks to my cousins Jomo and Mahdi (Lil Charles), I was always on the cutting edge of hip hop culture. They both were DJs, and Jomo was the illest b-boy in Memphis. We wanted to be like hip hop heads in NYC and devoured the culture from afar. I created a massive collage of my favorite rappers cut out from *Word Up!* magazine on one my bedroom walls, and I dreamed of being an MC. My first favorite group was Run-D.M.C., and the first album my dad bought me was their self-titled studio LP when I was ten years old. After hearing Stetsasonic's debut LP *On Fire* in 1986, I wanted to be a DJ and producer like Prince Paul. I made my first pause tape in 1987, looping "The 900 Number" by DJ Mark the 45 King for more than thirty minutes so my boys and I could bust rhymes over it. My hip hop career didn't pan out, but I've been studying and collecting vinyl for decades.

I was inspired to include music in my books by Dr. Jessica B. Harris, who suggests musical genres, singers, and groups to go along with menus in her classic cookbook *The Welcome Table: African American Heritage Cooking*. Here, I include the entire playlist so you can see all the songs in one place. If you read the headnotes to each recipe and meditate on the dish, you may get the connection to the song suggested at the end. If not, all good. Just eat and enjoy the sounds. Big-up to Edward and Margie Bryant and all their children. Big-up to my cousins. Big up to my pops. Big-up to my former piano teacher, Mrs. Harris. Big-up to Dr. Jessica Harris. Big-up to all the founding fathers and mothers of hip hop for setting this ish off.

"You Don't Want to Go to War (feat. Soulja Slim)" by Rebirth Brass Band from *Hot Venom*

"Golden Lady" by Stevie Wonder from *Innervisions* and "Isn't She Lovely" by Stevie Wonder from *Songs in the Key of Life*

"You Can't Blame the Youth" by Bob Marley & The Wailers from *Talkin' Blues*

"Hot Thursday" by Bei Bei & Shawn Lee from *Into the Wind*

"Hager Fiker" by Mulatu Astatke from *Sketches of Ethiopia*

"Tenement Yard" by Jacob Miller from *Song Book: Chapter a Day*

"Three Changes" by The Good, the Bad & the Queen from *The Good, the Bad & the Queen*

"TYAF" by Nick Hakim from *Green Twins*

"Sage Up (feat. Stic, Matene Strikesfirst, and DJ Cavem Moetavation)" by Xiuhtezcatl from *Break Free*

"Rize" by Steel Pulse from *Mass Manipulation*

"Succotash" by Herbie Hancock from *Inventions & Dimensions*

"Happy Talk" by Cannonball Adderley and Nancy Wilson from *Nancy Wilson & Cannonball Adderley*

"La La" by Lil Wayne from *Tha Carter III*

"Wanyinyin (feat. Angélique Kidjo)" by MHD from *MHD*

"Bucktown" by Smif-N-Wessun from *Dah Shinin'*

"Afro-Cu (Bembé)" by Mongo Santamaria from *What Do You Mean*

"Keep It 100" by DJ Cavem Moetavation from *Biomimicz*

"Live Your Life" by Yuna from *Yuna*

"The Capitalist Blues" by Leyla McCalla from *The Capitalist Blues*

"Parallax (feat. The Palaceer Lazaro)" by Shabazz Palaces from *Quazarz: Born on a Gangster Star*

"Addis Black Widow" by Mulatu Astatke & The Heliocentrics from *Inspiration Information 3*

"On Green Dolphin Street" by Miles Davis from *Kind of Blue*

"Boogie Chillen" by John Lee Hooker from *The Legendary Modern Recordings 1948-1954*

"Sing Out" by Dezarie from *Nemozian Rasta*

"II B.S." by Charles Mingus from *Mingus Mingus Mingus Mingus Mingus*

"Chonkyfire" by OutKast from *Aquemini*

"Hello Africa" by Blitz the Ambassador from *Diasporadical*

"Voodoo" by The Dirty Dozen Brass Band from *Voodoo*

"Swamp Thing" by Hiatus Kaiyote from *Choose Your Weapon*

"Sometimes It Snows in April" by Meshell Ndegeocello from *Ventriloquism*

"Lavender (feat. Kaytranada)" by BADBADNOTGOOD from *IV*

"Feather" by Little Dragon from *Machine Dreams*

"Milky Cereal" by LL Cool J from *Mama Said Knock You Out*

"They Say I'm Different" by Betty Davis from *They Say I'm Different*

"Melody Maker" by Keith Hudson from *The Hudson Affair: Keith Hudson and Friends*

"Dust (Reimagined)" by Van Hunt from *Trim (The Reimagined Van Hunt)*

"Melting Pot" by Booker T. & the M.G.'s from *Melting Pot*

"Big Rings" by Drake and Future from *What a Time to Be Alive*

"Big Kids Don't Play" by Grand Puba from *Reel to Reel*

"La Vida Es un Carnaval" by Angélique Kidjo from *Celia*

"Wu-Tang Forever" by Drake from *Nothing Was the Same*

"Cold Sweat" by James Brown from *20 All-Time Greatest Hits!*

"Flat of the Blade" by Massive Attack from *Heligoland*

"Kajo Golo Weka" by The Eagles Lupopo from *Kenya Special*

"Peter Piper" by Run-D.M.C. from *Raising Hell*

"Summertime (UFO Remix)" by Sarah Vaughan from *Verve Remixed*

"Tempo de Amor" by Smokey & Miho from *The Two EPs*

'Jumpin' Jive' by Cab Calloway from *Hi De Ho Man: Cab Calloway Classics*

"Al Salam Alena" by Mounira Mitchell from *Chili Houritki*

"Dub Money" by Horace Andy from *Dubbed in Kingston (Bunny "Striker" Lee 50th Anniversary Edition)*

"Back on My Regimen" by stic.man from *The Workout*

"Forbidden Knowledge" by Raury from *All We Need*

'Jah Jah Dub' by Ronnie Davis from *Ronnie Davis in Dub*

"Stay Flo" by Solange from *When I Get Home*

"Keep Your Hand on the Plow" by Mahalia Jackson from *Gospels, Spirituals, and Hymns*

"Been in the Storm" by Ranky Tanky from *Ranky Tanky*

"Ou Fe'M" by Riva Nyri Précil from *Perle De Culture*

"A Nickel and a Nail" by Don Bryant from *Don't Give Up on Love*

"Wubit" by Mulatu Astatke & Black Jesus Experience from *Cradle of Humanity*

"Bourbon Street Jingling Jollies" by Duke Ellington from *New Orleans Suite*

"Contronatura" by Stereolab from *Dots and Loops*

"I Own the Night (feat. Saul Williams)" by Christian Scott aTunde Adjuah from *Ancestral Recall*

"Gumbo" by Zion I from *The Take Over*

"Pynk" by Janelle Monáe from *Dirty Computer*

"Tasty (feat. Seneca B)" by Omaure from *Square One*

"Fool Forever" by Thao & The Get Down Stay Down from *A Man Alive*

"Manteca" by Quincy Jones from *You've Got It Bad Girl*

"Le Bien, Le Mal (feat. MC Solaar)" by Guru from *Guru's Jazzmatazz, Vol. 1*

"Africa Speaks (feat. Buika)" by Santana from *Africa Speaks*

"Nautilus" by Bob James from *One*

"New Jack Bounce (Interlude)" by Christian Scott aTunde Adjuah from *Diaspora*

"Portrait of Wellman Braud" by Duke Ellington from *New Orleans Suite*

"All I Blow Is Loud" by Juicy J from *Stay Trippy*

"No Indictment (feat. King Keon)" by SOL Development from *The Sol of Black Folk*

"Strange Piano" by Quasimoto from *The Further Adventures of Lord Quas*

"Fantastic Freaks at the Dixie" by Fantastic Freaks from *Wild Style Original Soundtrack*

"Scenario (Remix)" by A Tribe Called Quest from *The Love Movement*

"The Festival (feat. Little Dragon)" by Mac Miller from *GO:OD AM*

"Party Isn't Over/Campfire/Bimmer" by Tyler, The Creator (feat. Laetitia Sadier, Frank Ocean)

"Fever" by Junior Byles from *Curly Locks*

"Over the Rainbow" by Israel Kamakawiwo'ole from *Alone in IZ World*

"Candy" by Cameo from *Word Up!*

"Ego Trippin' (Original 12" Version)" by Ultramagnetic MC's from *Critical Beatdown*

"Young Black Men and Prison" by Angela Davis from *The Prison Industrial Complex*

"40 Acres and My Props" by Showbiz & A.G. from *Runaway Slave*

"Do I Need You" by Ann Peebles from *I Can't Stand the Rain*

"Insieme" by Vhelade from *AfroSarda*

"Cold Coffee and Cocaine" by Prince from *Piano & a Microphone 1983*

"Unstoppable (feat. Santigold & Lil Wayne)" by Drake from *So Far Gone*

"Hard Times" by Baby Huey & The Baby Sitters from *The Baby Huey Story: The Living Legend*

"Here Comes the Floods" by JoshuaGabriel from *21st Century Blues*

"The Sacred Bird" by Blitz the Ambassador from *The Burial of Kojo (Original Motion Picture Soundtrack)*

"Sour Mango" by Gabriel Garzón-Montano from *Jardín*

"Brokenfolks" from Georgia Anne Muldrow from *VWETO II*

"Is You Is or Is You Ain't My Baby? (Rae and Christian Remix)" by Dinah Washington from *Verve Remixed*

"Food Fight (feat. stic.man)" by J. Bless and Seasunz from *Earth Amplified*

"Hunter" by Björk from *Homogenic*

"Mango Walk" by The Senior Allstars from *DUB from Jamdown: Darker Than Blue*

"Higher" by Oh No from *Dr. No's Experiment*

"Atari" by Hiatus Kaiyote from *Choose Your Weapon*

"Ma colère" by Françoiz Breut from *Françoiz Breut*

"Spit Game" by Nappy Nina from *The Tree Act*

"Takuta (feat. Babatunde Olatunji)" by Youssou N'Dour from *History*

"Guerrilla" by Leon Fanourakis from *Chimaira*

"Focus" by H.E.R. from *H.E.R.*

"Don't Try to Use Me" by Horace Andy from *Wicked Dem a Burn: The Best of Horace Andy*

"RST (feat. DOOM & Mach-Hommy)" by Your Old Droog from *It Wasn't Even Close*

"Glowed Up (feat. Anderson .Paak)" by Kaytranada from *99.9%*

seeds

beans

tempura green beans   18

warm butter bean salad with roasted
bell peppers   21

haricot vert and mushroom stew   23

dry yardlong beans with broken rice   24

peas

pea shoot and peanut salad   27

smashed peas and creamy cauliflower   28

spicy spring pea sauce   30

chilled green soup   32

sweet corn

sweet corn relish   34

cornbread muffins   37

grilled corn on the cob   38

corn, red pepper, and blackened
tempeh chowder   40

tempura green beans

creole seasoning · charred lemon juice

makes 4 servings

Nagasaki meets New Orleans in these light, crispy, and delicious green beans. I know that starting this book with a recipe for tempura–a Japanese dish of deep-fried battered vegetables–is a bold choice, but I figured we'd jump right into the deep end. Frying can be tricky for a lot of people, and I offer general tips for doing it well in the sidebar on the opposite page. Making tasty tempura is next-level frying that requires specific skills to get it right. To be clear, this technique requires practice–took me about a dozen or so times to feel like I nailed it. Follow these tips and you will be frying up crispy and delicious tempura at home in no time:

- Mix the batter right before frying your veggies, so the coating is light and crispy.

- Do not overmix the batter, or your tempura will be doughy. It's fine if there are some lumps.

- Add cold, highly carbonated seltzer or sparkling water to the batter to give it airiness. I use our sparkling water machine to make some fresh right before mixing tempura batter.

I understand that a lot of people striving to maintain a healthy diet avoid fried foods altogether. I get it. I don't eat them often. But I try to steer clear of extremes and instead walk the middle way of moderation, giving myself room to indulge every once in a while. You should, too. This recipe will comfortably feed four people if you are snacking on the green beans like you would popcorn. I imagine they could feed double that amount if served as nibbles at a summer party. Don't be shy about dusting these with Creole seasoning and spraying them with skillet-charred lemon juice right before serving to really get the party buck jumping.

1 large lemon, halved

4 to 6 cups sunflower oil, for frying

1¼ cups cake flour

3 tablespoons arrowroot powder

1 teaspoon baking powder

½ teaspoon Creole Seasoning (page 239), plus more for dusting

½ teaspoon fine sea salt

⅛ teaspoon freshly ground black pepper

1 cup chilled club soda

1 pound green beans, trimmed

Preheat the oven to 200°F.

Heat a large cast-iron skillet over high heat. Place the lemon halves in the skillet, cut-side down, and cook until they are charred on the bottom, 2 to 3 minutes. Transfer the lemon halves to a plate. Remove the skillet from the heat and wipe out any charred lemon bits.

Pour about 1 inch of sunflower oil into the skillet. Heat the oil over medium-high heat to 375°F. Fill a large bowl one-third full with ice and water and set it nearby.

While the oil is heating, whisk together the flour, arrowroot, baking powder, Creole seasoning, salt, and pepper in a bowl.

Add the club soda and 2 ice cubes to the flour mixture and gently stir with a spoon until the batter just comes together, being careful not to overmix (a few lumps are fine). Place the bowl of batter in the bowl of ice water to keep the batter cold.

Working in batches of 6 to 8, dip the green beans into the batter and let the excess drip off. Add them to the hot oil and fry, moving them around with a wire spider to ensure even cooking, until the batter just starts to turn light golden and crisp, 2 to 3 minutes. Using the spider, transfer the beans to a paper towel–lined plate to drain. Place the plate in the oven to keep the green beans warm. Repeat to fry the remaining green beans.

To serve, arrange the green beans on a large platter, dust with Creole seasoning, and serve with the charred lemon halves.

"You Don't Want to Go to War (feat. Soulja Slim)" by Rebirth Brass Band from *Hot Venom*

frying

The first key to frying is ensuring that your oil is the perfect temperature. If the fat isn't hot enough, the food will absorb too much of it, and you will have a greasy end product. Obviously, if the fat is too hot, the surface of your food will burn and the inside won't thoroughly cook. Using a deep-fry thermometer is the best way to make sure you hit that sweet spot, but you don't necessarily need one. Adding a few test pieces to the oil will let you know if it is ready to fry a full batch. As soon as you slide a piece into the oil, it should start bubbling steadily. If the oil bubbles too vigorously, it is too hot and needs to cool down slightly. Also, make sure all the pieces are roughly the same size so everything cooks evenly. Lastly, fry in batches so you don't overcrowd the pan. The temperature of the fat will drop once you add food, so be sure to let the oil get hot again between batches to ensure proper cooking.

warm butter bean salad with roasted bell peppers

wilted arugula · pili pili oil · lemon juice

makes 4 servings

Smoky roasted peppers provide a bright contrast to the delicate, buttery flavor of big lima beans in this dish. The pili pili oil adds the subtlest kick–you'll notice it, but it doesn't overpower. Peppery arugula adds freshness, and a squeeze of lemon brightens everything. I created this recipe for a collaboration with Williams-Sonoma in 2019. My family had a Father's Day cookout with some friends (hi, Maisha, David, and Naya) that was shot by my buddy photographer Erin Scott, and Williams-Sonoma featured the images in their catalog, on their blog, and across their social media platforms. That was a meaningful partnership, since Father's Day is my favorite holiday of the year. While I'm appreciative of gifts, Father's Day is about expressing gratitude to my family for the love they show me every single day. When I was working on this book, I spent more than a year testing recipes and writing almost every weekend (and a lot of holidays). My wife and daughters supported me wholeheartedly throughout that process. On Father's Day weekend, I celebrate them for the privilege of being a husband and Baba.

1 pound dried large white lima beans, soaked in water and 3 tablespoons kosher salt overnight

1 bay leaf

1 large yellow onion: half diced, half left intact

5 garlic cloves: 3 cut in half, 2 minced

1 dried red chile

1½ teaspoons kosher salt, plus more as needed

2 large red bell peppers

2 large yellow bell peppers

2 large orange bell peppers

2 tablespoons extra-virgin olive oil

2 tablespoons Pili Pili Oil (page 232), plus more for drizzling

Freshly ground white pepper

8 ounces baby arugula (about 12 loosely packed cups), washed and spun dry

1 lemon, halved, for garnish

Flaky sea salt, for finishing

Drain the beans, put them into a large saucepan, and add water to cover by 2 inches. Bring the water to a boil over high heat. Skim off any foam and decrease the heat to medium-low. Add the bay leaf, onion half, halved garlic cloves, and dried chile. Partially cover and simmer, stirring occasionally, until just tender, adding water as needed to keep the beans covered, 1 to 1½ hours (the cooking time will greatly depend on the freshness of the beans). Once the beans are just tender, add 1 teaspoon of the salt and simmer for 10 more minutes. Drain the beans. Remove the bay leaf, onion, garlic, and chile and discard them. Set the beans aside.

While the beans are cooking, roast the bell peppers using one of the methods on page 22. Seed and thinly slice the bell peppers. Set aside.

In a large saucepan, warm the oil over medium-high heat until shimmering. Add the diced onion and cook, stirring occasionally, until soft and just starting to brown, 5 to 7 minutes. Add the minced garlic and remaining ½ teaspoon salt and cook, stirring, until it smells fragrant, 2 to 3 minutes. Add the lima beans, bell peppers, and pili pili oil

warm butter bean salad with roasted bell peppers, continued

to the pan. Raise the heat to high and cook for 1 minute, gently stirring to combine and warm the ingredients through. Turn off the heat and season aggressively with white pepper. Taste and season with salt. Divide the lima bean mixture evenly among four plates.

Add the arugula and 2 tablespoons water to the same pan. Set the pan over low heat, cover, and cook for 2 to 3 minutes, until the arugula wilts.

Place a handful of arugula over each serving, then drizzle with more pili pili oil and a squeeze of lemon. Finish with a sprinkle of flaky salt and serve.

"Golden Lady" by Stevie Wonder from *Innervisions* and "Isn't She Lovely" by Stevie Wonder from *Songs in the Key of Life*

roasting peppers

There are a few methods for roasting peppers. I prefer placing them directly over a burner on a gas stove and turning them with tongs until the skin is blackened and blistered all over. Maybe it's the nostalgia of first learning this procedure in culinary school, but the process is fulfilling. If you have an electric stove, you'll need to use the broiler or grill to achieve the same outcome—just be sure to turn them occasionally to char the skin on all sides. After they are properly charred, the peppers are placed in a heatproof container and covered for 15 minutes, until they have cooled and their skins have loosened up. Peel off the charred skin (avoiding washing the peppers or you will lose some of the flavor), then cut off the stem end, remove the core and seeds, and cut the flesh of the peppers into strips or as directed in the recipe. If you're not using the roasted peppers immediately after prepping them, simply place them in a bowl, toss with olive oil, and refrigerate until ready to use.

haricot vert and mushroom stew

sweet potato · russet potato ·
coconut-tomato broth

makes 4 to 6 servings

Haricots verts, French for "green beans," are legit one of my favorite vegetables. No matter when I have them, they take me back to raucous family gatherings (what's up, cousins?) in the days of my youth, since these green beans would often be a part of holiday spreads. This dish is inspired by run down, a stew popular in Jamaica, Tobago, and other Caribbean countries. Typically, the foundation of run down is fish and other sea creatures. My version includes roasted, firm, and meaty cremini mushrooms that pair well with the starchy sweet potatoes and russet potatoes. After sweating the aromatics, I add Xinjiang spice mix—a blend of flavors from the traditional Turkic cuisine of the Uighur people of Central and East Asia—to lend warm, peppery flavor to the rich, creamy coconut-tomato broth. I also add a whole Scotch bonnet or habanero chile to the stew while simmering to add more flavor and subtle heat. Be sure not to remove the stem or pierce the chile so it doesn't impart too much heat. The delicate, delicious haricots verts are added right before serving so they stay crisp-tender. Of course, if you can't find haricots verts, you can use regular green beans. Serve this stew on cool summer nights along with an aromatic grain dish, a side of fried green plantains, a leafy salad, and a rum-based cocktail.

3 tablespoons
coconut oil

8 ounces cremini
mushrooms, quartered

4 ounces sweet potato,
peeled and diced

4 ounces russet potato,
peeled and diced

1½ teaspoons
kosher salt, plus
more as needed

3 cups medium-diced
yellow onions

1 tablespoon
minced garlic

1½ teaspoons Xinjiang
Spice Mix (page 240)

1¾ cups canned
crushed tomatoes,
with their juices

¾ cup unsweetened
canned coconut milk

2 cups vegetable stock
(page 230)

1 Scotch bonnet or
habanero chile, stem on

8 ounces haricots
verts, cut in half on
an angle

¼ cup fresh cilantro
leaves, for garnish

Preheat the oven to 375°F. Line a rimmed baking sheet with parchment paper.

In a large skillet, warm 1 tablespoon of the coconut oil over medium-high heat until shimmering. Add the mushrooms and cook, stirring often, until they release their liquid, then cook until all the liquid has evaporated, 3 to 5 minutes. Transfer to a bowl. Add the sweet potato, russet potato, another tablespoon of the coconut oil, and ½ teaspoon of the salt and toss to combine. Transfer to the prepared baking sheet, spreading the vegetables in a single layer. Roast until the mushrooms are brown and the potatoes are starting to soften, about 30 minutes.

In a medium saucepan, warm the remaining 1 tablespoon coconut oil over medium heat until shimmering. Add the onions and sauté until soft, 5 to 7 minutes. Add the garlic, Xinjiang spice mix, and the remaining 1 teaspoon salt and sauté until the garlic is fragrant, 2 to 3 minutes. Add the tomatoes and their juices and simmer, stirring often, until starting to thicken, about 10 minutes. Add the coconut milk, stock, chile, and the roasted vegetables. Decrease the heat to low and simmer, partially covered, stirring occasionally, for about 30 minutes, until the stew has thickened. Remove the chile and set it aside. For a tamer stew, remove the habanero after 10 minutes.

Ladle a heaping cup of the stew into a blender, puree until smooth, and return the pureed stew to the saucepan. Season with salt to taste. Stir in the haricots verts and cook until just tender, about 2 minutes.

To serve, ladle the stew into bowls and garnish with the cilantro. For extra heat, squeeze the liquid from the chile into the stew before serving.

"You Can't Blame the Youth" by Bob Marley & The Wailers from *Talkin' Blues*

dry yardlong beans with broken rice

shoyu-vinegar sauce · pickled mustard greens · grated peanuts

makes 4 servings

Yardlongs are some of my favorite green beans to eat during the summer. They are perfect for pan-frying since cooking them in too much liquid tends to bog them down; I typically sauté them in sesame oil and garlic and leave it at that. When my brother-in-law, Jando, returned from a trip to China with a bag of fiery Szechuan peppercorns, I decided to cook a batch of yardlongs Szechuan-style. I got inspiration for this recipe from Omnivore's Cookbook, one of my favorite websites about Chinese cooking. The combination of shoyu-vinegar sauce, peppercorns, and pickled mustard greens makes this an intensely flavorful dish, so I serve it with a simply prepared broken rice, which is commonly used in Southeast Asian and West African cooking. Look for broken rice at Asian and African markets or buy it online. If you can't find yardlong beans at your local farmers' market, look for them at Asian specialty markets.

pro tip When grating the peanuts with a Microplane, watch your fingers. It's best to grate three-quarters of the nut, then pop the rest in your mouth.

broken rice

1 cup broken jasmine rice, soaked in water overnight

Kosher salt

1 teaspoon peanut oil

shoyu-vinegar sauce

2 tablespoons shoyu (Japanese-style soy sauce)

2 tablespoons unseasoned rice vinegar

1 teaspoon toasted sesame oil

1 teaspoon coconut palm sugar

1 dried chile pepper, broken apart to expose the seeds

yardlong beans

3 tablespoons peanut oil

1 pound yardlong beans, tough ends removed, sliced into 2-inch-long segments

1 tablespoon minced garlic

¼ teaspoon kosher salt, plus more as needed

½ teaspoon whole Szechuan peppercorns

½ cup Pickled Mustard Greens (page 140)

3 tablespoons finely grated roasted unsalted peanuts (grated with a Microplane; see Pro Tip)

Make the rice: Dump the rice into a fine-mesh strainer and rinse it thoroughly for 2 to 3 minutes. Combine the rinsed rice and 1 cup water in a small saucepan. Add a generous pinch of salt and the peanut oil. Bring to a boil over medium-high heat, then quickly decrease the heat to medium-low. Cover and simmer, undisturbed, until all the water has been absorbed, about 10 minutes. Remove from the heat and set aside to steam. Before serving, fluff the rice with a fork.

Make the sauce: In a small bowl, combine the shoyu, vinegar, sesame oil, and sugar and stir with a fork to combine. Add the chile (with its seeds), then set aside.

Make the yardlong beans: In a large cast-iron skillet, warm 2 tablespoons of the peanut oil over medium-high heat until shimmering. Add the beans and cook, tossing occasionally, until they start to brown and shrink a bit, about 5 minutes. Remove from the heat and transfer to a plate.

In the same pan, combine the remaining 1 tablespoon peanut oil, the garlic, salt, and peppercorns. Sauté over medium-low heat, stirring often, until the garlic smells fragrant, 2 to 3 minutes. Add the mustard greens and the sauce and return the beans to the pan. Raise the heat to high and cook, stirring, until well combined, about 2 minutes.

Transfer everything to a large serving plate, garnish with the peanuts, and serve with the rice.

"Hot Thursday" by Bei Bei & Shawn Lee from *Into the Wind*

pea shoot and peanut salad

red cabbage · crispy garlic ·
creamy ginger dressing

makes 4 servings

If you can't find pea shoots at your local market or store, don't fret. They are easy to grow at home, and take about two weeks to mature once you plant them. A quick search on Al Gore's internet will tell you everything you need to know about growing pea shoots. A popular way to prepare them is quickly stir-frying, but you can also eat them raw, like in this refreshing salad. It's inspired by a dish at my friend Tiyo Shibabaw's Burmese restaurant in Oakland, Teni East Kitchen. The bright flavors of the dressing combined with delicate pea shoots balance heavier dishes. Pea shoots have a chewy-grassy mouthfeel that may put some people off, but if you like watercress (which can be substituted for the pea shoots if they aren't available), this is your salad.

Make the dressing: In a blender, combine the ginger, shallot, garlic, vinegar, miso, agave, and tofu and blend briefly to combine. With the machine running, pour in the safflower oil through the hole in the lid and blend until smooth. Season with salt and pepper to taste.

Make the salad: In a large bowl, combine the pea shoots, cabbage, cilantro, peanuts, and crispy garlic. Sprinkle lightly with salt and squeeze some lemon juice over the top. Toss to combine. Add enough dressing to coat and toss well. Season with pepper and serve immediately.

"Hager Fiker" by Mulatu Astatke from *Sketches of Ethiopia*

creamy ginger dressing

1 tablespoon minced fresh ginger

1 teaspoon minced shallot

1/2 teaspoon minced garlic

2 tablespoons unseasoned rice vinegar

1 teaspoon white miso paste

1 teaspoon light agave nectar

2 tablespoons silken tofu

1/4 cup safflower oil

Kosher salt and freshly ground pepper

salad

10 ounces tender pea shoots

1/2 (2-pound) red cabbage, cored and thinly sliced (2 lightly packed cups)

7 cilantro sprigs

1/2 cup chopped roasted unsalted peanuts

1/4 cup Garlic Chips (page 232)

Kosher salt

1/2 lemon

Freshly ground pepper

smashed peas and creamy cauliflower

charred lemon–thyme oil · thyme ·
nigella seeds · flaky sea salt

makes 4 servings

The idea for this recipe came from mushy peas, the classic British dish that traditionally accompanies fish and chips. The simplest way to prepare fresh-from-the-shell peas is to blanch them in generously salted boiling water for about 2 minutes. If you are going to take advantage of fresh peas during their relatively short season, let them shine without doing too much to them. I think of my Creamy Cauliflower as a blank canvas on which to add more prominent flavors. The mild flavor of that dish perfectly balances the sweetness of the peas. The herbaceous, warm, and oniony nigella seeds and grassy charred oil make this a lively side dish that bridges winter and spring.

1 tablespoon
kosher salt

2½ cups shelled fresh
peas (a little over
2 pounds in the pod)

Creamy Cauliflower
(page 102)

Charred Lemon-Thyme
Oil (page 232), for
drizzling

2 teaspoons minced
fresh thyme, for garnish

1 tablespoon nigella
seeds, for garnish

Flaky sea salt

Fill a medium bowl with ice and cold water and set aside.

In a medium pot or saucepan, bring 1 quart water to a boil over high heat. Add the salt and gently pour the peas into the pot. Blanch until just tender, about 2 minutes. Drain then add to the ice water bath. Drain well after 5 minutes.

Transfer ¾ cup of the peas to a food processor and process until completely smooth, scraping down the bowl as necessary. Add the remaining peas to the processor and pulse a few times to create a chunky mixture with some whole and split peas remaining.

To serve, smear the creamy cauliflower over a large serving platter. Spoon the peas around and on top of the cauliflower. Drizzle with the lemon-thyme oil and sprinkle with the thyme, nigella seeds, and flaky salt to taste. Serve.

"Tenement Yard" by Jacob Miller from *Song Book: Chapter a Day*

spicy spring pea sauce

jalapeño · lemon juice

makes about 1 cup

This delicious pureed sauce really highlights the flavor of fresh English peas–the dish has only four other ingredients, and the peas are barely blanched (to brighten their color and remove the raw flavor). I love this sauce with Smashed Fried Potatoes (page 172), but it also goes nicely with other vegetables or pasta (hey, kids! look at the fun green sauce on your penne!). Use fresh green peas when you can, as the point of this dish is serving up some spring magic in a bowl, though you can make do with frozen when peas are not in season.

2¼ teaspoons kosher salt, plus more as needed

1 pound fresh spring peas in their pods

½ teaspoon minced seeded jalapeño

¼ teaspoon fresh lemon juice, plus more as needed

Freshly ground white pepper

In a medium pot or saucepan, bring 1 quart water to a boil over high heat. Add 2 teaspoons of the salt and gently pour the peas into the pot. Blanch until just tender, about 3 minutes. Drain the peas in a colander and rinse with cold water.

Transfer the peas to a blender. Add ½ cup water, the remaining ¼ teaspoon salt, the jalapeño, and the lemon juice and puree until smooth, adding more water if necessary (the mixture should be viscous but pour fairly easily from the blender).

Pour the pureed peas into a serving bowl, scraping the blender jar with a rubber spatula if necessary. Season with salt, white pepper, and lemon juice to taste.

"Three Changes" by The Good, the Bad & the Queen from *The Good, the Bad & the Queen*

blend your veggies

Throughout this book, you will find lots of vegetable purees. I use them as dips, spreads, and smears onto which I pile other vegetables, legumes, and the like. I started experimenting with different vegetable blends when we had our first daughter. After we introduced her to solid foods, we would blend any and every vegetable–beets, broccoli, butternut squash. You name it, we pureed it. In fact, we were very intentional about not introducing fruits for almost six months after she started eating solid foods because we wanted her to fall in love with the diversity of colors, flavors, and textures of vegetables. We quickly discovered that when using farm- and garden-fresh vegetables, we did not have to add a lot to the blends to enhance their flavor. Initially, we would just blanch or boil vegetables, then mix them with mashed grains like rice, quinoa, or millet. After a few months, we started roasting the veggies to deepen their flavor and bring out their natural sugars. Eventually, we began mixing in a hint of herbs, a touch of tamari, or a smattering of spices to amplify the flavor of our blends. Even though we imagined these combinations as "baby food," we enjoyed them just as much as our daughter did. I hope that making my vegetable purees will empower you to experiment with fresh, seasonal, and nutrient-dense vegetables to make your own combinations.

chilled green soup

lemongrass peanuts · thai basil oil · basil

makes 4 to 6 servings

I try to clean up my diet during the spring. After months of eating warming soups, hearty stews, and lots of comfort foods, I reset by eating ample seasonal green vegetables, including raw salads, every day. I hydrate by drinking lots of water, green juices, and vegetable smoothies. I also try to eat smaller meals for dinner, like this quick and easy chilled soup I created using spinach and Thai basil from our home garden, asparagus from the Friday farmers' market in Old Oakland, and green peas from Farmer Joe's, an independent supermarket in Oakland. When I end the day with this soup, I wake up the next morning feeling light. Although the soup requires just a tablespoon or two of lemongrass peanuts for garnishing, I make a lot more so I can eat the rest as a snack.

lemongrass peanuts

2 cups raw peanuts

1 thin lemongrass stalk

2 tablespoons peanut oil

1/2 teaspoon kosher salt

1/4 teaspoon raw cane sugar

2 makrut lime leaves, finely chopped

1 Thai chile, stemmed, seeded, and minced

soup

2 tablespoons extra-virgin olive oil

1 cup finely diced yellow onion

1/2 teaspoon kosher salt, plus more as needed

4 cups vegetable stock (page 230)

1 pound asparagus, tough stems trimmed, tips removed and reserved, stalks cut into 1/2-inch pieces

8 ounces baby spinach

1 1/2 cups shelled fresh peas (about 1 1/4 pounds in the pod)

1 tablespoon champagne vinegar

Finely ground white pepper

Thai Basil Oil (page 233), for drizzling

2 tablespoons minced fresh basil, for garnish

Make the peanuts: Preheat the oven to 350°F. Line a baking sheet with parchment paper.

Spread the peanuts in an even layer on the prepared baking sheet and bake, stirring every 5 minutes to ensure even cooking, until they are starting to crisp and smell fragrant, about 20 minutes.

Meanwhile, with a sharp knife, cut off and discard the lower bulb and upper end of the lemongrass stalk. Remove the tough outer layers until you get to the pale yellow inner core, and discard them. Thinly slice the lemongrass, then chop it as finely as possible.

In a small skillet, warm the peanut oil over medium-high heat until shimmering. Add the salt and sugar and cook, stirring frequently, until dissolved, about 1 minute. Add the lemongrass, lime leaves, and chile and cook until the lime leaves and lemongrass are crispy, about 3 minutes. Scrape all the ingredients into a heatproof bowl and set aside.

When the peanuts are done, pour them into the bowl with the lemongrass mixture, mix well, and let cool for 15 minutes. Spread the peanuts over a clean paper towel and give them a nice squeeze to soak up any excess oil before serving.

Make the soup: In a medium saucepan, warm the olive oil over medium heat until shimmering. Add the onion and the salt and sauté, stirring often, until translucent but not browning, about 7 minutes. Add the stock and bring to a boil. Add the asparagus (reserving the tips for later), reduce the heat to medium-low, and simmer until just tender, about 7 minutes. Add the spinach and peas and cook for an additional 2 minutes, until the spinach is wilted and the peas are just tender. Stir in the vinegar. Quickly remove from the heat and set aside to cool slightly.

Working in batches if necessary, carefully transfer the soup to a blender and puree, adding water as needed to reach the desired consistency. Refrigerate until fully chilled before serving.

To serve, thin the soup with water as needed (it should pour easily from a spoon), then season with salt and white pepper to taste. Ladle into bowls and garnish each serving with the reserved asparagus tips, a drizzle of basil oil, a sprinkle of the lemongrass peanuts, and a generous pinch of fresh basil.

"TYAF" by Nick Hakim from *Green Twins*

sweet corn relish

cherry tomatoes · red onion ·
green bell pepper · jalapeño

makes 2 pints

I channeled my maternal grandmother, Margie
Bryant, when I created this recipe. It reminds me
of the relish she made using fresh corn from farm
trucks parked in downtown Memphis. In fact, corn
relish was a traditional dish eaten throughout the
South and stored in the larder for leaner months.
I created it to top Smashed Fried Potatoes
(page 172), but my family quickly found multiple
uses for this tangy condiment: stuffing it into
tacos, serving it atop beans, and simply sautéing
it to serve as a side dish. Don't bother processing
this in a hot water bath; just store it in the refrigerator. It will be gone within a few days.

3 large ears sweet corn

12 ripe cherry
tomatoes, cut into
$\frac{1}{8}$-inch-thick slices

$\frac{1}{2}$ cup finely diced
red onion

$\frac{1}{2}$ cup finely diced
green bell pepper

2 tablespoons minced
jalapeño

2 garlic cloves, ends
cut off

$\frac{3}{4}$ cup rice vinegar

$\frac{1}{4}$ cup raw cane sugar

1 tablespoon brown
mustard seeds

2 teaspoons cumin
seeds

$\frac{1}{2}$ teaspoon kosher salt

$\frac{1}{2}$ teaspoon whole
black peppercorns

$\frac{1}{4}$ teaspoon ground
turmeric

Sterilize two 1-pint canning jars and their lids and
rings (see sidebar, opposite page) and set aside.

Fill a large bowl with ice and cold water and
set aside.

Bring a large pot of water to a boil over high heat.
Add the corn, bring the water back to a boil, and
blanch for 1 minute. Drain the corn in a colander
and immediately transfer it to the ice water for
5 minutes. Drain the corn and slice the kernels
from the ears.

Evenly divide the corn kernels, tomatoes, onion,
bell pepper, jalapeño, and garlic between the
canning jars and set aside.

In the pot you used for the corn, combine the
vinegar, $\frac{1}{4}$ cup water, the sugar, mustard seeds,
cumin seeds, salt, peppercorns, and turmeric and
bring to a simmer over medium-high heat. Cook
until the liquid is hot to the touch and the sugar
has completely dissolved, about 3 minutes.

Divide the liquid evenly between the canning
jars and let cool. Seal the jars and refrigerate the
relish for at least one day to develop the flavor.
The relish will keep in the fridge for up to 1 year.

"Sage Up (feat. Stic, Matene Strikesfirst, and DJ Cavem
Moetavation)" by Xiuhtezcatl from *Break Free*

canning and pickling

The most vivid memory I have of my maternal grandmother's kitchen is of the seven-foot-tall cupboard where she kept all her pickles and preserves. I loved helping her prepare fruits from her mini orchard and vegetables from her garden for the larder. My jobs were simple—pouring sugar over the fruits for her jams, filling the jars with food, and twisting the canning rings over the jars to hold the lids in place before they were processed. Mostly, I just loved spending time with Ma'Dear. If you have surplus produce from your garden or simply want to preserve seasonal vegetables at the peak of their ripeness for leaner months, canning and pickling are practices that you should employ.

First, you will need to get mason jars with lids and rings if you are planning to actually process foods and put them away in a cupboard, pantry, or the like. It is essential that you sterilize your jars before storing any food in them. If you are sealing the jars, it is important that you sterilize any utensils you will be using during the process. Sterilization is pretty simple: just simmer everything—jars, lids, and rings—in water for a few minutes. I usually transfer everything to a clean baking sheet and hold it in the oven set to the lowest temperature possible until I'm ready to fill and seal the jars.

Once you fill the jars, they can be stored in the refrigerator for short-term storage or processed in a bath of hot water to seal them for longer storage. Once they're sealed, store them in a cabinet, pantry, or similar dark, cool storage space. Unless a recipe states that the pickles, preserves, or the like can be stored in the pantry, simply refrigerate it. Foods processed for longer storage have to include the right amount of sugar and salt to ensure they're preserved safely and properly.

cornbread muffins

hot pepper jelly · whipped sweet corn

makes 9 muffins

My paternal grandfather lived through the Jim Crow South, so when he retired, all he wanted to do was praise the Lord, serve his community, spend time with his family, and tend his garden. He loved hanging out with his grandchildren, and I have fond memories of sitting with my Paw Paw at his kitchen table in the summer, eating a piece of cornbread slathered with butter while he drank buttermilk, sometimes crumbling cornbread into the milk and eating it like cereal. I carry on that tradition by feeding our girls my take on this special breakfast, usually on Saturdays. I remind them that this is not a dessert, and that Black folks in the South like their cornbread sweet because that's the way it's supposed to be eaten. Whipped sweet corn takes the place of butter, and we jazz it up with a heaping spoonful of hot pepper jelly—creating our own memories, with my Paw Paw at their heart.

cornbread muffins

3 tablespoons coconut oil, plus more for greasing

6 pitted Medjool dates

Boiling water

¾ cup medium-grind yellow cornmeal

¾ cup flour

2 tablespoons coconut palm sugar

1 tablespoon baking powder

½ teaspoon fine sea salt

2 heaping tablespoons freshly ground golden flaxseeds

1 cup unsweetened oat milk

whipped sweet corn

3 tablespoons vegan butter

¼ cup finely diced white onion

2 cups fresh corn kernels (from about 3 ears)

2 teaspoons coconut palm sugar

¼ teaspoon kosher salt, plus more as needed

½ cup Cashew Cream (page 231)

Fresh lemon juice

Freshly ground white pepper

Jalapeño Pepper Jelly (page 234), for serving

Make the muffins: Preheat the oven to 400°F. Generously coat nine wells of a standard muffin tin with coconut oil.

Put the dates in a small heatproof bowl and cover with boiling water. Let soak for about 5 minutes. Drain the dates, reserving the soaking liquid, and transfer them to a food processor. Add 1 tablespoon of the reserved soaking liquid and process, scraping down the sides and adding more of the reserved soaking liquid if necessary, until mostly creamy but with a few chunks remaining.

Place the prepared muffin tin in the oven to heat for 5 minutes.

Meanwhile, in a large bowl, sift together the cornmeal, flour, sugar, baking powder, and salt. Whisk until blended.

Put the flaxseeds and 6 tablespoons water in a medium bowl and whisk until well blended. Whisk in the pureed dates and the coconut oil until smooth. Whisk in the oat milk until well combined. Add the oat milk mixture to the cornmeal mixture and stir until just combined.

When the muffin tin is hot, remove it from the oven and immediately scrape the batter into the prepared muffin cups, distributing it evenly among them (they should be a little over three-quarters full).

Bake until the muffins are golden brown, 16 to 18 minutes. Let cool in the tin for about 10 minutes, then transfer to a wire rack to cool a bit more.

Make the whipped sweet corn: While the muffins are cooling, in a large skillet, melt the butter over medium heat. Add the onion and sauté, stirring often, until soft, 3 to 5 minutes. Add the corn, sugar, and salt and cook, stirring often, until the corn is just tender, about 5 minutes.

Scrape the contents of the skillet into a food processor. Add the cashew cream and process until silky smooth, adding water as necessary to reach the desired consistency. Taste and season with lemon juice, salt, and white pepper. Transfer to a serving bowl.

Serve the warm muffins slathered with whipped sweet corn and topped with pepper jelly.

"Rize" by Steel Pulse from *Mass Manipulation*

grilled corn on the cob

creamy cilantro sauce · cilantro · lime ·
charred habanero oil

makes 6 servings

Grilled corn appears at roughly 100% of our summer
cookouts. Most often, a simple mixture of olive oil,
salt, and pepper is the perfect coating, as it allows
the delicious, sweet kernels to shine. If I want the
corn to be the star of the meal, however, this is my
new go-to recipe. The key to any great corn dish is
choosing the freshest corn, so I'll offer these tips:

1. Look for cobs with moist, tight, bright green
   husks.
2. Squeeze the cob; it should be plump—if it feels
   scrawny, keep it moving.
3. Pull back the husks just far enough that you
   can check the kernels—you want them fat,
   milky, and bright.

It's a good idea to soak the cobs in water for
about 30 minutes before grilling them. This will
soften and moisturize the husks so they can
withstand the heat of the grill without burning or
catching fire. Serve the corn in a pool of creamy
cilantro sauce so the cobs can be dipped at your
leisure. A drizzle of habanero oil and a squeeze
of lime add just the right amount of heat and acid.

6 ears sweet corn,
husks intact

2 tablespoons
kosher salt

Creamy Cilantro Sauce
(page 235)

Charred Habanero Oil
(page 233), for drizzling

⅓ cup minced fresh
cilantro

1 lime, cut into wedges

Peel back the corn husks, but leave them attached
at the base of the corncob. Remove the corn silk,
then wrap the husks back around the corn. Put
the corn in a large pot and add the salt. Put a plate
on the corn to weight it down, ensuring it will stay
submerged, then add cold water to cover the corn.
Let soak for at least 30 minutes.

Heat a grill to medium-high.

Drain the corn. If necessary, tie the tops of the
corn husks with kitchen twine to keep them closed.

Put the corn on the grill, cover, and cook, turning
occasionally with tongs, until the husks are slightly
charred and the kernels are tender, about 25 minutes. Transfer the corn to a cutting board until
cool enough to handle, then fold back the husks
to expose the kernels.

To serve, spread some cilantro sauce over the
bottom of six medium plates. Place an ear of corn
to one side of each plate. Drizzle the corn with
habanero oil, garnish with the cilantro, and serve
with the lime wedges alongside.

"Succotash" by Herbie Hancock from *Inventions & Dimensions*

corn, red pepper, and blackened tempeh chowder

spring onions · charred jalapeños · marjoram

makes 4 to 6 servings

This is a simple corn chowder that really highlights fresh, seasonal corn and bell peppers. The tempeh makes it a hearty dish that can be enjoyed with crusty bread.

¼ cup Blackened Seasoning (page 239)

Safflower oil, for frying

1 (8-ounce) package tempeh, cut into ½-inch cubes

Fine sea salt

2 tablespoons extra-virgin olive oil

½ cup finely diced yellow onion

1 cup medium-diced red bell pepper (about 1 large)

2 cups medium-diced russet potato (about 1 large)

2 tablespoons arrowroot powder

3 cups unsweetened oat milk

3 cups corn stock (page 230)

4 cups fresh corn kernels (from 5 to 8 ears)

½ cup finely chopped spring onions (about 4)

Freshly ground white pepper

2 large jalapeños

Leaves from 5 marjoram sprigs

Line a baking sheet with paper towels. Pour the blackened seasoning into a paper bag and set aside.

Pour ½ inch of safflower oil into a Dutch oven. Heat the oil over medium-high heat until very hot but not smoking. Gently slide the tempeh into the pot in a single layer, decrease the heat to medium, and fry, stirring frequently, until golden brown, about 5 minutes. Immediately transfer the tempeh to the prepared baking sheet and sprinkle generously with salt. Transfer the tempeh to the paper bag, fold the bag over a few times to seal it, then shake vigorously to coat the tempeh with the seasoning. Set aside.

Set the pot aside to cool for about 10 minutes. Next, carefully pour the oil from the pot and discard it. Wipe out the pot with a clean paper towel.

Pour the olive oil into the pot and warm over medium heat until shimmering. Add the yellow onion, bell pepper, and potato and sauté, stirring occasionally, until the vegetables are soft, about 5 minutes. Whisk in the arrowroot and cook until it smells toasted, about 3 minutes. While whisking, slowly pour in the oat milk. Raise the heat to medium-high, bring to a simmer, then quickly decrease the heat to medium-low. Add the corn broth, corn kernels, and ½ teaspoon salt. Reduce the heat to low, cover, and simmer for about 10 minutes.

Ladle 2 cups of the chowder into a blender (try to scoop up mostly solids) and pulse a few times to break it up. Pour the blended portion back into the pot and simmer, partially covered, until the chowder has thickened, about 15 minutes. Stir in the spring onions and season with salt and white pepper.

While the chowder is simmering, roast the jalapeños using one of the methods on page 22. Seed and finely chop the roasted jalapeños.

To serve, divide the soup evenly among soup bowls and top with the fried tempeh and roasted jalapeños. Garnish with the marjoram leaves and serve.

"Happy Talk" by Cannonball Adderley and Nancy Wilson from *Nancy Wilson & Cannonball Adderley*

making soups and stews

One of the food hacks my family uses to help our weeks go smoothly is making a big batch of veggie stock and a double or triple batch of vegetable soup on Sundays so we have go-to meals on hand throughout the week. We often make enough stock to freeze so we can skip a week of making it, and when we make a triple batch of soup, we freeze a large portion for later. Both the stock and the soup will keep in the freezer for up to 3 months.

Since we eat a lot of soup noodles at our house, we simply stir in a slurry of miso to our stock, blanch fresh veggies, and boil noodles for a 30-minute meal. On other days, we make a grain or toast bread to go with our vegetable soup, and we are eating within 15 minutes of getting home.

The first step to making a flavorful vegetable soup is slow-cooking your aromatics (onions, carrots, celery, garlic, and the like) in a good-quality fat. This is when you can add spices to punch up the flavor. If you add spices to soup after you pour in stock, they will most likely get lost in the liquid. The only exception is salt. While you want to add a little salt while sautéing aromatics, don't go too heavy on it at the start. You can always season with salt and freshly ground pepper toward the end of cooking to ensure that the flavor of the soup is right where you want it. It's important to taste throughout the cooking process to make sure the flavor is heading in the right direction.

As with roasting, make sure you cut your vegetables into similar-size pieces so they cook evenly. Bite-size pieces are ideal so folks don't struggle chewing them.

bulbs

dill-pickled fennel

dill seeds · raw cane sugar · rice vinegar · orange peel

makes 1 quart

I'm not sure about other parts of the country, but in Memphis when I was growing up, eating whole dill pickles stuffed with sugar-sweet candy was a thing that Black kids did. I think it was an inventive way for young people to combine different foods to create a new trend. I remember the first time my big cousin Latrice let me try a bite of pickle with a peppermint stick stabbed in the middle—I must have been around seven years old. At that age, I found the flavor of dill pickles too intense to enjoy by itself, but I liked the interplay of the pickle's juicy, crunchy, and intensely sour flavor with the refreshing, cooling sensation of peppermint. I thought it was even more awesome to spike dill pickles with an orange Jolly Rancher or two. Inspired by that combination, I add orange peel and a touch of organic raw cane sugar to the brine I use for pickling fennel to give it citrusy sweetness. I mostly eat these pickles on sandwiches, but they also work well atop some grain-based salads and make a nice addition to party cheese boards.

2 medium fennel bulbs, trimmed, halved lengthwise, and cored

2½ tablespoons kosher salt

1 cup unseasoned rice vinegar

2 tablespoons raw cane sugar

1 teaspoon dill seeds

6 whole black peppercorns

¼ teaspoon mustard seeds

Pinch of ground cinnamon

1 (2-inch) strip orange peel

2 large garlic cloves

1 bay leaf

Thinly slice the fennel halves lengthwise on a mandoline. Transfer the fennel to a medium bowl, toss with 1 tablespoon of the salt, and set aside for 10 minutes, tossing every 2 minutes. Transfer the fennel to a colander, place the colander over the bowl, and let rest for 45 minutes to draw out excess liquid.

While the fennel is resting, sterilize a 1-quart canning jar and its lid and ring (see page 35) and set aside.

In a small saucepan, combine the vinegar, 1 cup water, the sugar, dill seeds, peppercorns, mustard seeds, cinnamon, orange zest, and remaining 1½ tablespoons salt. Bring to a simmer over medium-high heat and simmer until the liquid is hot to the touch and all the salt has dissolved.

Pack the fennel into the sterilized jar. Add the garlic and bay leaf, then pour the pickling liquid into the jar. Set aside to cool. Seal the jar and refrigerate for at least 1 day before using.

Like most pickles, these taste more delicious as the days go by. They should keep in the refrigerator for up to a year.

"La La" by Lil Wayne from *Tha Carter III*

fennel and citrus salad

almonds · dates · orange zest ·
citrus vinaigrette · flaky sea salt

makes 4 to 6 servings

This salad mashes up two memorable dishes from different periods of my life. I enjoyed the first one back during my college years, when my friend Gigi and I visited a restaurant in Milan that specialized in southern Italian cuisine. We must have spent two hours in that place stuffing our faces. When the waiter brought us a simple salad of fennel, blood oranges, and vinaigrette, I waved my hand no. He left it anyway. Gigi and I dug in, and it was the perfect ending to a rich meal. I ate the second dish in February 2019 at my friend Monifa Dayo's Oakland-based supper club. For the second course, she presented a life-changing salad that brilliantly melded the flavors of tart-sweet, perfectly ripe citrus fruits, bitter black olives, candy-sweet dates, and buttery almonds and almond oil. I could never replicate the brilliance of either of those moments, but I hope this salad brings a little sunshine (and raspberry-forward flavors from the blood oranges, plus subtle hints of sweet grapefruit from the Cara Caras) to your table during the winter months, when citrus fruits are at their peak.

1 small fennel bulb, trimmed, halved lengthwise, and cored

1 large shallot, minced

½ cup apple cider vinegar

2 teaspoons kosher salt, plus more as needed

1 cup extra-virgin olive oil

¼ cup coarsely chopped toasted almonds

2 large navel oranges

2 large Cara Cara oranges

4 large or 8 small blood oranges

1 teaspoon amber agave nectar

1 teaspoon Dijon mustard

Freshly ground black pepper

Light gray Celtic sea salt, for finishing

4 large dates, pitted and torn into small pieces

7 cilantro sprigs

Fill a large bowl with ice and water. Using a mandoline or sharp knife, thinly slice the fennel halves lengthwise and transfer to the bowl of ice water to chill for about 10 minutes before draining.

Put the shallot in a small heatproof bowl and set aside. In a small saucepan, combine the vinegar and the kosher salt and bring to a simmer over medium-high heat. Simmer, stirring, until all the salt has dissolved, about 30 seconds. Pour the vinegar over the shallot and set aside.

In the same saucepan, warm the olive oil over medium heat until just starting to shimmer. Remove from the heat, add the almonds, and set aside.

Finely grate 1 teaspoon of the zest from 1 navel orange and set aside.

Using a sharp knife, cut a slice off the top and bottom of each navel orange so they sit flat. Working with one orange at a time, stand the fruit on a cutting board and, using a sharp knife, slice off all the peel and white pith, following the curve of the fruit and reserving the trimmings. Set a strainer over a medium bowl and squeeze the trimmings over the strainer to extract their juice. Discard the trimmings. Thinly slice the oranges crosswise and transfer them to a bowl. Repeat with the Cara Cara oranges. Set aside.

Cut the sections from the blood oranges using the technique on page 46, catching the juice in the bowl with the navel and Cara Cara orange juices. Set the sections aside.

Drain the almonds through a fine-mesh sieve set over a bowl, reserving the olive oil, and set aside.

Transfer all but ¼ cup of the citrus juice to a small bowl to save for another use. Add the orange zest, agave, and mustard. While whisking, pour in 2 tablespoons of the reserved olive oil and whisk until emulsified. Taste and season the dressing with kosher salt and pepper.

▶

To serve, arrange the orange slices and segments on a large plate and sprinkle with Celtic sea salt. Spoon the dressing over the citrus, then artfully arrange the fennel over the orange slices and segments. Top with the dates and the almonds, then lightly drizzle with some of the reserved olive oil. Garnish with the cilantro sprigs and finish with Celtic sea salt.

"Wanyinyin (feat. Angélique Kidjo)" by MHD from *MHD*

cutting sections from oranges

While it might seem like a lot of trouble to cut segments from your citrus fruits, this method removes the bitter pith so you can enjoy the ambrosial, juicy fruit without any distraction. Plus, those beautiful sections of citrus take the presentation of your dish to the next level. While it takes practice to perfect, this technique can be easily mastered with patience. Before you get started, it is important to have a really sharp paring knife or chef's knife. There is no way you're cutting through the membrane with a dull knife. You can find dozens of videos online that demonstrate how to cut oranges and other citrus into segments, but I will give you a primer here.

To start, slice off both the stem and blossom ends of a citrus fruit and stand the fruit on one of its cut ends. Cut the peel and pith from the fruit, following the curve of the fruit from the top down, being sure to remove all the bitter white pith. Set a strainer over a bowl to catch the juices (I drink them or reserve them for vinaigrette). Holding the fruit over the strainer, slice between the membrane and one side of a segment of the fruit to remove the segment. Lift the segment out with the blade of the knife, set it aside in a separate bowl, and repeat until you've removed all the segments. Squeeze any remaining juice from the membranes into the bowl.

chickpeas, fennel, and potatoes

lime juice · cilantro sauce · cilantro

makes 4 to 6 servings

I first moved to Brooklyn in 1997 to attend graduate school at NYU. My homeboy from college, Mike Molina, and I got an apartment in Crown Heights on Schenectady Avenue near the Utica stop on the MTA's 3/4 line. Coming from New Orleans, where we went to college, a Black neighborhood in Brooklyn was the perfect place for us to land in NYC. Most of the folks living in our building were from the Caribbean, and there were lots of independently owned West Indian businesses, including a plethora of Rastafarian-owned health food stores and juice bars. Feeling stuffed the day after late-night munchies? A shot of ginger juice from down the block would take care of that. Wanting to alkalinize/energize before a long day on campus in Manhattan? A large green smoothie with ginseng from the juice spot by the subway, please. There were also lots of good, fast, and cheap Caribbean restaurants in the neighborhood. My two favorite quick bites were veggie patties stuffed inside warm coco bread from any number of Jamaican spots around the way and doubles—fried flatbreads with a curried chickpea filling—at a hole-in-the-wall Trinidadian restaurant on Utica Avenue.

REGGAE AIR HORN BLASTING

At that same Trini spot, I would sometimes get chana and aloo, a mixture of chickpeas and potatoes simmered in curry sauce, and it was delicious. This recipe is my ode to that dish. I incorporate fennel, using it like I would an onion, to add its subtly sweet anise flavor. The cilantro sauce takes this to the next level. Eat it with a green salad to balance everything out.

¾ cup dried chickpeas, picked through and soaked overnight in water plus 3 tablespoons kosher salt

1 bay leaf

½ large white onion

5 garlic cloves: 3 cut in half, 2 minced

1 dried red chile

Coarse sea salt

1 pound Yukon gold potatoes, peeled and cut into ½-inch cubes

3 tablespoons extra-virgin olive oil

Freshly ground white pepper

1 teaspoon ground turmeric

1 teaspoon coriander seeds

¾ teaspoon cumin seeds

¾ teaspoon fenugreek seeds

¼ teaspoon brown mustard seeds

¼ teaspoon ground cinnamon

1 whole clove

1 (8- to 10-ounce) fennel bulb, trimmed (fronds reserved), quartered, cored, and finely chopped

¼ teaspoon to 1 tablespoon seeded minced habanero chile

2 tablespoons tomato paste

3 cups vegetable stock (page 230)

1 cup Cashew Cream (page 231)

Cilantro Sauce (page 235)

½ cup chopped fresh cilantro leaves plus ¼ cup packed whole leaves

Fresh lime juice, for finishing

Preheat the oven to 450°F. Line a baking sheet with parchment paper.

Drain the chickpeas and pour them into a medium saucepan or Dutch oven. Add water to cover by 3 inches. Bring the water to a boil over high heat, then lower the heat to medium and add the bay leaf, onion, halved garlic cloves, and dried chile. Partially cover and simmer until just tender, 45 minutes to 1 hour. Add 1 tablespoon salt and simmer for 5 minutes more. Drain the beans, remove the bay leaf, onion, garlic cloves, and chile, and discard.

While the chickpeas are cooking, in a large bowl, combine the potatoes, 1 tablespoon of the olive oil, ½ teaspoon salt, and a few turns of white pepper and toss well with clean hands to combine. Spread the potatoes over the prepared baking sheet in one layer and roast until tender and starting to turn golden on the edges, 25 to 30 minutes. Remove from the oven and set aside.

In a small skillet, combine the turmeric, coriander, cumin, fenugreek, mustard seeds, cinnamon, clove, and ¾ teaspoon salt. Toast the spices over medium heat, shaking the pan so they don't burn, until fragrant, about 1 minute. Immediately scrape the spices into a mortar or spice grinder. Grind into a fine powder and set aside.

In the pot you used to cook the chickpeas, warm the remaining 2 tablespoons olive oil over medium-high heat. Add the fennel and sauté until it begins to soften, 4 to 5 minutes. Add the minced garlic and the habanero and sauté until the garlic is fragrant, 3 to 4 minutes. Stir in the spice blend and cook, stirring, until well combined, about 2 minutes. Stir in the tomato paste until well combined. Pour in the stock and cashew cream and add the potatoes and chickpeas. Stir well to combine, decrease the heat to medium-low, partially cover, and simmer, stirring and scraping the bottom of the pan occasionally, until the flavors have melded and the curry has thickened, about 20 minutes. Season with salt to taste.

To serve, spoon the chickpeas, fennel, and potatoes into bowls. Top with cilantro sauce and garnish with chopped cilantro, whole cilantro leaves, and a smattering of the reserved fennel fronds, if you like. Give the whole thing a big squeeze of lime juice and serve.

"Bucktown" by Smif-N-Wessun from *Dah Shinin'*

cooking beans

While I'm not totally opposed to using canned beans, I tend to avoid them and cook dried beans from scratch instead. Cooking beans from scratch gives me control over their texture, seasonings, and the like, and they taste far superior to canned. I encourage you to make beans from scratch for the recipes in this book to ensure you're getting the best flavor in every dish.

Before cooking dried beans, it's important to pick through them for foreign objects. I know this seems tedious, but just spread the beans across a baking sheet and make sure there are no pebbles or debris among them. Also, get rid of any shriveled beans.

Rinse the beans a few times in cold water, place them in a pot, and add enough cold water to cover them by at least 2 inches, so they have room to expand. I soak my beans with 3 tablespoons of kosher salt to help flavor them, so add some before covering the pot and putting the beans in the refrigerator overnight. The next day, discard any beans that have floated to the top of the water. (If you're in a rush, use this quick-soaking method: Simply cover the dried beans with cold water by 2 inches, add 1 tablespoon of kosher salt, and bring to a boil. Cover the pot with a lid, turn off the heat, and let them sit for 1 hour, then continue as directed below.)

Before cooking, drain the soaked beans and return them to the pot. Add fresh water to cover the beans by about 3 inches. Also, I typically add a bay leaf, onion, garlic, and a dried chile to boost the flavor of my beans while simmering them. Bring the water to a boil, decrease the heat to medium, and simmer for the time suggested in the recipe. Check on the beans periodically and add more water as needed to keep them covered. One last thing: I was always taught to add salt just as the beans turn tender for further seasoning. Don't add too early or you risk slowing down their cooking time.

citrus and garlic-herb braised fennel

sunchoke cream · plantain powder ·
fennel fronds · olive oil · fleur de sel

makes 4 servings

Yes, this is the recipe that I talked about in the intro. Pan-seared fennel alone is yummy, but mojo-inspired citrus and garlic-herb sauce, umami-rich plantain powder, delicate anise-flavored fennel fronds, rich sunchoke cream, and a drizzle of really good olive oil elevate this to a standout dish. While layered, this is a fairly simple dish to make. The key is preparing some of the components (i.e., the plantain powder and sunchoke cream) ahead of time so you don't get bogged down making garnishes. Trust me, the payoff is BIG. If my persnickety five-year-old likes this dish, you will love it.

citrus and garlic-herb sauce

1 cup fresh orange juice

¼ cup fresh lime juice

1 tablespoon white vinegar

5 garlic cloves, minced

1 tablespoon minced fresh parsley leaves

½ teaspoon ground cumin

¼ teaspoon kosher salt

fennel

2 large fennel bulbs with fronds

5 tablespoons olive oil

Fine sea salt

¼ cup torn fresh parsley leaves

½ cup Plantain Powder (page 238)

Freshly ground black pepper

1 tablespoon orange zest

Sunchoke Cream (page 191), for serving

Extra-virgin olive oil, for drizzling

Fleur de sel, for finishing

Make the sauce: In a small bowl, whisk together all the ingredients for the sauce. Set aside at room temperature for 1 hour.

Make the fennel: Cut the tops off the fennel bulbs, setting aside the fronds for garnish. Trim the bottoms. Quarter the fennel bulbs through the core, leaving some of the core intact so the pieces don't fall apart as they cook.

In a large skillet, warm the olive oil over medium-high heat. When it starts to shimmer, add the fennel quarters, cut-side down, and cook, turning the fennel with tongs, until all the cut sides are golden brown, about 20 minutes. Sprinkle with salt, then use the tongs to carefully transfer the fennel to a plate.

Decrease the heat to medium-low. Pour in the sauce and bring it to a simmer. Cook for a few minutes just to warm through. Carefully transfer the fennel back to the skillet and simmer, basting and flipping the pieces every few minutes, until tender, about 10 minutes. Remove from the heat.

To serve, spoon a little of the sauce onto each of four small plates and top each plate with two pieces of fennel. Garnish each with 1 tablespoon of the parsley, a *generous* dusting of plantain powder, a few turns of black pepper, a pinch of orange zest, and a few of the reserved fennel fronds. Add a dollop of sunchoke cream. Drizzle with extra-virgin olive oil, sprinkle with fleur de sel, and serve.

"Afro-Cu (Bembé)" by Mongo Santamaria from *What Do You Mean*

spicy lacto-fermented leeks

berbere spice blend

makes about 1 quart

This has become my go-to condiment when I want to add some spicy umami. These leeks add heat and tang to crackers, toast, sandwiches, soups, stews, vegetable dishes, and grains. They pretty much elevate the flavor of everything. The berbere spice blend gives them an Ethiopian flavor profile, but feel free to experiment with your favorite fiery spice blend.

Note: You will need a 2-quart mason jar or a fermentation crock for this recipe.

2½ tablespoons kosher salt

3 cups filtered water

6 cups thinly sliced leeks (about 1½ pounds/3 large leeks, white and tender green parts only)

2 teaspoons minced garlic

2 teaspoons Berbere Spice Blend (page 238)

In a small saucepan, combine 1 tablespoon of the salt and the filtered water. Heat over medium heat, stirring, until the salt has completely dissolved. Refrigerate the brine until completely cool.

While the brine is cooling, put the leeks in a large bowl and sprinkle with the remaining 1½ table-spoons salt. With clean hands, massage the leeks until they begin to release liquid, 3 to 5 minutes. Transfer the leeks to a colander in the sink and rinse the bowl clean. Set a plate on top of the leeks and weight it down (a 28-ounce can of tomatoes works well for this). Let the leeks stand for 1 hour to release more liquid.

Transfer the leeks back to the bowl, add the garlic and berbere spice blend, and mix well with clean hands. Transfer the mixture to a clean 2-quart mason jar or fermentation crock. Pack the leeks in as tightly as possible and place something over the leeks to weight them down. Add just enough of the chilled brine to cover the leeks. It's important that they stay submerged. Cover the jar with cheesecloth and set it aside at room temperature to ferment for at least 1 week.

Once the leeks have fermented to your taste, cover the jar and refrigerate. They will keep in the refrigerator for up to 3 months.

"Keep It 100" by DJ Cavem Moetavation from *Biomimicz*

cleaning leeks

Because leeks are grown in sandy soil, it is important to thoroughly clean them before cooking them. First scrub them to remove any visible soil. Cut off and discard the root of the leeks. Remove the dark green tops of the leeks and save for stock (or making my Warm Beluga Lentils with Roasted Leek Tops and Kale, page 58). Slice each leek in half length-wise, then fan them out under cool running water to rinse all the soil and sand from their inner layers.

creamy sweet potato leek soup

puffed black ginger rice · cilantro · coconut cream

makes 4 to 6 servings

This tasty and rich soup is fairly easy to make, though the puffed black ginger rice takes some time (worth it!). The star is undoubtedly the sweet potatoes—a staple of African American cooking. The leeks play a supporting role, deepening the flavor of the soup. A smattering of cashew cream adds a velvety texture to the base of the soup, and a drizzle of coconut cream adds both flavor and visual interest. The idea for the topping comes from my wife's sizzling rice soup, Chinese vegetables in a light veggie broth sprinkled with crispy rice. Here ginger-scented, deep-fried Forbidden Rice adds texture and gives the soup a boost of flavor. To save time, boil and bake the rice in advance, then deep-fry it just before serving so it's hot and puffy. Of course, you can skip the rice and enjoy the soup with toasted bread.

puffed black ginger rice

1 cup black Forbidden Rice, soaked in water overnight and drained

1 tablespoon ginger juice (from ½ cup coarsely shredded fresh ginger; see sidebar, page 54)

¾ teaspoon kosher salt

sweet potato leek soup

1 tablespoon olive oil

2 cups chopped leeks (2 or 3 medium, white parts only)

½ teaspoon kosher salt, plus more as needed

5 cups vegetable stock (page 230), plus more as needed

1¼ pounds sweet potatoes, peeled and thinly sliced

¼ cup Cashew Cream (page 231)

1 tablespoon unseasoned rice vinegar

Freshly ground white pepper

to finish

1 cup coconut oil, for frying

½ cup minced fresh cilantro

Coconut Cream (page 231)

Flaky sea salt, for finishing

Start the rice: In a small saucepan, combine the rice, ginger juice, salt, and 2 cups water. Bring to a boil over high heat, quickly decrease the heat to low, cover, and cook until the rice has absorbed the water, about 25 minutes. Remove from the heat and set aside, covered, to steam for 20 minutes.

Preheat the oven to 300°F. Line a baking sheet with parchment paper.

With a fork, transfer the rice from the saucepan to the prepared baking sheet. Spread it in an even layer, separating the rice grains as much as possible with the fork. Bake, stirring occasionally, until the rice dries, 20 to 30 minutes. Set aside until ready to deep-fry.

Make the soup: In a medium saucepan, warm the oil over medium-high heat until shimmering. Add the leeks and the salt, decrease the heat to medium-low, and cook, stirring occasionally, until the leeks are meltingly tender but not brown, about 20 minutes.

Add the stock and sweet potatoes. Raise the heat to high, bring to a boil, then decrease the heat to medium. Simmer, partially covered, until the sweet potatoes are tender, about 30 minutes.

creamy sweet potato leek soup, continued

In batches, carefully transfer the soup to a blender and puree until smooth. Return the soup to the pot and stir in the cashew cream and vinegar. Taste and season with salt and white pepper. Gently warm through over low heat; do not allow the soup to come to a boil. Add additional broth or water as needed to thin the soup (it should easily pour from a spoon).

Finish the rice: Just before serving the soup, line a plate with paper towels. In a wok or small saucepan, heat the coconut oil over medium-high heat to 375°F (if you don't have a deep-fry thermometer, drop in one grain of rice to see if it puffs up—if it does, the oil is ready). Working in batches, add the rice to the hot oil and fry until it puffs up, floats to the top of the oil, and has a brownish hue, 15 to 20 seconds. With a stainless steel spider, transfer the rice to the paper towel–lined plate to drain. Repeat to fry the remaining rice. Transfer the rice to a medium bowl and stir in the cilantro. Mix well.

To serve, ladle the soup into bowls, drizzle with coconut cream, and generously top with the puffed rice and cilantro. Finish with a sprinkle of flaky salt and serve.

"Live Your Life" by Yuna from *Yuna*

juicing ginger

The easiest way to get juice from ginger is feeding it into an electric juicer, but here is another way if you don't have a juicer: First, grate ginger knobs on a box grater (the coarse side with the big holes works well). You can also pulverize the ginger in a food processor to yield ginger pulp. Next, wrap the pulp in cheesecloth and squeeze to extract as much juice as possible. You can also squeeze the pulp with your hands (skipping the cheesecloth), in batches, and then strain the juice of any solids afterward.

caramelized leek and seared mushroom toast

mustard–pine nut spread · pine nuts · thyme · tarragon

makes 4 servings

My wife and I are saving up for a bigger house, so I had to ease up on buying expensive avocado toast. (Because buying avocado toast is the only thing slowing us down from sizing up in one of the most expensive cities in the world during a historical moment where the wealthiest 1 percent of American households own 40 percent of the country's wealth while a record number of people toil in poverty and debt *Stanley from *The Office* eye roll*.) Anyway, I get down with fancy toast sometimes when I'm eating out, and I wanted to offer a make-at-home alternative. Off the top, you must start with really good rustic bread–if you have some, you're halfway there. If you don't want to make it yourself, find the hardworking bakers in your area and show them some love. Next, you need a creamy spread. Pile on some farm-fresh toppings and good salt, and you are golden. The mustard–pine nut spread can be used on any number of sandwiches, but it plays off earthy mushrooms perfectly. Serve with a raw salad for a light meal.

mustard–pine nut spread

¾ cup pine nuts

¼ cup extra-virgin olive oil

2½ tablespoons whole-grain mustard

1 teaspoon dark agave nectar

Fine sea salt and freshly ground white pepper

toast

1 pound wild mushrooms, such as maitake, chestnut, or chanterelle

2 tablespoons extra-virgin olive oil, plus more for brushing the bread

Kosher salt

1 cup finely chopped leek (about 1 medium)

1 tablespoon minced fresh thyme

4 thick slices sourdough or other rustic bread

1 tablespoon chopped fresh tarragon

Flaky sea salt

Freshly ground white pepper

Make the spread: In a small skillet, toast the pine nuts over medium-high heat, shaking the pan for even cooking, until they are starting to turn golden, about 3 minutes. Transfer the nuts to a mortar and pound into a fine paste with the pestle. Add the olive oil, mustard, agave, a pinch of salt, and a few turns of white pepper and stir well to combine. Set aside.

Make the toast: Clean the mushrooms (see page 162). Remove any tough stems and, depending on what type of mushrooms you are using, chop larger mushrooms to ensure all the pieces are fairly uniform in size.

In a cast-iron skillet, warm 1 tablespoon of the olive oil over medium heat. When the oil shimmers, add the mushrooms and a generous pinch of salt, being careful not to overcrowd the pan. Cook, stirring often and scraping the pan, until the liquid released by the mushrooms has fully evaporated and the mushrooms are starting to brown, 7 to 10 minutes. Turn off the heat, transfer the mushrooms to a medium bowl, and set aside.

In the same skillet, warm the remaining 1 tablespoon olive oil over medium-low heat until shimmering. Add the leek and cook until softened, about 5 minutes. Add the thyme and a pinch of salt and cook until the leek is browning and smells fragrant, 2 to 3 minutes. Transfer to a small bowl and set aside.

Position an oven rack about 6 inches from the broiler heat element and preheat the broiler to high.

Arrange the bread on a baking sheet and broil until golden brown. Flip the bread and broil for about 30 seconds on the second side; take it out of the oven quickly so it doesn't burn.

To serve, arrange one slice of toast on each of four small plates and brush with olive oil. Generously slather on the mustard–pine nut spread, top it with the leek mixture, then evenly distribute the mushrooms over that. Garnish each with a tiny bit of tarragon (just enough for a few pops of flavor), then season with flaky salt and a few turns of white pepper and enjoy.

"The Capitalist Blues" by Leyla McCalla from *The Capitalist Blues*

warm beluga lentils with roasted leek tops and kale

creamy sun-dried tomato broth · thyme

makes 4 to 6 servings

Writing this book forced me out of my comfort zone in many regards. Before testing this recipe, I had never attempted to cook with the tough leek tops. I always composted them and stuck with the tender base. In the spirit of zero-waste cooking, I experimented with different ways of cooking leek tops before settling on this recipe. Briefly blanching softens them a bit, and roasting further tenderizes them and deepens their flavor. This process turns them pale green, so I mixed them with kale for a nicer presentation. This is a fairly involved recipe, so I wouldn't be mad if you used store-bought hot pepper vinegar in lieu of making it from scratch.

roasted vegetables

1 tablespoon plus ¼ teaspoon kosher salt

Dark green tops and light green outer leaves from 2 leeks, scrubbed and sliced on an angle into ½-inch-thick strips (about 6 cups)

4 ounces lacinato kale, rinsed, stemmed, halved crosswise, and sliced into long strips

1 tablespoon extra-virgin olive oil

lentils

1 tablespoon extra-virgin olive oil

½ small yellow onion, finely diced

2 garlic cloves, minced

Leaves from 2 thyme sprigs, minced

1 cup black beluga lentils, picked over and rinsed

1½ cups tomato puree

1 cup vegetable stock (page 230)

¼ cup Cashew Cream (page 231)

3 tablespoons Sweet Hot Pepper Vinegar (page 234), plus more as needed

Kosher salt

Freshly ground black pepper

sun-dried tomato broth

2 sun-dried tomato halves, or 2 tablespoons packed julienned sun-dried tomatoes

Boiling water

¼ cup extra-virgin olive oil

10 large garlic cloves, thinly sliced

2 (1-inch) thyme sprigs

2 tablespoons fresh lemon juice

2 tablespoons Sweet Hot Pepper Vinegar (page 234)

¾ teaspoon kosher salt

Freshly ground black pepper

Roast the leeks and kale: Preheat the oven to 350°F.

Bring a large pot of water to a boil over high heat. Season with 1 tablespoon of the salt. Gently drop the leeks into the water. Bring back to a boil and cook until the leeks are just starting to soften, about 2 minutes. Add the kale and boil for 30 seconds. Drain the vegetables in a colander. Lay a clean kitchen towel on a work surface, spread the vegetables over it, and gently pat dry. Transfer the vegetables to a large bowl.

Add the olive oil and remaining ¼ teaspoon salt and use your hands to evenly coat the vegetables with the oil. Divide them between two rimmed baking sheets and roast until crisp, about 30 minutes. Be sure to stir the vegetables every 10 minutes, then shake the pans to even them out before returning the pans to the oven.

Make the lentils: While the vegetables are roasting, in a medium saucepan, warm the olive oil over medium heat. When the oil shimmers, add the onion and cook, stirring frequently, until softened, 5 to 7 minutes. Add the garlic and thyme and cook until aromatic, 1 to 2 minutes. Add the lentils, stir to coat in the oil, then pour in the tomato puree and the stock.

Increase the heat to medium-high and bring to a boil. Reduce the heat to medium-low and simmer until the lentils are just tender, 20 to 25 minutes. Remove from the heat. Scoop out 2 tablespoons of the cooking liquid and set aside for the broth. Stir in the cashew cream and the vinegar. Taste and season with salt and pepper. Cover to keep warm.

Make the broth: Put the sun-dried tomatoes in a small heatproof bowl and add boiling water to cover. Let soak while you cook the garlic.

In a medium skillet, warm the olive oil over medium-low heat. Add the garlic and thyme and cook, stirring occasionally, until crisp and golden brown, 8 to 10 minutes. Strain the garlic oil through a fine-mesh sieve into a bowl; set the oil aside. Discard the thyme and set aside the garlic chips for garnish.

Drain the sun-dried tomatoes and transfer to a blender. Add the lemon juice, vinegar, reserved 2 tablespoons lentil cooking liquid, and the salt and process until smooth. With the blender running, slowly pour in the garlic oil through the hole in the lid and blend until emulsified.

To serve, divide the warm lentils among individual bowls. Drizzle with about 1 tablespoon of the broth and top with the roasted vegetables. Garnish with the garlic chips and a few turns of black pepper. Serve warm.

"Parallax (feat. The Palaceer Lazaro)" by Shabazz Palaces from *Quazarz: Born on a Gangster Star*

grilled spring onions with lemon-thyme oil

stewed red lentils · creamy cauliflower · thyme

makes 4 servings

When spring onions are available in late spring and summer, I char them on my grill as often as possible. Most of the time, I don't have a vision for how they will be used in the meal, but that always seems to work itself out. I usually toss them with peanut oil first, but for this recipe, an herby thyme oil packed with lemon zest reigns. I once topped my version of misir wot, a signature Ethiopian dish made with red lentils, with some chopped spring onions grilled in lemon-thyme oil, and my wife said it felt like a flavor explosion in her mouth. I trust that this re-creation of that combination will lead to a similar experience for you. Make sure you soak two 8-inch wooden skewers in water for half an hour before grilling to prevent them from burning. If you can't grill the spring onions, simply warm the lemon-thyme oil in a large skillet and cook them until they just start to brown, about 1 minute.

spring onions

2 tablespoons plus ⅛ teaspoon kosher salt

12 spring onions or large scallions, trimmed

1 teaspoon Charred Lemon-Thyme Oil (page 232), plus more for oiling the grill

Flaky sea salt

stewed red lentils

3 tablespoons extra-virgin olive oil

¾ cup finely chopped yellow onion

½ teaspoon minced garlic

1 tablespoon Berbere Spice Blend (page 238)

1 cup tomato puree

½ teaspoon kosher salt, plus more as needed

2½ cups vegetable stock (page 230)

1 cup red lentils, rinsed and picked over

Creamy Cauliflower (page 102), for topping

3 (2-inch) thyme sprigs, for garnish

Grill the spring onions: Fill a large bowl with ice and water and set aside. Bring a large pot of water to a boil over high heat. Add 2 tablespoons of the kosher salt and the spring onions and boil for 1 minute. Using tongs, remove the spring onions and immediately plunge them into the ice water to stop the cooking and set their color. Transfer the spring onions to a clean kitchen towel, gently pat dry, and set aside.

Heat a grill to medium-high and lightly oil the grill grates with charred lemon-thyme oil.

In a large bowl, combine the charred lemon-thyme oil and remaining ⅛ teaspoon kosher salt and mix well. Add the spring onions and toss well to coat. Line up the spring onions side by side on a cutting board and thread about 5 skewers, one at a time, crosswise through all the spring onions at even intervals. Grill the spring onions, turning them a few times, until starting to char, about 5 minutes. Transfer to a plate and sprinkle with flaky salt. When cool enough to handle, remove the skewers.

Make the lentils: In a medium saucepan, warm the olive oil over medium-low heat until shimmering. Add the yellow onion and cook, stirring occasionally, until just starting to brown, about 10 minutes. Add the garlic and cook, stirring occasionally, until fragrant, 2 to 3 minutes. Dump in the berbere spice blend, tomato puree, and salt and stir until thoroughly incorporated.

Stir in the stock, followed by the lentils. Raise the heat to high, bring to a boil, then quickly decrease the heat to medium-low and cook until the lentils are tender and the mixture is thick, 30 to 45 minutes. Season with salt to taste.

To serve, place the spring onions on a large serving platter. Place the lentils in a bowl, and smear some creamy cauliflower on top of them (or top with a mounded scoop of creamy cauliflower) along with the thyme sprigs. Serve alongside the grilled spring onions.

"Addis Black Widow" by Mulatu Astatke & The Heliocentrics from *Inspiration Information 3*

spinach-avocado dip with scallions

serrano chiles · parsley

makes about 2 cups

This dish happened by accident. The morning after one of my family's "taco nights," I made a quick-and-dirty lunch, warming beans, frying tortillas, and steaming baby spinach. I topped my tacos with guacamole that my wife had made with scallions, since we were out of onions. It was good! I thought, *Let's double down on the East Asian flavor profile*—since scallions are one of the most important fresh ingredients in Chinese cooking—and added shoyu for saltiness and rice vinegar for acid. In this recipe, I actually skip the shoyu to ensure that the dip is bright in color. Plus seasoned rice vinegar gives this dip a complex flavor and makes adding shoyu for saltiness largely unnecessary. While similar to guacamole in spirit, the texture of this recipe is smooth after whipping it in a food processor. This allows it to easily pivot from dip to sandwich spread. In fact, I used it to make toast for a collaboration with Williams-Sonoma, smearing it on country bread and topping it with daikon, scallions, gomasio (a Japanese condiment made of unhulled sesame seeds and salt), Aleppo pepper, and borage flowers.

2 teaspoons
avocado oil

1 tablespoon
minced garlic

8 ounces baby spinach

4 ripe Hass avocados,
pitted and peeled

¼ cup seasoned
rice vinegar

Coarse sea salt

¼ cup thinly
sliced scallions

¼ cup minced
fresh parsley

3 tablespoons diced
seeded serrano chiles

Fresh lemon juice

In a medium skillet, combine the avocado oil and garlic and sauté over medium heat, stirring often, until the garlic smells fragrant and just starts to turn golden, 3 to 5 minutes. In stages, fill the pan with spinach, stirring to facilitate wilting, and cook until all the spinach is wilted. Remove from the heat and transfer the spinach mixture to a food processor. Process until finely chopped, scraping down the sides as necessary. Scrape the spinach puree into a medium bowl and set aside.

Return the bowl and blade to the food processor. Add the avocados and vinegar and process until smooth. Scrape the avocado into the bowl with the spinach mixture and season with salt to taste. Fold in the scallions, parsley, and serrano. Taste and add just enough lemon juice to brighten up the dip, then serve.

"On Green Dolphin Street" by Miles Davis from *Kind of Blue*

scallion-teff biscuits

mushroom gravy · microgreens

makes 10 to 12 biscuits and about 2½ cups gravy;
5 to 6 servings

Here's the thing: these scallion biscuits are a
standout on their own. But I wanted to pair them
with umami-rich mushroom gravy so they could
be eaten as a meal. This is the type of breakfast
that my dad likes to have on vacation or on one of
his "cheat days." I agree with Pops. It's a dish that
requires a leisurely day to make and enjoy.

gravy

2 tablespoons
extra-virgin olive oil

4 ounces button
mushrooms, stemmed
and diced

4 ounces cremini
mushrooms, stemmed
and diced

2 tablespoons
millet flour

1 cup unsweetened
oat milk

1 cup mushroom stock
(page 230)

½ teaspoon kosher salt,
plus more as needed

Freshly ground
white pepper

biscuits

1¼ cups unbleached
all-purpose flour

¾ cup teff flour

1 tablespoon raw
cane sugar

2 teaspoons baking
powder

¾ teaspoon fine
sea salt

½ teaspoon
baking soda

7 tablespoons coconut
oil, chilled for at least
15 minutes

½ cup thinly sliced
scallions (about 8)

1 cup unsweetened
oat milk

1 tablespoon apple
cider vinegar

Microgreens, for garnish

Make the gravy: In a medium saucepan, warm
1 tablespoon of the olive oil over medium heat. Add
the mushrooms and sauté, stirring often, until the
liquid they release has evaporated, 5 to 7 minutes.
Stir in the flour and remaining 1 tablespoon olive oil
until well combined. Decrease the heat to low and
cook, stirring often, until the flour starts to brown,
about 10 minutes.

While whisking, add the oat milk, stock, and salt.
Increase the heat to medium-high and bring to a
simmer, then decrease the heat to medium-low
and simmer, whisking very frequently, until thickened, about 15 minutes. Season with salt and white
pepper to taste; cover to keep warm while you
make the biscuits.

Make the biscuits: Preheat the oven to 425°F. Line
a baking sheet with parchment paper.

In a large bowl, sift together the flours, sugar,
baking powder, salt, and baking soda. Whisk until
well blended. Add the coconut oil and use two
butter knives or your fingers to cut it into the flour
until the mixture is the size of small peas. Stir in
the scallions.

In a small bowl, stir together the oat milk and vinegar. Make a well in the center of the flour mixture
and pour in the oat milk mixture. Stir just until the
dough comes away from the sides of the bowl.

Use an ice cream scoop and a spoon (if needed)
to portion out 10 to 12 mounds of dough, with
2 inches between them, on the baking sheet, each
2 to 2½ inches in diameter. Bake until golden brown
on the bottom, 16 to 18 minutes.

To serve, place two hot biscuits on each plate and
top with a generous ladle of the gravy. Garnish with
microgreens. Serve.

"Boogie Chillen" by John Lee Hooker from *The Legendary
Modern Recordings 1948-1954*

farro and kidney beans with burnt scallions

coconut milk · thyme · parsley

makes 4 to 6 servings

This recipe (see photo on page 67) is inspired by the rice and peas (or rice and beans) dish that's found throughout the Caribbean but is most closely associated with Jamaica. Depending on whom you ask, the "peas" are pigeon peas or kidney beans–I use the latter in this recipe, and farro instead of the traditional long-grain white rice. Farro, one of the first crops to be cultivated in the Middle East's Fertile Crescent, was used for thousands of years in the Near East and parts of Africa until modern wheat varieties took over. Now the grain is most associated with Italian cooking. One of my favorite things about farro is its chewiness. Think about the difference between overcooked and al dente pasta. In this dish, the bite that you get from farro is so much more satisfying than rice. Farro has a much more complex flavor than rice, too–nutty and slightly sweet–adding an even more distinctive taste to this recipe.

¾ cup dried kidney beans, picked over and soaked in water overnight (see page 48)

1 bay leaf

½ large white onion

3 garlic cloves, cut in half

1 dried red chile

Coarse sea salt

1 cup farro, soaked in water plus 1 tablespoon vinegar overnight

1 cup unsweetened canned coconut milk

2 allspice berries

2 tablespoons coconut oil

2 bunches scallions (about 7 ounces total), thinly sliced

2 large garlic cloves, minced

½ teaspoon smoked paprika

2 tablespoons minced fresh thyme

¼ teaspoon cayenne pepper, or more to taste

White wine vinegar

½ cup chopped fresh parsley

Drain the kidney beans, put them in a medium saucepan, and add water to cover by 3 inches. Add the bay leaf, onion, garlic halves, and chile and bring to a boil over high heat. Reduce the heat to low and simmer until the beans are just tender, 45 to 60 minutes. Add ½ teaspoon salt and simmer for 5 minutes more. Drain the beans and remove and discard the bay leaf, onion, garlic, and chile.

While the beans are cooking, drain the farro and put it in a large saucepan. Add 1½ cups water, the coconut milk, allspice berries, and ½ teaspoon salt. Bring to a rolling simmer over medium-high heat, then quickly decrease the heat to medium-low, cover, and simmer until the farro is al dente (taste a few grains to test for doneness). Drain the farro, reserving the cooking liquid, and return the farro to the saucepan; set the cooking liquid aside.

While you've got the beans and the farro cooking, in a medium skillet, warm the coconut oil over medium-low heat. Add the scallions and cook, stirring often to prevent them from sticking, until they start to crisp and almost blacken around the edges, about 20 minutes. Add the minced garlic and paprika and cook until the garlic is fragrant, about 3 minutes. Remove from the heat.

Add the beans, scallion-garlic mixture, thyme, cayenne, and ½ teaspoon salt to the saucepan with the farro and toss with a fork to combine. Add some of the reserved farro cooking liquid to create a risotto-like texture. Season to taste with white wine vinegar and additional salt, if necessary. Serve topped with the parsley.

"Sing Out" by Dezarie from *Nemozian Rasta*

soaking grains

I typically soak my grains before cooking, as it shortens their cooking time and makes them more digestible. Soaking most grains in filtered water with a little acid (lemon, vinegar, or the like) for 8 hours or overnight is sufficient for breaking down the hard-to-digest components of grains (phytic acid) and releasing beneficial nutrients (phytase).

cooking farro

Cooking farro can be tricky. A lot of people have expressed anxiety about over- or undercooking it. It took me years to figure out the most effective way of preparing it. First, I put it in a pot, add water to cover and a tablespoon of vinegar, and let it soak in the refrigerator for 8 hours or overnight. Then I drain it, return it to the pot, and add 2 ½ cups liquid for every 1 cup farro. I bring the liquid to a boil, then reduce the heat to maintain a simmer; after 25 minutes, I start checking it by tasting a few grains and continue to cook as needed until it reaches my desired texture, typically al dente.

stems

shaved asparagus salad

sweet meyer lemon vinaigrette ·
lemon zest · grated walnuts · dill

makes 4 to 6 servings

There is something about the combination of
asparagus and lemon that keeps me coming back
for more. This recipe has a similar flavor profile to
the Asparagus with Lemon-Pepper Marinade on
page 72, but don't fret; this dish serves a different
purpose than that one. I imagine the grilled
asparagus in the second recipe being served on
paper plates in a crowded, smoke-filled backyard
with Outkast, UGK, and the Hot Boys bumpin'
through speakers. I see this salad being served
on matte gray ceramic plates in your partner's
parents' dining room when you're meeting them
for the first time, with Charles Mingus playing
softly in the background so y'all can have polite
conversation. I'm just BS'ing. This is a quick and
easy salad that helps you make the most of farm-
fresh asparagus during its short peak season. I
know you can probably get asparagus year-round,
but you can't beat the flavor of those beautiful
stalks in April and May. The key to really killing this
salad is using a mandoline or a vegetable peeler
to slice the asparagus into delicate strips that
easily soak up the dressing. If you can't access
Meyer lemons, Eureka or other varieties will work
just fine. And feel free to experiment with other
spring vegetables or with any number of shaveable
vegetables such as beets, radishes, or fennel.
I promise, everyone from your parents to your
patnas will be smiling while eating this.

¼ cup fresh Meyer
lemon juice

1 teaspoon minced
shallot

¼ teaspoon whole-
grain mustard

½ teaspoon
minced garlic

1 teaspoon raw
cane sugar

1½ teaspoons kosher
salt, plus more as
needed

6 tablespoons
walnut oil

Freshly ground
white pepper

2 pounds large
asparagus

1 Eureka lemon,
cut in half

1 teaspoon finely grated
Meyer lemon zest

⅓ cup walnuts, toasted
and finely grated with
a Microplane

¼ cup chopped
fresh dill

In a blender, combine the Meyer lemon juice, shallot,
mustard, garlic, sugar, and ½ teaspoon of the salt.
With the blender running, slowly pour in the walnut
oil through the hole in the lid. Taste and season with
salt and white pepper. Set aside.

Using a vegetable peeler, shave the asparagus into
long, thin strips and transfer to a large bowl. Sprinkle
the remaining 1 teaspoon salt over the asparagus,
then squeeze the juice from the Eureka lemon over
the top. Toss gently to combine.

Add enough of the dressing to lightly coat the
asparagus, drizzling it around the rim of the bowl to
allow it to sink to the bottom. Gently toss to coat.
Garnish with the lemon zest, grated walnuts, and
the dill, then serve.

"II B.S." by Charles Mingus from *Mingus Mingus Mingus
Mingus Mingus*

asparagus with lemon-pepper marinade

lemon juice · lemon zest · black and white pepper

makes 4 to 6 servings

I created this recipe after watching the second episode of the first season of *Atlanta*. I've never had lemon pepper wings, but when Darius and Paper Boi drooled over the light emanating from their chicken-filled box, it was clear that I needed to see what all the hype was about. After an afternoon of testing, while bumpin' OutKast's *Southernplayalisticadillacmuzik*, I landed on a marinade that combines tangy lemon juice, bright lemon zest, and pungent black pepper. Instead of creating a recipe for ranch dressing, which is typically served alongside wings, I blended the marinade with silken tofu to give it depth and creaminess. I finished the dish with a hit of earthy-floral white pepper and more lemon zest. This for all my people grinding and hustling in ATL, the Bluff City, MIA, North Cakalak, and the Big Easy. As Andre 3000 said at the Source Awards in 1995, "It's like this though, I'm tired of them closed-minded folks. It's like we got a demo tape but don't nobody want to hear it, but it's like this: the South got something to say! That's all I got to say."

1 cup silken tofu

1 tablespoon plus 2 teaspoons finely grated lemon zest

2 tablespoons olive oil

2 tablespoons water

2 tablespoons unseasoned rice vinegar

1/4 cup fresh lemon juice, plus more as needed

1 teaspoon plus 2 tablespoons kosher salt, plus more as needed

1 teaspoon freshly ground black pepper

1 pound thick asparagus, trimmed

Freshly ground white pepper

In a blender, combine the tofu, 1 tablespoon of the lemon zest, the olive oil, water, rice vinegar, lemon juice, 1 teaspoon of the salt, and the black pepper and puree until smooth, adding more lemon juice if necessary until the mixture is runny. Pour into a shallow dish, using a rubber spatula to scrape out all the sauce. Set aside.

Fill a large bowl with ice and cold water. In a large pot, bring 2 quarts water to a boil over high heat. Add the remaining 2 tablespoons salt and the asparagus and blanch for 30 seconds to brighten the color. Using tongs, remove the asparagus from the pot and quickly plunge it into the ice water. Let cool for 5 minutes. Drain the asparagus, pat dry with a clean kitchen towel, and transfer to the shallow dish with the dressing. Toss well and set aside for 1 hour.

Heat a grill to high.

Grill the asparagus, turning with tongs to ensure even cooking, until tender and blistered in spots, 3 to 5 minutes.

To serve, place the asparagus on a serving plate, drizzle with the lemon-pepper sauce, and sprinkle with the remaining 2 teaspoons lemon zest. Season with salt and white pepper to taste, then serve.

"Chonkyfire" by OutKast from *Aquemini*

salad basics

Whether I'm using spring and summer varieties like butter, red leaf, and romaine or fall and winter bitter leaves like radicchio, chicory, and frisée, I incorporate salad greens into hearty salads throughout the year. These leaves are all great bases, and the possibilities are limitless from there. Add other cooked and raw vegetables, dried fruits, and proteins to take them to the next level. Croutons, nuts, and seeds are great finishers that add texture and visual interest. Experiment with different homemade dressings and vinaigrettes for a final coat. To get the most flavor from your dressing, sprinkle your salad with salt and give it a generous squeeze of fresh lemon juice right before lightly tossing with the dressing.

red rice with spring vegetables

asparagus · spring peas · sugar snap peas

makes 4 to 6 servings

In case you don't know, there is some serious debate among West Africans about the origins and supremacy of jollof rice (there is a particularly fierce rivalry between Ghanaians and Nigerians). I keep my Black American a** out of that dispute. In fact, I refuse to call my version "jollof." I stick with the neutral "red rice" to play it safe. This is my latest iteration of a jollof-inspired rice. I like it a little wet, so I include ample tomato juice and stock. This version is a distinctly spring dish, with bright, just-tender peas and asparagus topping the rich, tangy, umami-filled rice.

1 cup brown basmati rice, rinsed and soaked in water overnight

3 tablespoons peanut oil

1 cup finely diced yellow onion

1 green bell pepper, finely diced

1 large habanero chile, seeded and finely diced

1 tablespoon minced garlic

1/2 teaspoon paprika

1/2 teaspoon chili powder

3/4 teaspoon kosher salt

1 cup tomato paste

1 tablespoon Bragg Liquid Aminos

1 1/2 cups canned diced tomatoes, with their juices

2 1/2 cups vegetable stock (page 230)

8 ounces asparagus, trimmed and sliced on an angle into 1-inch pieces

1 1/3 cups shelled fresh spring peas (a little over 1 pound in their pods)

4 ounces sugar snap peas, trimmed and sliced in half on an angle

1 teaspoon Pili Pili Oil (page 232), for drizzling

1 large lemon, halved

Drain the rice and set it aside.

In a medium saucepan, warm the peanut oil over medium heat until shimmering. Add the onion and bell pepper and sauté, stirring often, until well caramelized, 10 to 15 minutes. Add the habanero and garlic and cook until the vegetables are soft and the garlic smells fragrant, 3 to 5 minutes. Add the paprika, chili powder, and 1/2 teaspoon of the salt and stir well for a minute or so to combine. Add the tomato paste and the liquid aminos and cook, stirring often, until well combined, about 3 minutes. Add the diced tomatoes and their juices and cook, stirring often, until the sauce just starts to thicken, 5 to 7 minutes. While stirring, slowly pour in the stock. Raise the heat to high and bring the mixture to a boil, then lower the heat to medium. While the stock is simmering, add the asparagus, spring peas, and sugar snap peas. Simmer the vegetables for 1 minute, then remove them with a spider or skimmer and transfer to a bowl. Sprinkle with the remaining 1/4 teaspoon salt and drizzle with the pili pili oil, toss well to combine, and set aside.

Add the rice to the saucepan, cover, decrease the heat to low, and cook for 45 minutes, until most of the liquid has been absorbed. Remove from the heat and let the rice steam, covered, for 15 minutes.

To serve, fluff the rice with a fork and transfer to a serving bowl. Squeeze lemon juice over the rice, place the vegetables over the rice, and serve.

"Hello Africa" by Blitz the Ambassador from *Diasporadical*

roasted sweet potato and asparagus po'boy

creole rémoulade · heirloom tomato · dill-pickled fennel

makes 4 sandwiches

When I lived in New Orleans, ordering a vegetarian po'boy meant you would get bread, mayonnaise, iceberg lettuce, and bland tomatoes. This recipe is the type of sandwich that I wish my crew and I could have eaten back in the day. I started conceiving of this recipe in 2012 when I sandwiched some leftover candied sweet potatoes from my book *The Inspired Vegan* between bread for lunch. While sweet, the Garnet yams also had a savory essence from the miso, molasses, sesame oil, and tamari in the marinade (in case there is any confusion, while labeled "yams," Jewel and Garnet yams are actually sweet potatoes). Since most folks can't imagine a po'boy without some deep-fried element, I was reluctant to share a recipe for one that was stuffed with sweet potatoes. That changed when I ran across a po'boy on the *Food & Wine* website created by chef Kevin Nashan that included roasted sweet potatoes dusted with Cajun seasoning. I coat mine in blackened seasoning instead, and before roasting, I parboil them. In culinary school, I learned that this method yields a sweeter, creamier roasted sweet potato. I imagine this sandwich sitting at the crossroads of winter and spring, so I add roasted asparagus to the mix. The dense, sweet-savory Garnet yams and the delicate, earthy asparagus are a perfect match. The piquant Creole rémoulade brings everything together. While this sandwich may not visually read as a po'boy in the way that most people envision them, you best believe it has the spirit of a classic New Orleans "dressed" po'boy.

2 tablespoons plus ¾ teaspoon kosher salt, plus more as needed

8 ounces asparagus, trimmed and sliced into ¾-inch pieces

1 pound Garnet yams, peeled and sliced into ½-inch-thick rounds

3 tablespoons extra-virgin olive oil

2 teaspoons molasses

2 teaspoons Bragg Liquid Aminos

1 tablespoon Blackened Seasoning (page 239)

2 (15-inch) loaves soft-crusted French or Italian bread

Creole Rémoulade (page 237), for dressing

2 large heirloom tomatoes, cut into ¼-inch-thick slices

Freshly ground white pepper

1 cup Dill-Pickled Fennel (page 44)

2 cups shredded little gem lettuce

In a large pot, bring 3 quarts water to a boil over high heat. Add 2 tablespoons of the salt and the asparagus. Remove from the heat and let the asparagus sit for 30 seconds. With a spider or tongs, transfer the asparagus to a colander and set aside. Gently slide the yams into the hot water, cover, and set aside for 1 hour. Drain the yams in a colander and set aside to dry for 30 minutes. Transfer to a large bowl.

Preheat the oven to 400°F. Line two baking sheets with parchment paper.

In a small bowl, combine 2 tablespoons of the olive oil, the molasses, liquid aminos, blackened seasoning, and ½ teaspoon of the salt and mix well. Pour the mixture over the yams and gently toss to coat. Gently transfer the yams to one of the prepared baking sheets, spread them in an even layer, and roast until tender, about 50 minutes, flipping the rounds once after 25 minutes to ensure even cooking.

In a medium bowl, combine the asparagus with the remaining 1 tablespoon olive oil and ¼ teaspoon salt. Toss well and transfer to the other prepared baking sheet. After you flip the yams at the halfway mark, place the baking sheet with the asparagus in the oven. Roast for 25 minutes, until tender and crisp.

roasted sweet potato and asparagus po'boy, continued

Remove both sheets of vegetables from the oven and set aside.

Halve the bread crosswise then lengthwise and place the slices in the oven for 4 to 5 minutes, or until just lightly toasted.

This is my suggestion for serving, but feel free to play around with a method that works for you. Spread the cut sides of the bread *generously* with rémoulade (I'm talking about a messy slather). Divide the yam rounds evenly between the bottom halves of the bread. Top the yams with a few spears of asparagus. Top the asparagus with the tomato slices, then sprinkle with salt and a few turns of white pepper. Top the tomatoes with the pickled fennel, then top the fennel with a handful of lettuce. Cover with the top halves of the bread, and enjoy.

"Voodoo" by The Dirty Dozen Brass Band from *Voodoo*

simple celery salad

charred lemon oil · salt · white pepper · parsley

makes 4 servings

I'll admit, I jumped on the celery juice craze in the beginning of 2019 and drank a tall glass of it every day for two weeks. I was surprised to hear a lot of people commenting about how radiant my skin looked, and I lost five pounds over that period. I eased up on my daily routine (just got tired of it), but I still blend a few stalks with water a few times a week and sip on it during the day. In March 2019, my friend Anya Fernald posted a picture on Instagram of a chopped celery salad and wrote a caption about it being a staple in her home. Since I had literally ten bunches of celery in the deli drawer of my fridge, I made a salad inspired by hers. Now I eat it at least once a week. Sometimes I just want a clean, raw, and crunchy green salad, and this always does the trick.

10 celery stalks, strings removed (see sidebar), thinly sliced on an angle, plus ½ cup celery leaves for garnish

1½ tablespoons Charred Lemon Oil (page 232)

Kosher salt and freshly ground white pepper

2 tablespoons minced fresh parsley

In a large bowl, combine the celery and lemon oil. Toss to combine. Season with salt and white pepper, then garnish with the parsley and celery leaves and serve.

"Swamp Thing" by Hiatus Kaiyote from *Choose Your Weapon*

removing the strings from celery

One of the first skills I learned in culinary school was how to remove the tough strings, or ribs, running along the outside lengths of a celery stalk. Sounds fun, right? Unless celery is cut into paper-thin slices, I don't like eating it if the tough strings haven't been removed. They're chewy. They get stuck in my teeth. They're a pain. I'll admit, when I'm home and don't care much about presentation, I will use a Y-shaped peeler to remove a thin layer of the celery, thus removing the strings. Don't be like me. De-string your celery like a grown-up by using a paring knife to get beneath the strings and pulling them off. It will take longer than my lazy way, but yours will look nicer in the end.

crunchy, bitter, and tart salad with sweet mustard vinaigrette

celery · granny smith apple · radicchio · frisée · toasted walnuts

makes 4 to 6 servings

People most often associate salads with summertime, but I need *clap* my *clap* bitter *clap* leaves *clap* during the colder months. Belgian endive, curly endive, radicchio, frisée, escarole. Give me all the chicories! I think it might be more accurate to describe these as bitter*sweet* greens, since they often have a subtly sweet earthy flavor that follows their initial bite. This salad (see photo on page 80) is my ode to winter roughage. I know this might sound dramatic, but there is a symphony in my mouth when I'm eating this dish—the title says it all. If you aren't into bitter vegetables, this salad might change your mind. Bitter is an underappreciated flavor in the American palate. Plus, the assertive dressing balances the acerbic flavor of the leaves. In all my recipes, I encourage you to use what is freshest and most easily accessible. In that spirit, feel free to use your favorite bittersweet greens for this salad. And stretch beyond the common Chioggia radicchio, most often found at supermarkets, and include heirloom varieties such as Treviso Tardivo and Castelfranco, if you have access to them.

sweet mustard vinaigrette

2 tablespoons apple cider vinegar

1 tablespoon fresh lemon juice

2 teaspoons light agave nectar

1½ teaspoons coarse-grain mustard

Kosher salt and freshly ground white pepper

5 tablespoons walnut oil

salad

5 ounces radicchio (1 small head), cored and torn into bite-size pieces

3 ounces frisée (1 medium head), white and light green parts only, torn into bite-size pieces

2 celery stalks, strings removed (see sidebar, opposite page), thinly sliced on an angle, plus ½ cup celery leaves for garnish

1 Granny Smith apple, cored and thinly sliced using a mandoline or sharp knife

Kosher salt

½ large lemon

½ cup walnut halves, toasted, for garnish

Freshly ground black pepper

Make the vinaigrette: In a blender, combine the vinegar, lemon juice, agave, mustard, a pinch of salt, and a few turns of white pepper. With the blender running, slowly pour in the walnut oil through the hole in the lid and blend until emulsified. Taste and season with salt and white pepper and set aside.

Make the salad: In a large bowl, combine the radicchio, frisée, celery, and apple. Sprinkle with salt, then squeeze the juice from the lemon half over the top. With clean hands, toss the salad leaves. Add just enough vinaigrette to lightly coat the leaves, then toss.

To serve, divide the salad evenly among individual plates, sprinkle with the walnuts, and garnish with the celery leaves. Drizzle with more vinaigrette, give each salad a few turns of black pepper, and serve.

"Sometimes It Snows in April" by Meshell Ndegeocello from *Ventriloquism*

wheat berry salad with creamy ginger dressing

celery · fuyu persimmons · dried cherries · pecans

makes 4 servings

This grain-based salad is healthy, hearty, and delicious. I took inspiration from the classic Waldorf salad, one of my favorites growing up (the apples and grapes made it fun). I use wheat berries, the whole form of the wheat grain, since they are highly nutritious and make this a more substantial meal, and I include persimmons to celebrate fall. This salad would work well as a light lunch or as a side at dinner. If persimmons aren't available, you can substitute a firm plum or apple instead.

creamy ginger dressing

⅓ cup silken tofu

1 teaspoon finely grated lemon zest

2 tablespoons fresh lemon juice

2 tablespoons unseasoned rice vinegar

1 teaspoon Dijon mustard

1 tablespoon coconut palm sugar

2 tablespoons minced fresh ginger

½ teaspoon minced garlic

¼ teaspoon kosher salt

2 tablespoons extra-virgin olive oil

Freshly ground white pepper

wheat berry salad

1 cup whole wheat berries, soaked in water plus 1 tablespoon vinegar and refrigerated overnight

¼ teaspoon kosher salt

2 large Fuyu persimmons

1 large celery stalk, strings removed (see page 78), cut on an angle into ¼-inch slices

½ cup coarsely chopped toasted pecans

¼ cup unsweetened dried cherries

½ cup chopped fresh flat-leaf parsley, for garnish

Make the dressing: In a blender, combine the tofu, lemon zest, lemon juice, vinegar, mustard, sugar, ginger, garlic, and salt. With the blender running, slowly pour in the oil through the hole in the lid and blend until emulsified. Season with white pepper and set aside.

Make the salad: Drain the wheat berries, transfer them to a medium saucepan, and add 3 cups water. Bring the water to a boil over high heat. Add the salt and decrease the heat to low. Cover and simmer until the wheat berries are tender but chewy, about 1 hour. Remove from the heat and let steam, covered, for 15 minutes. Drain the wheat berries in a colander, then rinse under cold water for 2 minutes.

In a large bowl, combine the persimmons, celery, pecans, and cherries. Dump the wheat berries into the bowl, add the dressing, and combine everything with clean hands or a mixing spoon.

Garnish with the parsley and serve.

"Lavender (feat. Kaytranada)" by BADBADNOTGOOD from *IV*

braised artichoke hearts with celery root–carrot puree

herbed croutons and bread crumbs

makes 6 servings

This is a simple and delicious dish that uses a silky celery root and carrot puree as the bed for artichokes braised in a bright liquid of wine, lemon juice, and fat. A topping of herbed croutons and bread crumbs adds a delicious layer of texture, making this a standout dish. Big thanks to Monifa Dayo for advice on making this dish shine.

herbed croutons and bread crumbs

6 tablespoons olive oil

1 tablespoon minced fresh rosemary

1 tablespoon minced fresh thyme

1 tablespoon minced garlic

1 loaf sourdough bread, ripped into 1-inch pieces

Kosher salt

braised artichoke hearts

1 lemon, halved

6 medium artichokes

1 cup dry white wine

½ cup extra-virgin olive oil

2 tablespoons fresh lemon juice

2 tablespoons kosher salt

1 bay leaf

1 habanero chile, stem intact

2 garlic cloves, cut in half lengthwise

celery root–carrot puree

1 medium celery root (about 1 pound), peeled and cut into ½-inch dice

1 large carrot (about 4 ounces), peeled and thinly sliced

3 large peeled garlic cloves

1 cup unsweetened coconut milk

1 tablespoon olive oil

¾ teaspoon kosher salt, plus more as needed

Freshly ground white pepper

Flaky sea salt

Make the herbed croutons and bread crumbs: Preheat the oven to 325°F and line a baking sheet with parchment paper.

In a large bowl, combine the olive oil, rosemary, thyme, and garlic and mix well. Transfer the bread to the bowl, sprinkle with salt to taste, and toss to coat the bread. Spread the bread in one even layer on the baking sheet. Bake, shaking the pan and stirring every 5 minutes to ensure even toasting, until crunchy, 20 to 30 minutes.

Transfer half of the croutons to a food processor and pulse quickly to form bread crumbs. Set the bread crumbs and croutons aside.

Make the artichoke hearts: To prevent the artichokes from browning, fill a large bowl with water and squeeze juice from the lemon halves into it (drop the lemon halves in as well). Throughout the process of trimming the artichokes described below, dip the artichokes into the lemon water to prevent browning.

Using a paring or chef's knife, trim the stem of an artichoke. Next, snap off the tough outer leaves until you reach the tender interior leaves (they should be pale white-green-yellow). Using a paring knife, clean up the stem and the outside of the base of the artichoke by trimming around it. Using a serrated knife, trim the top inch or so of the artichoke, then, using a soupspoon, scoop out the fuzzy innards of the artichoke heart. Put the trimmed artichoke into the lemon water and repeat the process with the remaining artichokes.

In a large pot or Dutch oven over medium-high heat, combine the wine, olive oil, lemon juice, salt, bay leaf, habanero, garlic, and 7 cups water. Bring the liquid to a boil. Gently slide in the artichokes, lower the heat to medium, and simmer until tender, 30 to 45 minutes, removing the habanero after cooking for 15 minutes. Remove the artichokes with a slotted spoon and set aside.

**braised artichoke hearts with
celery root–carrot puree, continued**

Make the celery root–carrot puree: While the
artichokes are simmering, combine the celery
root, carrot, and garlic in a medium saucepan. Add
enough water to cover by 2 inches and place over
medium-high heat. Bring to a simmer, decrease
the heat to medium-low, and simmer until tender,
about 40 minutes. Drain in a colander, reserving
the cooking liquid. Transfer the celery root, carrot, and garlic to a blender. Add the coconut milk,
olive oil, and kosher salt. Puree the mixture, adding
the reserved cooking water if necessary, to form
a spreadable puree. Season with kosher salt and
white pepper to taste.

To serve, smear the celery root-carrot puree onto
a serving platter, top with the artichokes, and
garnish with the croutons and bread crumbs.
Season with flaky sea salt to taste.

"Feather" by Little Dragon from *Machine Dreams*

apple and kohlrabi coleslaw

napa cabbage · red cabbage

makes 4 to 6 servings

This is one of my favorite salads in this book. Since the crunchy apple and kohlrabi are so refreshing, it would make the perfect palate cleanser between heavier courses at dinner, but most often I eat it for a light lunch.

1 cup shredded napa cabbage

1 cup shredded red cabbage

2¼ teaspoons kosher salt, plus more as needed

2 cups kohlrabi matchsticks

2 cups Granny Smith (or other green apple) matchsticks

⅓ cup minced fresh parsley, plus ¼ cup whole leaves

¼ cup fresh lime juice

⅓ cup unseasoned rice vinegar

1 tablespoon shoyu

1 teaspoon coconut palm sugar

½ cup safflower oil

Freshly ground white pepper

Combine the cabbages in a large bowl. Sprinkle with 2 teaspoons of the kosher salt. With clean hands, massage the cabbage until soft and wilted, about 3 minutes. Transfer the cabbage to a colander set in the sink and rinse the bowl. Put a plate on top of the cabbage and weight it (a 28-ounce can of tomatoes works well for this). Let sit for 1 hour. Rinse the cabbage in cold water and let drain for 20 minutes. Wipe the bowl with a clean kitchen towel.

Return the cabbage to the bowl and add the kohlrabi, apples, and minced parsley. Toss well to combine. Set aside.

In a blender, combine the lime juice, vinegar, shoyu, sugar, and ¼ teaspoon salt. With the blender running, slowly pour in the safflower oil through the hole in the lid and blend until emulsified. Season with salt and white pepper to taste.

Pour enough of the dressing over the salad to lightly coat, toss, and garnish with the parsley leaves, then serve.

"Milky Cereal" by LL Cool J from *Mama Said Knock You Out*

kohlrabi kimchi

garlic · ginger · korean red chile powder

makes 1 quart

While I enjoy cabbage-based kimchi, I prefer the firm bite that I get from turnip much more. Inspired by turnip kimchi, I use kohlrabi for this bold and spicy version. You can find gochugaru–red chile powder used in Korean cooking–at Asian markets or online.

1 pound kohlrabi, peeled and cut into large dice

1 tablespoon minced garlic

1½ teaspoons minced fresh ginger

1½ tablespoons gochugaru (Korean red chile powder)

1½ tablespoons sea salt

In a large bowl, combine the kohlrabi, garlic, ginger, and gochugaru and toss together with clean hands. Pack the mixture into a clean quart-size canning jar and set aside.

In a small saucepan, combine the salt and 3 cups water. Bring to a simmer over medium-high heat and simmer until the salt has dissolved. Let cool, then pour the brine into the jar over the kohlrabi. Place fermentation weights or something similar atop the kohlrabi to ensure it stays covered with the brine. Cover with a lid and set aside on the counter for up to 72 hours (the longer it sits at room temperature, the quicker and deeper the fermentation). Transfer to the refrigerator and let the kohlrabi ferment for 1 week before eating. The kimchi will last up to 1 year refrigerated.

"They Say I'm Different" by Betty Davis from *They Say I'm Different*

kohlrabi and carrots

broken lime vinaigrette

makes 4 servings

This quick salad is inspired by do chua, a sweet and crunchy daikon-and-carrot pickle used to enhance Vietnamese bánh mì sandwiches. I toss the vegetables in a broken vinaigrette and top them with peanuts for crunch. Save the remaining dressing for another use.

1 pound kohlrabi, peeled, halved, and thinly sliced with a mandoline

1 pound carrots, peeled and thinly sliced into ribbons with a Y-shape vegetable peeler or mandoline

½ teaspoon minced garlic

1 teaspoon minced fresh ginger

½ cup unseasoned rice vinegar

2 tablespoons fresh lime juice

1 teaspoon minced shallot

1 tablespoon coconut palm sugar

2 tablespoons peanut oil

Kosher salt

½ cup peanuts, toasted, for garnish

Freshly ground white pepper

Transfer the vegetables to a large bowl. Fill the bowl with cold water and ice and set aside for 20 minutes. Drain the vegetables in a colander and set aside to dry for 20 minutes. Gently pat with a clean kitchen towel to absorb any remaining moisture. Dry the bowl and return the vegetables to it.

In a small bowl, whisk together the garlic, ginger, vinegar, lime juice, shallot, sugar, and peanut oil until combined. Season with salt to taste.

To serve, pour enough dressing over the salad to lightly coat and toss. Divide the salad among four plates and top with the peanuts. Season with pepper and serve.

"Melody Maker" by Keith Hudson from *The Hudson Affair: Keith Hudson and Friends*

whole charcoal-roasted kohlrabi

peanut sauce · crushed peanuts · fresno chiles · parsley

makes 4 servings

A lot of people have never heard of kohlrabi, and those who have are often reluctant to try it since it looks a little like an alien when the bulb is held upright and the stems and leaves are hanging below it. I've experimented with many ways of preparing this cruciferous vegetable, but roasting it on charcoal is my favorite by far. Like the Ash-Roasted Sweet Potatoes on page 185, this kohlrabi (see photo on page 91) takes on the smokiness of the coals after sitting over them for at least an hour. Use chunk/lump charcoal as opposed to briquettes, as the latter typically have chemicals that you don't want near your food. If you aren't able to roast the kohlrabi over coals, place them on a baking sheet over a bed of kosher salt and roast them in the oven at 450°F until charred on the outside and tender on the inside, about 1½ hours.

I serve the kohlrabi with a chunky peanut sauce. You'll have enough to use elsewhere (it freezes well), but don't be stingy with it when serving this recipe. To make it a meal, pull together a green salad, fry some green plantains, and make my Farro and Kidney Beans with Burnt Scallions (page 64).

peanut sauce

1 tablespoon peanut oil

1 cup finely diced yellow onion

1 tablespoon minced garlic

½ teaspoon cumin seeds, toasted and ground

1 teaspoon kosher salt, plus more as needed

¼ cup tomato paste

1 tablespoon Bragg Liquid Aminos

¾ cup crunchy unsalted peanut butter

5 cups vegetable stock (page 230)

2 tablespoons ginger juice (see sidebar, page 54)

1 habanero chile, stem intact

kohlrabi

8 Fresno chiles, finely chopped

8 medium kohlrabi (6 to 9½ ounces each)

1 cup crushed roasted peanuts

¼ cup chopped fresh parsley

Flaky sea salt and freshly ground white pepper

2 tablespoons finely-grated lemon zest

Make the peanut sauce: In a Dutch oven, warm the peanut oil over medium-high heat until shimmering. Add the onion and cook until soft, 3 to 4 minutes, then add the garlic, cumin, and salt and stir well to combine. Decrease the heat to low, add the tomato paste and liquid aminos, and cook, stirring often, until the tomato paste starts to darken, about 5 minutes. Stir in the peanut butter and mix well to combine. While stirring, pour in the stock and ginger juice. Add the habanero and simmer, partially covered, stirring occasionally, for 1 hour. Remove and discard the pepper, season the sauce with salt, and set aside.

Make the kohlrabi: Position an oven rack as close as possible to the broiler heat element and preheat the broiler to high.

Place the chiles on a baking sheet, cut-side down, and broil until they are soft and starting to blacken, about 1 minute. Remove from the oven and set aside.

Arrange a generous pile of chunk/lump charcoal in one even layer at the bottom of a grill. Light the charcoal.

When the coals turn white, place the kohlrabi directly on the coals and roast, turning often to ensure even cooking, until the skin is blackened and the interior is tender, 1 to 1½ hours. Poke the kohlrabi with a metal skewer to judge doneness; it should slide in easily with very little resistance. Transfer to a plate to cool. Once the kohlrabi are cool enough to handle, peel them.

Right before serving, warm the peanut sauce over medium heat, adding water to loosen it if necessary.

To serve, generously spread peanut sauce over a serving plate, arrange the kohlrabi on top, then garnish with the chiles, peanuts, and parsley. Sprinkle with flaky salt and lemon zest, a few turns of white pepper, and serve.

"Dust (Reimagined)" by Van Hunt from *Trim (The Reimagined Van Hunt)*

flowers

broccoli, broccoli rabe, and broccolini

cauliflower

broccoli-dill sandwich spread

garlic · umami powder · lemon juice

makes 1¼ cups

Although this recipe is prepared in the way you would generally make a pesto, we will call it an awesome broccoli puree that can be used as a spread for sandwiches like the Pan-Seared Summer Squash Sandwich on Multigrain Bread (page 121). You can also toss it with pasta; just add a little more oil. While this recipe does not use the broccoli stem, don't toss it out; thinly shave it for a veggie stir-fry.

1 tablespoon kosher salt, plus more as needed

1 medium broccoli head, cut into florets, stem reserved for another use

½ cup loosely packed fresh dill

⅓ cup Umami Powder (page 239)

1 large garlic clove, minced

⅓ cup extra-virgin olive oil, plus more as needed

Freshly ground white pepper

Fresh lemon juice

Bring a large pot of water to a boil over high heat. Add the salt and the broccoli. Cook until just tender, about 1 minute. Drain in a colander and run under cold water for a minute or so. Gently pat dry with a clean kitchen towel.

In a food processor, combine the broccoli, dill, umami powder, and garlic and process until finely chopped. Stop the machine and scrape down the sides of the bowl. With the processor running, slowly pour in the olive oil and process until the mixture is smooth. The mixture should be spreadable like a good hummus. If it is too thick, drizzle in additional oil, with the processor running, 1 tablespoon at a time.

Transfer to a bowl and season with salt and white pepper to taste. Add just enough lemon juice to brighten the spread a bit. Pour a thin layer of oil over the sauce and refrigerate, covered, until ready to use. It will last 5 to 7 days refrigerated and 3 to 4 months in the freezer.

"Melting Pot" by Booker T. & the M.G.'s from *Melting Pot*

big beans, buns, and broccoli rabe

royal corona beans · tomatoes · persillade

makes 6 servings

This recipe has everything I want in a good sandwich—toasted homemade bread, hearty protein, and broccoli rabe. That's right—I declare roasted broccoli rabe florets as the new default vegetable for sandwiches, lettuce be damned. My friend Soleil Ho, restaurant critic for the *San Francisco Chronicle*, would likely agree—in her words, "I hate lettuce, but I really hate hot lettuce." This recipe is inspired by bunny chow, a South African dish made by hollowing out a loaf of white bread and filling it with curry. Although the original version was vegetarian, it is more common to find bread stuffed with meaty curries these days. The first time I had bunny chow was at the now-closed South African restaurant Madiba in my old Brooklyn neighborhood. When I had it a second time, prepared by the People's Kitchen Collective at the Museum of the African Diaspora's first Diaspora Dinner, I was blown away.

The popular vegetarian version of bunny chow uses lima beans. I need a meatier and heartier bean for this dish, so I use corona beans—huge, thick-skinned beans with a creamy interior. They work even better than I could have imagined. If you can't find them, you can use cannellini beans instead, but do yourself a favor and order a bag of Royal Corona beans from Rancho Gordo. If you don't have time to make the buns, toasted vegan potato buns will work just fine. Lastly, while this is a sandwich, I imagine folks digging in with a fork and knife.

bread

3 cups unbleached all-purpose flour

¼ cup teff flour

¼ cup almond flour

2 tablespoons raw cane sugar

2 teaspoons instant yeast

¾ teaspoon fine sea salt

1 cup warm water

¼ cup melted coconut oil, plus more for greasing the bowl and work surface and brushing the buns

broccoli rabe

1 teaspoon kosher salt, plus more as needed

1½ pounds broccoli rabe, thick stems trimmed

1 tablespoon extra-virgin olive oil

beans

1 cup dried corona beans, picked over and soaked in water overnight (see page 48)

1 teaspoon kosher salt, plus more as needed

2 tablespoons extra-virgin olive oil

1 cup finely diced yellow onion

1 garlic clove, minced

½ teaspoon minced fresh ginger

1 tablespoon Berbere Spice Blend (page 238)

1 tablespoon tomato paste

1 (14.5-ounce) can diced tomatoes, pureed in a blender

1½ cups diced peeled Yukon gold potatoes (1 large or 2 small)

½ cup Persillade (page 235), for garnish

Flaky sea salt and freshly ground white pepper

Make the bread: In a large bowl, whisk together the flours, sugar, yeast, and salt. Pour in the warm water and the coconut oil. Starting with a wooden spoon and then using your hands, mix to form a shaggy dough. Transfer to a clean countertop and knead to form a soft, stretchy ball of dough, 5 to 7 minutes.

With a towel, wipe the bowl clean, then lightly grease it with oil. Place the dough in the bowl, loosely cover with a clean kitchen towel, and set aside in a warm area until the dough doubles in size, about 1 hour.

Lightly grease a clean work surface. Turn the dough out onto the surface and gently punch it down to deflate it. Divide the dough into six equal pieces and roll each into a taut ball.

Lightly grease a baking sheet and space the balls of dough evenly across the pan. Gently flatten the tops of the dough, cover with a clean kitchen towel, and set aside until the buns have doubled in size, about 1½ hours.

Preheat the oven to 350°F.

Bake the risen buns until golden brown, about 25 minutes. Brush the buns with coconut oil and transfer to a wire rack to cool. Increase the oven temperature to 425°F.

Make the broccoli rabe: Line a baking sheet with parchment paper.

Fill a medium saucepan a little over halfway with water and bring it to a boil over high heat. Add the salt and the broccoli rabe and simmer for 1 minute. Quickly remove from the heat and drain. Dump the broccoli rabe onto a clean kitchen towel and gently squeeze to absorb some of the moisture. Transfer the broccoli rabe to a large bowl, add the olive oil and a pinch of salt, and toss. Transfer to the prepared baking sheet and roast until the florets are tender and the leaves are starting to crisp slightly at the edges, about 20 minutes.

Make the beans: Drain and rinse the beans. Place them in a medium saucepan and add enough water to cover by 4 inches. Bring to a boil over medium-high heat. Remove the lid, decrease the heat to medium-low, and simmer until the beans are softening but still slightly firm, 1 to 1½ hours. Stir in the salt and simmer for 10 minutes more.

Remove from the heat and let the beans cool in their liquid for 1 hour.

Drain the beans, reserving the cooking liquid, and set both aside.

While the beans are cooling, in a large skillet over medium heat, warm the olive oil until shimmering. Add the onion, season with salt, and sauté until starting to brown, 7 to 10 minutes. Add the garlic and ginger and cook until fragrant, 3 to 4 minutes. Add the berbere spice blend and tomato paste and stir to thoroughly combine. Add the tomato puree, potatoes, beans, and 2 cups of the reserved bean cooking liquid. Simmer, partially covered, until the potatoes are fork-tender, about 45 minutes.

To serve, slice the buns in half horizontally, then toast them to your liking. Place the bottom half of each bun on an individual plate. Pile a handful (about ¼ cup) of the broccoli rabe on the bun, spoon a heaping serving of the beans on top of the broccoli rabe, and garnish with persillade. Sprinkle with flaky salt and white pepper, then serve.

"Big Rings" by Drake and Future from *What a Time to Be Alive*

grilled broccoli rabe

charred lemon and spinach sauce ·
aleppo pepper · grilled bread

makes 4 to 6 servings

The day I was testing this recipe, my friend Mark Bittman posted a picture on Instagram of his buddy Daniel grilling in the snow—head enveloped in smoke. Below the picture Mark asked, "Who decided that the most acceptable time to stand next to a giant box of fire is when it's 90 degrees outside?" That was a question I had been thinking about often. While we don't get much snow in Oakland, I spent a lot of time standing in the winter rain testing recipes for this book. It started as a necessity, but after a few times, I really enjoyed the process of grilling while it was drizzling. I could write a few sentences describing how I was subconsciously fostering a connection with the natural world, but that would be a lie. The reality is, when I grilled in the rain, nobody bothered me. No wife. No kids. Just me and a glass of mescal for an hour or so.

Anyway, this is a simple recipe with a big payoff. Two pounds of broccoli rabe might seem like a lot, but once it has been blanched and grilled, it shrinks down a bit. If the stems seem too tough, cut them off and eat just the florets. You could always roast the broccoli rabe in the oven at 425°F until the leaves are crisping and the stems are tender, 10 to 12 minutes, and skip the spinach sauce if you are pressed for time, but do yourself a favor and enjoy that green on green the first time you make this.

1 tablespoon plus
¼ teaspoon kosher salt

2 pounds broccoli rabe,
tough stems trimmed

1 teaspoon extra-virgin
olive oil

1 cup Charred Lemon
and Spinach Sauce
(page 154)

Aleppo pepper,
for garnish

Grilled bread,
for serving

Fill a large bowl with ice and water. Bring a large pot of water to a boil over high heat. Add 1 tablespoon of the salt and the broccoli rabe. Blanch for about 2 minutes. With tongs, transfer the broccoli rabe to the ice water and let cool. Drain and pat dry with a clean kitchen towel.

Heat a grill to high.

In a large bowl, combine the olive oil and remaining ¼ teaspoon salt. Add the broccoli rabe and toss to coat. Grill the broccoli rabe, turning once or twice, until lightly charred, 5 to 7 minutes.

To serve, smear the sauce over a serving plate, pile the broccoli rabe on top, and sprinkle with Aleppo pepper. Serve with grilled bread on the side.

"Big Kids Don't Play" by Grand Puba from *Reel to Reel*

charred brassicas

tahini · chermoula · pomegranates ·
fleur de sel · olive oil

makes 4 to 6 servings

This recipe was contributed by one of the most
talented chefs I know, Monifa Dayo. I invited her to
join a crew of folks I put together to cater Angela
Davis's seventy-fifth birthday party in 2019. The
whole meal was impressive, but this dish was
undoubtedly a standout. It's pretty simple; cauliflower and Romanesco are charred in the oven,
then placed atop a flavorful tahini sauce and
drizzled with chermoula. The dish is finished with
pomegranate seeds, fleur de sel, and olive oil.

tahini sauce

1 cup tahini

Juice of 2 large lemons

½ teaspoon kosher salt

chermoula

2 shallots, finely diced

1 cup apple cider
vinegar

2 tablespoons
kosher salt

3 walnut-size knobs
fresh ginger, peeled

1 serrano chile

1 green garlic stalk

1 bunch parsley,
coarsely chopped

1 bunch cilantro,
coarsely chopped

1 bunch marjoram,
coarsely chopped

Zest and juice of
2 large lemons

Extra-virgin olive oil

brassicas

1 cauliflower head,
cored and cut into
florets

1 Romanesco head,
cored and cut into
florets

Extra-virgin olive oil

Kosher salt and freshly
ground black pepper

2 tablespoons
fleur de sel

Fresh lemon juice

Seeds from
2 pomegranates

Marash chile flakes,
for dusting

Make the tahini sauce: In a small bowl, combine the
tahini, lemon juice, and salt and stir well. Set aside.

Make the chermoula: Place the shallots in a small
mason jar, add enough of the vinegar to cover
them, and stir in the salt. Set aside for 1 hour.

With a Microplane, shave the ginger and serrano
into a bowl. In a mortar, pound the green garlic into
a paste with the pestle. Add it to the bowl with the
ginger and serrano. Drain the shallots, reserving the
vinegar, and add them to the bowl. Add the parsley,
cilantro, marjoram, lemon zest, lemon juice, and
1½ tablespoons of the reserved vinegar. While
whisking, pour in enough olive oil until the mixture
pours easily from a spoon. Set aside.

Prepare the cauliflower and Romanesco: Position
an oven rack as close as possible to the broiler
heat element and preheat the broiler to high. Line
a baking sheet with parchment paper.

Place the cauliflower and Romanesco florets in
a large bowl, drizzle liberally with olive oil, and
aggressively season with salt and black pepper.
Evenly spread the florets on the prepared baking
sheet. Broil until charred and tender, 3 to 5 minutes.
Set aside to cool briefly before serving.

To serve, pour a pool of the tahini sauce onto a
serving plate. Place the brassicas over the sauce.
Spoon more tahini sauce on top of the brassicas
and drizzle with the chermoula. Drizzle with olive
oil, sprinkle with the fleur de sel, and squeeze lemon
juice over the top. Sprinkle with the pomegranate
seeds, dust with chile flakes, and serve.

"La Vida Es un Carnaval" by Angélique Kidjo from *Celia*

creamy cauliflower

olive oil · salt · lemon juice

makes 4 to 6 servings

This is a quick and easy side dish that my five-year-old would eat every day if she could. The cauliflower puree alone is proper, but sometimes I fold in whipped potatoes to create a lighter, fluffier cousin of mashed potatoes. You can prepare this as a silky-smooth side dish by adding a little more water, or serve it as a mounded scoop atop rich and spicy dishes (like my Stewed Red Lentils on page 60) to round them out, like one might use sour cream.

1 medium cauliflower head (about 1 pound), cored and coarsely chopped

¾ teaspoon kosher salt, plus more as needed

5 tablespoons extra-virgin olive oil

Fresh lemon juice

Freshly ground black pepper

In a food processor, pulse the cauliflower until it is broken down into small, grainlike pieces about the size of raw couscous.

In a medium saucepan, bring ½ cup water to a boil over high heat. Add the cauliflower, decrease the heat to medium, and partially cover. Steam, stirring occasionally, until the cauliflower is tender and most of the water has evaporated, about 10 minutes. Remove the lid and cook, stirring frequently with a rubber spatula, until the cauliflower no longer loses liquid when pressed with the spatula, about 5 minutes more. The cauliflower should now have the texture of fluffy steamed couscous.

Rinse out the food processor bowl and return the cauliflower to it. Add the salt. With the processor running, slowly pour in the olive oil through the feed tube until it is pureed but thick. At this point, the cauliflower is at a good consistency for topping another dish or serving in mounded scoops. If you'd like a thinner puree to spread across a plate, with the food processor running, slowly add 3 to 4 tablespoons water through the feed tube. Transfer to a medium bowl.

Before serving, taste the puree and season with lemon juice, pepper, and additional salt.

"Wu-Tang Forever" by Drake from *Nothing Was the Same*

hot sauce–soaked cauliflower over whole-wheat bread

apple and kohlrabi coleslaw · dill-pickled fennel

makes 4 servings

I was hesitant to include this recipe. Over the years, I have avoided replicating trendy dishes through a vegan lens, but I had to go there with this one, which is my take on Nashville Hot Chicken. It has all the elements that make that dish so popular: crispy cauliflower soaked in a fiery hot sauce, a cooling side slaw, tart pickles, and a simple piece of bread for sopping up the sauce. This is bar food that would go well with a beer. My technique for frying the cauliflower is a modified version of one that my friend Samin Nosrat introduced in the *New York Times Magazine*.

1⅓ cups white rice flour

⅔ cup tapioca flour

2 tablespoons plus ½ teaspoon kosher salt, plus more as needed

2 teaspoons Louisiana hot sauce, plus more to taste

2 small cauliflower heads (about 1 pound each), trimmed and cut into four ½-inch-thick steaks

½ cup safflower oil, plus more for frying

2 teaspoons minced garlic

2 teaspoons cayenne pepper

2 teaspoons chili powder

2 teaspoons smoked paprika

1 teaspoon coconut palm sugar

4 slices whole-wheat bread, toasted

Apple and Kohlrabi Coleslaw (page 87)

Dill-Pickled Fennel (page 44)

Preheat the oven to 200°F. Place a cooling rack in a rimmed baking sheet.

In a large bowl, whisk together the flours, 2 tablespoons of the salt, and hot sauce. Whisk in 1¾ cups water, adding more as needed, to form a mixture that is the consistency of a wet pancake batter. Season to taste with additional hot sauce and salt.

Place two of the cauliflower steaks in the batter and turn to coat. Let marinate while you heat the oil.

Pour about ½ inch of oil into a deep cast-iron skillet or Dutch oven. Place over medium-high heat and bring oil to 350°F.

When the oil is hot, remove the cauliflower steaks from the batter, gently shaking off excess, and carefully transfer to the hot oil. Let fry until deeply browned on the first side, 8 to 10 minutes. Flip and fry until deeply browned on the second side, 4 to 6 minutes.

Meanwhile, move the remaining two cauliflower steaks to the bowl with the batter and turn to coat.

When the first two steaks are done frying, transfer them to the prepared rack on the baking sheet. Place in the oven to keep warm. Fry the remaining two cauliflower steaks in the same way as the first.

While the last two steaks are frying, prepare the spicy oil: In a small skillet, combine the ½ cup safflower oil and the garlic and set the pan over medium heat. Whisk in the cayenne, chili powder, paprika, sugar, and remaining ½ teaspoon salt and simmer until the garlic starts to smell fragrant and turns golden. Remove from the heat.

Once all of the cauliflower is done frying and transferred to the oven, warm the spicy oil over medium-high heat, whisking to combine the spices. Remove from the heat.

Remove the cauliflower from the oven, then, still on the rack, brush each steak on all sides with the spicy oil. Use as much or as little as you and your guests can handle.

To serve, divide the bread among four plates, top each with a cauliflower steak, and serve with coleslaw and pickled fennel alongside.

"Cold Sweat" by James Brown from *20 All-Time Greatest Hits!*

dirty cauliflower

tempeh · porcini mushrooms ·
cremini mushrooms · scallions · parsley

makes 4 to 6 servings

Yeah, I know. You've had "cauliflower rice" before and it sucked. Well, this ain't that. Although I employ the method of pulsing cauliflower in a food processor to yield ricelike pieces, think of this as a complexly flavored cauliflower recipe that could easily be a main. It's actually a grain-free reinvention of my Dirty Millet from *Afro-Vegan*, but even better. The cauliflower is sautéed quickly so it still has a little bite, the tempeh and mushrooms add a "meaty" texture and loads of umami, and the scallions and parsley brighten each bite.

pro tip If you are trying to infuse plant-based dishes with umami, use dried porcini mushrooms.

½ ounce dried sliced porcini mushrooms

2 cups boiling water

½ (2½-pound) cauliflower head, leaves removed, chopped into small pieces

5 tablespoons extra-virgin olive oil

8 ounces cremini mushrooms, cut into ½-inch-thick slices

Kosher salt

5 ounces tempeh, crumbled

1 cup finely diced yellow onion

1 cup finely diced green bell pepper

½ cup finely diced celery

¼ teaspoon cayenne pepper

½ teaspoon minced garlic

1 tablespoon tamari

Freshly ground black pepper

3 scallions, green parts only, thinly sliced on an angle, for serving

⅓ cup chopped fresh flat-leaf parsley, for serving

Put the porcini mushrooms in a small heatproof bowl and pour in the boiling water, making sure it covers the mushrooms. Use a small plate or the like to weight down the mushrooms to ensure they stay submerged. Soak for 20 minutes, then drain through a fine-mesh sieve set over a bowl, reserving the soaking liquid. Finely chop the porcini mushrooms and set them aside. Strain the soaking liquid to remove any grit and set aside.

While the porcini are soaking, in a food processor, pulse the cauliflower until it is broken down into small, grainlike pieces, using five to ten 1-second pulses. Transfer to a medium bowl.

Line a plate with paper towels and set it nearby. In a large skillet, warm 2 tablespoons of the olive oil over medium-high heat until shimmering. Add the cremini mushrooms and cook, undisturbed, until brown and crisp on one side, about 5 minutes. Sprinkle with salt, then flip the mushrooms and cook until well browned and tender, about 3 minutes more. Transfer to the prepared plate and set aside.

Add the remaining 3 tablespoons olive oil to the skillet. Add the crumbled tempeh and cook over medium-high heat, stirring occasionally, until it begins to brown, 1 to 3 minutes. Lower the heat to medium; add the onion, bell pepper, celery, cayenne, and ½ teaspoon salt and sauté until the vegetables start to soften, about 5 minutes. Add the garlic and cook until fragrant, about 2 minutes. Drizzle the tamari over the mixture and stir to combine. Scrape the mixture into a medium bowl.

In the same skillet, combine the chopped porcinis and 1 cup of the reserved soaking liquid and bring to a simmer over high heat. Add the cauliflower and cook, stirring frequently, until the cauliflower is just tender, 3 to 5 minutes.

Transfer the cauliflower to the bowl with the vegetables and tempeh. Add the cremini mushrooms and toss to combine. Taste and season with salt and black pepper, transfer to a serving bowl, and garnish with the scallions and parsley before serving.

"Flat of the Blade" by Massive Attack from *Heligoland*

panko-crusted cauliflower and coconut curry

garlic oil · parsley

makes 4 servings

My Kenyan college buddy Kabui once described a chicken and coconut curry dish called kuku paka, originating from Kenya's coastal region. Here I adapted a coconut curry recipe that I created a few years ago with a nod to that conversation with Kabui. I pair it with roasted cauliflower topped with parsley-flecked panko bread crumbs.

coconut curry

3 tablespoons coconut oil

1 teaspoon yellow mustard seeds

1 cup finely diced yellow onion

1 tablespoon minced garlic

1 tablespoon minced fresh ginger

1½ teaspoons Garam Masala (page 239)

1 teaspoon chili powder

½ teaspoon ground turmeric

2 bay leaves

1 teaspoon kosher salt

1 (14-ounce) can diced tomatoes, with their juices

1 (14-ounce) can unsweetened coconut milk

1 (2-inch) cinnamon stick

cauliflower

2 large cauliflower heads (about 2 pounds each), leaves removed and stems trimmed so they sit flat

1½ teaspoons coarse sea salt

½ cup Garlic Oil, plus Garlic Chips (page 232)

1 cup panko bread crumbs

¾ cup packed fresh flat-leaf parsley leaves, plus more for garnish

Cooked black rice, for serving

Make the curry: In a sauté pan, warm the coconut oil over medium heat. Add the mustard seeds and cook until they pop, 2 to 3 minutes. Add the onion and sauté for 5 to 7 minutes, until soft. Add the garlic, ginger, garam masala, chili powder, turmeric, bay leaves, and salt and sauté for 2 minutes more. Remove from the heat, discard the bay leaves, and set aside.

Place the tomatoes and their juices in a large bowl. With clean hands, squeeze the tomatoes to break them into smaller pieces. Transfer them to the pan with the onion. Add the coconut milk, then fill the coconut milk can one-quarter full with water and stir it well to incorporate any leftover coconut milk. Add this to the pan along with the cinnamon stick and mix well. Simmer until the sauce has thickened, about 20 minutes, removing the cinnamon stick after 5 minutes.

Make the cauliflower: Preheat the oven to 450°F. Line a baking sheet with parchment paper. In a large pot, bring 4 quarts water to a boil over high heat. Stand one head of cauliflower on the stem end and, using a sharp chef's knife, cut two 1-inch-thick slices, cutting through the core so the slices hold together. Repeat with the other head (reserve the unused portions for another use).

Add 1 teaspoon of the salt to the boiling water and, one at a time, use tongs to gently lower the cauliflower slices into the water. Cover and cook for 2½ minutes. Using two slotted spoons, gently transfer the cauliflower slices to a colander to cool.

Gently transfer the cauliflower slices to the prepared baking sheet. Brush ¼ cup of the garlic oil over the slices, coating them on both sides. Roast until the cauliflower is browned, about 25 minutes.

While the cauliflower is roasting, in a food processor, combine the panko, parsley, and remaining ½ teaspoon salt and process until the mixture is well blended. Transfer the mixture to a small bowl and pour in the remaining ¼ cup garlic oil. Mix well.

Remove the baking sheet from the oven and spoon an even coating of the panko mixture over each slice of cauliflower. Switch the oven to broil on low, return the baking sheet to the oven, and broil until the panko mixture starts to bubble and brown.

To serve, ladle the curry into four shallow bowls, place a cauliflower slice in each bowl, and garnish with the garlic chips and some parsley. Serve with black rice.

"Kajo Golo Weka" by The Eagles Lupopo from *Kenya Special*

fruits

quick-pickled sweet peppers

rice vinegar · white vinegar · raw cane sugar

makes two ½-pint jars

This is a simple recipe to make use of mini sweet peppers. I often add them to sandwiches, and they are always a hit when I make vegan cheese boards for parties (Miyoko's vegan cheese for the win!). If you can't get mini sweet peppers from a farmers' market, I have seen mixed bags of them in the produce section of many conventional supermarkets.

8 ounces mini sweet peppers, thinly sliced into rings

½ cup unseasoned rice vinegar

¼ cup white vinegar

2 tablespoons raw cane sugar

1½ teaspoons kosher salt

1 large garlic clove, smashed

Divide the peppers evenly between two clean ½-pint canning jars, leaving ½ inch of headspace at the top. Set aside.

In a small saucepan, combine the vinegars, sugar, salt, garlic, and ¼ cup water and heat over medium heat, stirring occasionally, until the liquid is hot to the touch and the sugar has completely dissolved, about 3 minutes. Remove the garlic with a fork and discard. Divide the liquid evenly between the jars. Set aside to cool for 30 minutes, seal the jars, then refrigerate for at least 1 day before serving. The pickled peppers should keep in the refrigerator for up to 1 month.

"Peter Piper" by Run-D.M.C. from *Raising Hell*

spicy stewed peppers

bell peppers · sweet peppers · onions · hot pepper vinegar

makes 4 to 6 servings

Inspired by peperonata, a traditional Italian stew made of onions and bell peppers, this is one of my go-to dishes during the summer. Plus, it's a great recipe for using the surplus of bell peppers in our garden. While peperonata is often slow-stewed for over an hour, this is a quick and easy dish— once your ingredients are prepped, it takes just 15 minutes to cook. These peppers are perfect for cookouts, since they can be served at room temperature. Present them as a side dish or as a topping for crusty bread or crackers.

3 tablespoons extra-virgin olive oil

1 cup thinly sliced yellow onion

1 large red bell pepper, thinly sliced

1 large yellow bell pepper, thinly sliced

1 large orange bell pepper, thinly sliced

1 cup thinly sliced assorted mini sweet peppers

½ teaspoon kosher salt, plus more as needed

2 tablespoons Sweet Hot Pepper Vinegar (page 234), or to taste

Freshly ground white pepper

In a large skillet, warm the olive oil over medium heat until shimmering. Add the onion and cook until just starting to caramelize, about 10 minutes. Add the bell peppers and mini sweet peppers and cook until softened, about 5 minutes. Pour in ¼ cup water and add the salt. Simmer, partially covered, until the vegetables are meltingly tender, about 15 minutes. Remove from the heat and pour in the vinegar. Taste, season with salt and white pepper, and serve in a large bowl.

"Summertime (UFO Remix)" by Sarah Vaughan from *Verve Remixed*

blistered shishito pepper salad

creamy miso-ginger dressing · frisée · gomasio

makes 4 servings

One of my favorite fall snacks is blistered shishitos–Japanese chile peppers. They typically have a mild, sweet flavor that makes them delicious to eat on their own. In restaurants, they are often served with a simple shoyu sauce or something acidic like cut lemons and limes or a ponzu sauce. I prefer eating them with a creamy dipping sauce to chill out the heat of any hotter peppers, so I created this miso-ginger dressing to pair with them. You can serve the charred peppers and dressing as an appetizer, or complete this full recipe to level up to a bright salad. Since early fall is the peak season for shishito peppers and frisée–a small curly endive–they go together beautifully. The bittersweet taste of both vegetables is balanced by the vibrant dressing. A sprinkling of gomasio, a Japanese condiment made of unhulled sesame seeds and salt, adds another layer of flavor.

Make the dressing: In a blender, combine the tofu, miso, sugar, vinegar, lemon juice, garlic, and ginger. With the blender running, slowly pour in the peanut oil through the hole in the lid and blend until creamy. Season with the salt, if desired, and set aside.

Make the salad: Line a baking sheet with a paper towel and set it nearby. In a large cast-iron skillet, heat 2 tablespoons of safflower oil over medium-high heat until shimmering. Add enough peppers to fit comfortably in the pan and cook, shaking the pan occasionally for even blistering, until the peppers are charred and tender, about 4 minutes. Transfer to the prepared baking sheet. Repeat this, adding more safflower oil with each round, until all the peppers are blistered. Sprinkle the peppers with salt.

To serve, put the frisée in a medium bowl and add just enough of the dressing to lightly coat.

Smear a little dressing onto each of four plates, top each with a handful of peppers, and evenly divide the frisée among them. Drizzle a little more dressing on top, sprinkle with gomasio, and serve.

"Tempo de Amor" by Smokey & Miho from *The Two EPs*

creamy miso-ginger dressing

¼ cup silken tofu

1 heaping tablespoon white miso paste

½ teaspoon coconut palm sugar

1 tablespoon unseasoned rice vinegar

1 tablespoon fresh lemon juice

½ teaspoon minced garlic

2 teaspoons minced fresh ginger

2 tablespoons peanut oil

½ teaspoon kosher salt (optional)

salad

Safflower oil, for blistering the peppers

8 ounces shishito peppers

Kosher salt

6 ounces frisée (1 large head), white and light green parts only, torn into bite-size pieces

Gomasio, for garnish

hoppin' john–stuffed peppers

creamy red pepper sauce · scallion oil · fried and fresh scallions

makes 4 servings

I was inspired to make this recipe (see photo on page 116) after having a remarkable dinner at Hart's Restaurant in Brooklyn with my good friend, the brilliant filmmaker Shalini Kantayya. Hart's packed farm-fresh banana peppers with Hoppin' John—a black-eyed peas and rice dish popular in the South—and it spoke to my soul. Fresh banana peppers may be difficult for some to obtain, so I call for yellow bell peppers instead. If you have access to banana peppers, however, by all means use them.

hoppin' john

¾ cup black-eyed peas, picked over and soaked overnight in water plus 1 tablespoon kosher salt

1 bay leaf

1 large yellow onion: half diced, half left intact

5 garlic cloves: 3 cut in half, 2 minced

1 dried red chile

2½ teaspoons kosher salt

½ cup long-grain brown rice, rinsed and soaked overnight in water plus 1 tablespoon vinegar

2 tablespoons extra-virgin olive oil

2 tablespoons sun-dried tomato paste

¼ teaspoon cayenne pepper

2 tablespoons Bragg Liquid Aminos

2 cups vegetable stock (page 230)

red pepper sauce

6 tablespoons extra-virgin olive oil

1 cup diced yellow onion

½ teaspoon ground cumin

⅛ teaspoon cayenne pepper

2 teaspoons coarse sea salt

3 large garlic cloves, minced

1 teaspoon minced, seeded habanero chile

1½ cups canned whole tomatoes, with their juices

2 large red bell peppers, roasted (see sidebar, page 22), seeded, and coarsely chopped

½ cup Cashew Cream (page 231)

2 tablespoons fresh lemon juice

1 tablespoon apple cider vinegar

fried scallions

½ cup safflower oil

6 scallions, very thinly sliced on an angle

Coarse sea salt

bell peppers

4 large yellow bell peppers or banana peppers

1 tablespoon fine sea salt, plus more as needed

Scallion Oil (page 233), for serving

2 tablespoons minced fresh scallions, for serving

Flaky sea salt, for finishing

Freshly ground white pepper

Make the Hoppin' John: Drain and rinse the black-eyed peas. Put them in a medium saucepan and add enough water to cover them by 2 inches. Bring the water to a boil over high heat. Skim off any foam and decrease the heat to medium-low. Add the bay leaf, onion half, halved garlic cloves, and dried chile. Partially cover and simmer until just tender, 45 minutes to 1 hour (the cooking time will greatly depend on the freshness of the beans). Once the beans are just tender, add 1 teaspoon of the salt and simmer for 10 more minutes. Drain the beans. Remove the bay leaf, onion, garlic, and chile and discard them. Set the beans aside.

Drain the rice and place it in a small bowl.

In a large Dutch oven, warm the olive oil over medium heat until shimmering. Add the diced onion and the remaining 1½ teaspoons salt and cook, stirring often, until the onion starts to brown, 10 to 12 minutes. Add the tomato paste, minced garlic, cayenne, and rice and cook, stirring with a wooden spoon, until the rice starts smelling nutty, about 2 minutes.

Add the liquid aminos and stock and bring to a boil. Gently stir in the black-eyed peas. Return to a boil, decrease the heat to low, cover, and cook until most of the liquid has evaporated (the mixture should be slightly moist to yield moist finished peppers), about 50 minutes. Remove from the heat and let sit, covered, for 10 minutes to finish steaming the rice. Transfer the Hoppin' John to a large bowl and set aside. Clean the Dutch oven.

Make the red pepper sauce: While the Hoppin' John is cooking, in a medium saucepan, warm the olive oil over medium-low heat until shimmering. Add the onion, cumin, cayenne, and salt and sauté until the onion just starts to brown, 10 to 12 minutes.

Stir in the garlic and chile and sauté until fragrant, 3 to 4 minutes more, then transfer the mixture to a blender. Add the tomatoes with their juices, roasted peppers, cashew cream, lemon juice, vinegar, and ¾ cup water and puree until smooth.

Make the fried scallions: In a small skillet, heat the safflower oil over medium heat until shimmering. Add the scallions and fry, stirring frequently, until deeply browned and crisp, 3 to 5 minutes. Remove the skillet from the heat. Use a slotted spoon to transfer the scallions to a paper towel–lined plate and sprinkle with salt. Let cool completely before serving.

Make the peppers: Preheat the oven to 400°F.

In a large pot, bring 3 quarts water to a boil over high heat. Pour about 1 cup of the red pepper sauce into the Dutch oven.

Meanwhile, slice the bell peppers in half lengthwise and discard the ribs and seeds, scraping the ribs with a spoon to ensure a smooth interior. With a paring knife, cut two ½-inch slits in the sides of each pepper to allow the sauce to seep through when cooking.

Add the salt and the peppers to the boiling water and cook until just tender but still crisp, 3 to 4 minutes. With tongs, transfer the peppers to a cutting board or large plate. Lightly season the peppers with salt.

Fill each pepper with a heaping portion of Hoppin' John, packing the mixture in firmly. Place the peppers, filling-side up, in the sauce in the Dutch oven. They should fit snugly. Pour in additional red pepper sauce as needed to come three-quarters of the way up the sides of the peppers. Loosely cover the peppers with aluminum foil and bake until the peppers are tender and heated through, 45 minutes to 1 hour. Transfer the peppers to a plate.

Serve family style or spread about ¼ cup of the red pepper sauce over each of four plates and place two bell pepper halves on each plate. Drizzle each pepper with scallion oil and garnish with the fried scallions and some fresh scallions. Season with a sprinkle of flaky salt and white pepper and serve.

"Jumpin' Jive" by Cab Calloway from *Hi De Ho Man: Cab Calloway Classics*

oven-roasted zucchini

collard-peanut pesto · roasted peanuts

makes 4 servings; 1 cup pesto

Forks down, my favorite way of preparing summer squash is grilling. When that method isn't convenient, I use this simple oven-roasting technique instead. Good olive oil, salt, and pepper are enough to bring out the best of garden-fresh zucchini and other squashes, but I created a vibrantly colored, mouth-watering collard-peanut pesto to add a little flair to this dish. Rather than tossing the zucchini in the pesto, however, I simply add dollops of it to the bowl for people to incorporate as much as they like into their individual servings. This recipe is inspired by *courgettes avec des arachides* (French for "zucchini with peanuts"), a classic dish from the north-central African country Chad, but feel free to experiment with other summer squashes (pattypan, crookneck, zucchetta)–dealer's choice.

Make the pesto: In a food processor, combine the collards, peanuts, miso, and garlic and blend until it forms a chunky paste. While the food processor is running, slowly pour in the olive oil through the feed tube, adding more if needed to reach your desired consistency. Season with salt, pepper, and additional lemon juice to taste. Set aside.

Make the zucchini: Preheat the oven to 450°F. Line a baking sheet with parchment paper.

In a large bowl, toss the zucchini with the olive oil and salt, then spread the zucchini over the baking sheet in one even layer. Roast until the zucchini is brown around the edges, 18 to 20 minutes. To serve, transfer the zucchini to a bowl and give it a few turns of pepper. Next, drop in a few heaping dollops of pesto so that people can scoop as much as they'd like when serving themselves, adding more pesto to the bowl as needed. Pile the peanuts in a small serving bowl and present alongside the zucchini.

For any leftover pesto, pour a thin layer of olive oil over it, cover, and refrigerate for up to 1 week.

"Al Salam Alena" by Mounira Mitchell from *Chili Houritki*

collard-peanut pesto

2 cups loosely packed stemmed, chopped collard leaves

1/3 cup roasted peanuts

3 tablespoons white miso paste

1 teaspoon minced garlic

1 tablespoon lemon juice, plus more as needed

1/2 cup olive oil, plus more as needed

Kosher salt

Freshly ground black pepper

oven-roasted zucchini

4 medium zucchini (about 1 1/2 pounds total), cut into 1/2-inch dice

1 tablespoon extra-virgin olive oil

1/2 teaspoon kosher salt

Freshly ground black pepper

1/2 cup chopped roasted peanuts

yellow squash soup

coconut cream · crushed pecans ·
herbs and spices

makes 4 to 6 servings

This coconut milk–laced soup is a fun way to use crookneck or straightneck yellow squash during the summer. The flavor profile of the soup is inspired by herbs and spices that one would find in Jamaican jerk seasonings. Many of them are pureed into the soup. Others go into a topping that includes pecans, thyme, cinnamon, allspice, nutmeg, and salt. Sprinkle it on along with coconut cream and fresh cilantro to add texture and visual interest. You can certainly puree this soup in the pot using an immersion blender, but you need to ladle the soup into a high-powered blender and puree it if you want it to be ultra-silky smooth.

½ cup chopped
raw pecans

2 teaspoons fresh
thyme

¼ teaspoon
ground cinnamon

¼ teaspoon
ground allspice

¼ teaspoon freshly
grated nutmeg

¼ teaspoon flaky
sea salt

¼ cup coconut oil

1½ cups finely diced
yellow onions

1 teaspoon raw
cane sugar

1 teaspoon kosher salt,
plus more as needed

2 teaspoons
minced garlic

1 tablespoon finely
grated fresh ginger

½ teaspoon minced
seeded Scotch bonnet
or habanero chile

2 pounds crookneck
or straightneck yellow
squash, sliced into
1-inch-thick rounds

4 cups vegetable stock
(page 230)

1½ cups unsweetened
canned coconut milk

Freshly ground
black pepper

Coconut Cream
(page 231)

¼ cup minced fresh
cilantro, plus ⅓ cup
loosely packed
cilantro leaves

In a food processor, combine the pecans, thyme, cinnamon, allspice, nutmeg, and flaky salt and pulse until the pecans are coarsely ground.

Warm a medium skillet over medium heat. Tip in the pecan mixture and toast, stirring often to prevent burning, until fragrant, about 1 minute. Scrape the mixture into a bowl and set aside.

In a large saucepan, warm the coconut oil over medium heat. Add the onions, sugar, and kosher salt, decrease the heat to low, and cook, stirring often, until starting to caramelize, 15 to 20 minutes. Add the garlic, ginger, and chile and cook until the garlic is fragrant, about 3 minutes. Add the squash and the stock, raise the heat to medium-high, and bring to a simmer. Decrease the heat to low and simmer until the squash is tender, about 30 minutes.

Working in batches, carefully transfer the soup to a blender and puree until smooth, then return the soup to the saucepan (or blend the soup directly in the pan with an immersion blender). Add the coconut milk and warm through over low heat. Add a little water to thin the soup, if necessary (the soup should pour easily from a spoon). Taste and season with salt and pepper.

To serve, ladle the soup into bowls. Garnish with coconut cream, the spiced pecan mixture, and the cilantro. Serve.

"Dub Money" by Horace Andy from *Dubbed in Kingston*
(Bunny "Striker" Lee 50th Anniversary Edition)

pan-seared summer squash sandwiches on multigrain bread

broccoli-dill sauce · heirloom tomato · pickled sweet peppers · arugula

makes 2 servings

There's a bakery across from my gym that serves a pretty awesome veggie sandwich. It's seasonal, so the ingredients change accordingly, but the core elements are all the same: freshly baked bread, pesto, and fresh and pickled vegetables. Instead of spending $12 a pop, I started making my own at home. Get creative with the summer squashes you use, and feel free to throw in some Marinated Trumpet Mushrooms (page 162).

4 tablespoons extra-virgin olive oil	Broccoli-Dill Sandwich Spread (page 94)
1 medium zucchini (about 5 ounces), sliced lengthwise into ½-inch-thick slices	1 medium heirloom tomato, thinly sliced
1 medium yellow squash (about 5 ounces), sliced lengthwise into ½-inch-thick slices	1½ cups arugula
	¼ cup Quick-Pickled Sweet Peppers (page 110)
Kosher salt	Flaky sea salt and freshly ground black pepper
4 slices multigrain sandwich bread, toasted	

Line a baking sheet with paper towels or a clean kitchen towel.

In a large cast-iron skillet, warm 2 tablespoons of the olive oil over high heat until shimmering. Arrange a single layer of the zucchini and squash slices in the pan, sprinkle with kosher salt, and sear until golden brown, 3 to 5 minutes. Using a fork, gently flip the slices, lightly sprinkle with kosher salt, and cook until browned on the second side, about 2½ minutes. Transfer to the prepared baking sheet. Add the remaining 2 tablespoons olive oil to the skillet and repeat with the remaining zucchini and squash.

Lay 2 slices of the bread on a clean work surface. Generously spread each slice with broccoli-dill sauce. Divide the seared zucchini and squash between the slices, ensuring that each sandwich has a mix of the two. Top with the tomato slices, arugula, and pickled peppers. Sprinkle each sandwich with flaky salt and black pepper.

Top with the remaining bread and press down gently, then slice each sandwich in half and serve.

"Back on My Regimen" by stic.man from *The Workout*

tempura-fried squash blossoms with eggplant-almond stuffing

corn puree · sautéed corn and zucchini · basil · peach filfel chuma

makes 4 servings

Summer officially starts when you make this dish for a cookout. This is peak party food—seasonal, salty, colorful, crunchy, dredged, and delicious. The idea for this recipe came after I read an article about ancient Africans making cheese. The piece described how archeological scientists at the University of Bristol in the United Kingdom analyzed organic residuals on pottery in the Libyan Sahara and discovered the remains of dairy products made from cow's, goat's, and sheep's milk, dating back to between 7,200 and 5,800 years ago. Around the time I read the article, summer squash was at its peak. I saw some beautiful blossoms at the market and created this recipe, inspired by the classic cheese-stuffed squash blossoms. This flavorful eggplant-almond stuffing contrasts brilliantly with the crunchy coating on the blossoms. Keeping it seasonal, I serve the fried blossoms with a simply sautéed mixture of fresh sweet corn and zucchini.

corn puree

2 tablespoons extra-virgin olive oil

1 teaspoon minced garlic

3 cups fresh sweet corn kernels (from 4 large ears)

1 cup vegetable stock (page 230)

Kosher salt

Freshly ground black pepper

Juice of 1 large lemon

sautéed corn and zucchini

1 tablespoon extra-virgin olive oil

1½ cups diced zucchini

Kernels from 3 ears fresh sweet corn

Kosher salt

Freshly ground white pepper

squash blossoms

1 medium eggplant

1 cup slivered blanched almonds

2 tablespoons Umami Powder (page 239)

2 tablespoons minced basil

1 tablespoon yellow miso paste

1 tablespoon fresh lemon juice, plus more as needed

¼ teaspoon cayenne pepper

Kosher salt

12 large squash blossoms, stems intact, pistils removed

Vegetable oil, for frying

1¼ cups flour

¾ cup chilled club soda

Peach Filfel Chuma (recipe follows), for serving

Make the corn puree: In a saucepan over medium heat, combine the olive oil and garlic and cook, stirring often, until the garlic smells fragrant, 2 to 3 minutes. Add the corn and cook, stirring often, until tender, about 5 minutes. Add the vegetable stock and stir well to combine.

Transfer the contents of the saucepan to a blender and puree until smooth. Pour back into the sauce-pan and simmer over medium-low heat, stirring occasionally, until the puree starts to thicken, 10 to 15 minutes. Add the lemon juice and season with salt and pepper to taste and set aside.

Make the corn and zucchini: In a Dutch oven over medium heat, warm the oil until shimmering. Add the zucchini, cover, and cook, shaking the pan occasionally, until the zucchini is tender, about 5 minutes. Add the corn and continue cooking, stirring often, until the corn is heated through and most of the liquid has evaporated, about 3 minutes. Season with salt and pepper to taste. Transfer the

corn and zucchini to a serving bowl. Wipe the pot clean with a kitchen towel.

Make the squash blossoms: Preheat the oven to 425°F. Place the eggplant on a baking sheet and roast until very soft, about 45 minutes. Let cool for about 10 minutes.

Slice the eggplant in half, then scoop out its flesh into a fine-mesh strainer set over a medium bowl. Press the eggplant with a spatula or the back of a spoon to extract as much of its liquid as possible. You should have about 1 cup of eggplant. Transfer to a food processor and add the almonds, umami powder, basil, miso, lemon juice, cayenne, and ¾ teaspoon salt. Process until well blended. Season to taste with additional salt and lemon juice.

Gently open the petals of each blossom and stuff a heaping tablespoon of the eggplant mixture down toward the base. Twist the tops of the petals together and transfer to a plate.

Fill the Dutch oven you used for the corn and zucchini with vegetable oil to a depth of about 2 inches and heat the oil over medium-high heat to 350°F. Line a plate with paper towels and set it nearby.

In a large bowl, whisk together the flour and 1 teaspoon salt. When the oil is close to the right temperature, add the club soda to the flour mixture and whisk until just combined. Some small lumps are fine; be careful not to overmix.

Dip a few of the stuffed blossoms into the batter to coat. Gently shake off any excess batter, then transfer the blossoms to the hot oil and fry until golden brown all over, about 90 seconds per side. Transfer to the paper towel–lined plate and sprinkle with a little salt. Repeat to batter and fry the remaining blossoms.

Divide the corn puree between four shallow bowls and place three squash blossoms and a scoop of zucchini and corn over the puree. Serve with the Peach Filfel Chuma for dipping.

"Forbidden Knowledge" by Raury from *All We Need*

peach filfel chuma

makes about 1 cup

1 tablespoon extra-virgin olive oil	½ teaspoon red chile flakes
3 tablespoons minced garlic	½ teaspoon finely grated lemon zest
1 teaspoon cumin seeds, toasted and ground	½ cup diced frozen or fresh peaches
1 teaspoon caraway seeds, toasted and ground	¼ cup water
3 tablespoons sweet paprika	3 tablespoons fresh lemon juice
	Kosher salt
	Freshly ground white pepper

Combine the oil and garlic in a small saucepan and warm over medium-low heat until the garlic is fragrant, 2 to 3 minutes. Scrape into a blender. Add the cumin, caraway, paprika, chile flakes, lemon zest, peaches, water, and lemon juice. Puree until smooth. Season with salt and pepper to taste. Use immediately or transfer to a small jar and cover with olive oil. It will keep, covered and refrigerated, for 2 weeks.

baked acorn squash

jerk marinade

makes 4 servings

I wanted to open the section on winter squashes with a simple roasted squash recipe. I use acorn squash here, but you could substitute any number of winter squashes–butternut, buttercup, kabocha, delicata. The idea for slathering the squash with jerk marinade came from an image that Erin Alderson posted on her Instagram account (@naturallyella) of a roasted red kuri squash smeared with "a jerk seasoning blend!" Winner!

| 1 large acorn squash, quartered | Jerk Marinade (page 235) |

Preheat the oven to 375°F.

Remove the seeds and strings from the squash, reserving the seeds for another use (see page 127). Arrange the squash on a rimmed baking sheet, cut-side up. Add enough water to fill the baking sheet by ¼ inch. Cover with aluminum foil and bake until the squash is tender when pierced with a fork, about 35 minutes. Remove the foil and generously slather the squash with the jerk marinade. Switch the oven to broil on high, put the squash back in the oven, and broil until the sauce is bubbling, about 3 minutes.

"Jah Jah Dub" by Ronnie Davis from *Ronnie Davis in Dub*

winter squash

With the diversity of winter squashes available, it would be a shame not to incorporate them into lots of meals during peak season. In this book I employ a number of techniques for cooking winter squash–from roasting to pureeing–so I want to offer a few tips for preparing it. First, thoroughly wash and dry your squash before cooking. Next, use a sharp knife instead of a peeler to peel winter squash. Finally, save winter squash seeds instead of discarding them. They can be tossed in a little fat and seasonings and then oven-roasted to be eaten as a snack or used as a garnish.

mashed kabocha

coconut palm sugar · ground cinnamon ·
flaky sea salt

makes 4 to 6 servings

Sometimes doing less is more. Kabocha squash—
or Japanese pumpkin as it is often called—has a
sweet, earthy flavor and a lower water content
than many other winter squashes, making it ideal
for simple preparation like oven-roasting. In this
recipe, I roast and then mash the squash along
with coconut palm sugar, cinnamon, and oat milk
for creaminess. While I mostly make this as a side
dish, we sometimes have it for breakfast.

1 (1½-pound) kabocha squash, quartered	¼ teaspoon ground cinnamon
1½ tablespoons coconut oil	1 cup unsweetened oat milk, warmed
2 teaspoons coconut palm sugar	Flaky sea salt

Preheat the oven to 375°F.

Remove the seeds and strings from the squash,
reserving the seeds for another use (see below).
Arrange the squash on a rimmed baking sheet,
cut-side up. Add enough water to reach ¼ inch up
the sides of the baking sheet. Cover with aluminum
foil and bake until the squash is tender when
pierced with a fork, about 35 minutes. Remove
from the oven.

Using a spoon, scrape the flesh of the squash
from the skin and transfer it to a medium bowl.
Compost the skin. With a fork, mash the squash.
Add the coconut oil, sugar, and cinnamon. While
stirring with the fork, slowly pour in the oat milk
and stir until the mixture is smooth. Sprinkle with
flaky salt and serve.

"Stay Flo" by Solange from *When I Get Home*

roasting winter squash seeds

Don't discard the seeds from winter squash.
Roast them. After that, they can be used as a
garnish or eaten as a snack. You simply need
to add enough oil to lightly coat them, toss with
your choice of dried spices, and then roast in
a 275°F oven until golden, about 15 minutes.

butternut squash and sesame seed hand pies

sweet potato–sage cream ·
fried sage leaves · lemon

makes 6 hand pies

This recipe was inspired by the compact portable foods originally made for laborers that we find in many traditional cultures: bunny chow in South Africa, patties in Jamaica, zongzi in China, hand pies in the southern United States. The combination of butternut squash and sesame seeds alone makes a fun and filling side (feel free to go there), but this duo stuffed inside a flaky shell makes these hand pies a pick-up-and-go food that kids love. Serving them with silky sweet potato–sage cream makes this a super snack. A touch of acid is required to make this dish really pop, so serve them with lemon halves and encourage folks to spray some juice on each bite.

filling

2½ cups diced peeled butternut squash

3 teaspoons melted coconut oil

¼ teaspoon ground cinnamon

⅛ teaspoon plus ¼ teaspoon kosher salt, plus more as needed

½ cup toasted sesame seeds

2 tablespoons pure maple syrup

Freshly ground white pepper

pastry

1¾ cups unbleached all-purpose flour

1 cup whole-wheat pastry flour

2 teaspoons ground turmeric

½ teaspoon fine sea salt

¾ cup coconut oil

2 teaspoons apple cider vinegar

½ cup plus 2 tablespoons ice water

2 tablespoons unsweetened oat milk

1 tablespoon dark agave nectar

sweet potato–sage cream

¼ cup safflower oil

6 fresh sage leaves plus 2 tablespoons minced fresh sage

Coarse sea salt

1¼ pounds sweet potatoes, peeled and cut into ½-inch cubes

¼ cup Cashew Cream (page 231)

1 teaspoon coconut palm sugar

2 tablespoons pure maple syrup

3 large lemons, cut in half

Make the filling: Preheat the oven to 425°F. Line a large rimmed baking sheet with parchment paper.

In a bowl, combine the squash, the coconut oil, the cinnamon, and ⅛ teaspoon of the salt and toss until the squash is evenly coated. Transfer to the baking sheet and roast until tender and starting to brown on the edges, about 30 minutes, stirring once after 15 minutes.

Put the sesame seeds into a large bowl and set aside.

When the squash is finished cooking, transfer it to the bowl with the sesame seeds. Pour in the maple syrup and stir, mashing the squash with a fork. If needed, add water, 1 tablespoon at a time, so that the mixture is moist. Season with salt and pepper to taste. Set aside while you make the pastry.

Make the pastry: In a large bowl, combine 1½ cups of the all-purpose flour, the pastry flour, turmeric, and salt and mix well. Dollop the coconut oil into the flour mixture. Transfer the bowl to the refrigerator and chill until the coconut oil is firm, 20 to 30 minutes.

Using clean hands, rub the coconut oil into the flour mixture until the mixture resembles fine sand, about 10 minutes.

In a small bowl, combine the vinegar and ice water and mix well. While stirring, add the vinegar mixture to the flour mixture by the tablespoon just until the dough comes away from the sides of the bowl and begins to coalesce. You may not use all of the water mixture, but you should use most of it; do not overwork the dough. The dough should have the texture of slightly dry Play-Doh. Squeeze it into a tight ball, flatten the ball, cover in plastic wrap, and refrigerate for 1 hour. (Do not leave the dough in the refrigerator for much more than an hour.)

butternut squash and sesame seed hand pies, continued

Preheat the oven to 350°F. Line a baking sheet with parchment paper.

Lightly dust a clean work surface with the remaining ¼ cup all-purpose flour. Roll out the dough until it is about ⅛ inch thick. Cut six 6-inch circles from the dough, using a cereal bowl as a guide. If needed, gather the scraps, roll them out a second time, and cut more circles in order to get six total.

Spoon 2 heaping tablespoons of the filling onto one half of each circle, leaving about a ⅛-inch border. Fold the other half over to make a half-moon and press the edges to seal (if your dough is on the dry side, you may need to run wet fingers around the edge of the circles before folding them over the filling to help get a good seal). Crimp the edges using a fork.

In a small bowl, combine the oat milk and agave nectar and mix thoroughly. Set aside.

Transfer the hand pies to the prepared baking sheet and bake until golden brown, 35 to 40 minutes, brushing the oat milk-agave mixture onto the pastries 20 minutes into cooking to give them a beautiful brown color.

Make the sweet potato–sage cream: While the hand pies are baking, line a plate with a paper towel and set aside. Heat the safflower oil over medium-high heat in a small skillet. Fry the whole sage leaves until crisp, about 3 seconds. Remove the skillet from the heat and use a fork to immediately transfer the leaves to the plate. Sprinkle the leaves with salt to taste and set them and the oil aside.

Place the sweet potatoes in a medium saucepan and add enough water to cover them by ½ inch. Bring the water to a boil over high heat, immediately lower the heat to medium, and simmer, partially covered, until the sweet potatoes are fork-tender, 15 to 20 minutes. Drain well.

Transfer the sweet potatoes to a food processor and add the cashew cream, 2 teaspoons of the sage oil (reserving the remaining oil for another use), the sugar, maple syrup, and ¼ teaspoon salt. Process until smooth, adding enough water to make the mixture loose enough to smear across a plate. Transfer to a bowl and stir in the minced sage. Season to taste with salt.

To serve, smear the sweet potato–sage cream over one side of six plates, top each with a hand pie, and garnish with a fried sage leaf. You can also serve these "family style" by placing the pies on a platter and the sweet potato-sage cream in a bowl garnished with a couple of crispy sage leaves. Either way, serve with lemon halves or some other acid for adding to each bite.

"Keep Your Hand on the Plow" by Mahalia Jackson from *Gospels, Spirituals, and Hymns*

roasted delicata squash, black-eyed peas, and mustard greens

apple cider vinegar · pikliz

makes 4 to 6 servings

This is the type of food my grandparents made every day. They sourced fresh ingredients mostly from their home gardens; they let the vegetables and legumes shine through, seasoning them simply with salt and pepper; and they made sure that the dish was juicy with broth, so one could sop it up with cornbread.

black-eyed peas

2 tablespoons extra-virgin olive oil

1 cup finely diced white onion

½ cup finely diced carrot

½ cup finely diced celery

1 tablespoon minced garlic

1 tablespoon minced canned chipotle chile

1 bay leaf

1½ cups dried black-eyed peas, soaked in water with 1 tablespoon kosher salt overnight

1 teaspoon kosher salt, plus more to taste

1 tablespoon apple cider vinegar

Freshly ground white pepper

squash

2 medium delicata squash (about 1 pound each), halved lengthwise, seeded (reserved for another use), and cut into ¼-inch-thick slices

2 tablespoons extra-virgin olive oil

2 tablespoons light agave nectar

¼ teaspoon kosher salt

mustard greens

2 tablespoons extra-virgin olive oil

4 shallots, minced

2 teaspoons minced garlic

¼ teaspoon kosher salt, plus more as needed

1 pound mustard greens, ribs removed, leaves torn into bite-size pieces

1 tablespoon apple cider vinegar

Pikliz (page 134) or Pickled Mustard Greens (page 140), for serving

Make the black-eyed peas: In a large pot, warm the olive oil over medium-high heat until shimmering. Add the onion, carrot, and celery and sauté until the vegetables soften, 8 to 10 minutes. Add the garlic, chipotle, and bay leaf and cook until the garlic smells fragrant, 3 to 4 minutes. Drain the black-eyed peas, add them to the pot, and pour in enough water to cover them by 2 inches. Increase the heat to high and bring the water to a boil, then immediately decrease the heat to medium-low, skim off any foam, cover, and simmer until the black-eyed peas are just tender, about 45 minutes. Stir in the salt and cook for another 5 minutes. Drain the beans, reserving the cooking liquid, and discard the bay leaf.

Return the black-eyed peas to the pot, transferring 1 cup of them to a blender. Pour in 1½ cups of reserved cooking liquid and pulse until chunky but not fully pureed, about 30 seconds. Pour the mixture into the pot and bring to a boil over high heat. Reduce the heat to medium-low, stir in the vinegar, and season with salt and pepper to taste. Simmer for a few more minutes and then remove from the heat.

Make the squash: While the black-eyed peas are cooking, preheat the oven to 425°F. Line a baking sheet with parchment paper.

In a large bowl, combine the squash, olive oil, agave nectar, and salt and toss to combine. Spread the squash on the prepared baking sheet and roast until tender and browning, about 30 minutes.

Make the greens: In a Dutch oven, warm the olive oil over medium heat until shimmering. Add the shallots and sauté, stirring often, until soft, 2 to 3 minutes. Add the garlic and salt and cook until the garlic is fragrant, 2 to 3 minutes. Stir in the mustard greens and 2 cups of the reserved cooking liquid from the black-eyed peas. Decrease the heat to low and cook, partially covered, until the greens are meltingly tender, about 25 minutes. Stir in the vinegar and season with salt to taste.

To serve, present the black-eyed peas, squash, and mustard greens in bowls, pour in a little (about ¼ cup) of the reserved cooking liquid from the black-eyed peas, and generously top with pikliz or pickled mustard greens (and some of their liquid).

"Been in the Storm" by Ranky Tanky from *Ranky Tanky*

leaves

cabbage

dark leafy greens

parsley

spinach

pikliz

cabbage · carrot · habanero · white vinegar

makes 1 quart

A few years back at one of MoAD's galas, the museum auctioned off a private dinner curated by me. To make the meal, I hired my buddy Isaiah Martinez—a super-talented Afro-Caribbean chef now working in Eugene, Oregon. I had my friend Jaynelle—owner of Pietisserie—make pies for dessert, and I brought on the homie DJ Max Champ to spin records. The whole event was fresh, and Isaiah killed the food. Included in his Afro-Caribbean feast was pikliz, a condiment in Haitian cuisine made of pickled cabbage, carrots, bell peppers, and Scotch bonnet peppers. This brilliant combination of quick-pickled vegetables adds acid and heat to enhance flavor and punch up dishes from rice to rich stews. I pretty much incorporate pikliz in meals throughout the week these days.

2 cups finely chopped green cabbage

2¼ teaspoons kosher salt

½ cup ¼-inch diced white onion

½ cup ¼-inch diced peeled carrot

½ cup ¼-inch diced, seeded green bell pepper

1 teaspoon minced garlic

2 tablespoons minced seeded Scotch bonnet or habanero chile, or to taste

1 cup white vinegar

¼ cup fresh navel orange juice

2 tablespoons fresh lime juice

Combine the cabbage and 2 teaspoons of the salt in a large bowl. With clean hands, massage the cabbage until soft and wilted, about 3 minutes. Transfer to a colander set in the sink and rinse the bowl. Put a plate on top of the cabbage and weight it down (a 28-ounce can of tomatoes works well for this). Let sit for 1 hour.

Rinse the cabbage under cold water, then squeeze with clean hands to extract as much liquid as possible. Transfer the cabbage back to the bowl. Add the onion, carrot, bell pepper, garlic, chile, and remaining ¼ teaspoon salt. With clean hands, gently mix everything, then transfer to a sterilized 1-quart canning jar (see sidebar, page 35). Pour in the vinegar, orange juice, lime juice, and ¼ cup water, adding more water as needed to ensure the vegetables are completely submerged. Cover and refrigerate for at least 2 days to allow the flavors to develop before enjoying. It should keep for up to 1 year refrigerated.

"Ou Fe'M" by Riva Nyri Précil from *Perle De Culture*

memphis coleslaw

red and green cabbage ·
green bell pepper · carrot

makes 4 to 6 servings

I can get down with vinaigrette-coated slaws,
but this creamy version speaks to my soul. It
evokes some of my fondest childhood memories
and goes perfectly on my Cornmeal-Fried Oyster
Mushroom Po'Boy (page 165). This is the coleslaw
that I grew up eating. It is the coleslaw that my
dad made most "fish fry" Fridays at our home in
Memphis. It's the one that relatives would make
for large family gatherings during summers, and it
is the one that you will find at the innumerable rib
joints for which my home city is famous. So what
sets it apart from other slaws? I asked my dad
to share the keys to making good Memphis-style
coleslaw, and he said, "Lots of mayo and a touch
of sugar and vinegar." Before he could finish, my
mom chimed in, "Add a tiny bit of mustard and
some celery seeds." So there you have it.

½ small green cabbage
(about 1 pound), cored
and coarsely chopped

⅛ small red cabbage
(about ¼ pound), cored
and coarsely chopped

2 teaspoons kosher
salt, plus more as
needed

½ cup coarsely
grated carrot

1 cup thinly sliced
green bell pepper

½ cup thinly sliced
red onion

¾ cup vegan
mayonnaise

2 tablespoons
unseasoned rice
vinegar

2 tablespoons apple
cider vinegar

2 teaspoons raw
cane sugar

¼ teaspoon molasses

¼ teaspoon whole-
grain mustard

⅓ teaspoon
celery seeds

Freshly ground
white pepper

Combine the cabbages and 2 teaspoons of the
salt in a large bowl. With clean hands, massage
the cabbage until soft and wilted, about 3 minutes.
Transfer to a colander set in the sink and rinse the
bowl. Put a plate atop the cabbage and weight it
down (a 28-ounce can of tomatoes works well for
this). Let sit for 1 hour.

Rinse the cabbage under cold water, then transfer
it back to the bowl. Add the carrot, bell pepper,
and onion. With clean hands, mix well.

In a small bowl, whisk together the mayonnaise,
vinegars, sugar, molasses, and mustard. Pour just
enough of the dressing into the bowl to moisten
the slaw and mix well with clean hands. Add the
celery seeds, taste, and season with salt and
pepper. Cover and refrigerate for at least 1 hour.

Bring to room temperature and toss well before
serving, adding a tad bit more dressing, if desired.

"A Nickel and a Nail" by Don Bryant from *Don't Give Up on Love*

sautéed cabbage and roasted potatoes

carrot puree · ginger-habanero vinegar · parsley

makes 4 servings

The initial inspiration for this recipe was atakilt, a hearty Ethiopian dish of slow-cooked potatoes, cabbage, and carrots. Here I roast cubes of potatoes until just crisp so they remain firm and hold up while being sautéed with the cabbage. Rather than adding cut carrots to the mix, I smear a carrot puree onto the serving plate and pile the cabbage and potatoes on top. The carrot puree visually brightens the dish and adds a "saucy" element. To pull everything together, I created a spicy and acidic ginger-habanero vinegar. The vinegar has more of a Caribbean flavor profile, so I see this as an East-Africa-meets-West-Indies mash-up. When prepping, be meticulous about cutting the potatoes into equal-size ½-inch cubes (as precise as you can get them). This facilitates even roasting and provides consistency in each bite.

2 pounds Yukon gold potatoes, cut into ½-inch cubes

4 tablespoons extra-virgin olive oil

2 teaspoons coarse sea salt, plus more as needed

Freshly ground white pepper

1 pound carrots, thinly sliced

1 teaspoon red wine vinegar, plus more as needed

2 teaspoons brown mustard seeds

¼ to ½ teaspoon red pepper flakes

1 teaspoon raw cane sugar

8 ounces green cabbage, cored and thinly sliced

6 tablespoons vegetable stock (page 230) or water

Ginger-Habanero Vinegar (page 234)

½ cup loosely packed fresh flat-leaf parsley leaves, for garnish

Preheat the oven to 450°F. Line a baking sheet with parchment paper.

In a large bowl, combine the potatoes, 1 tablespoon of the olive oil, 1 teaspoon of the salt, and a few turns of white pepper and toss well with clean hands to combine. Spread the potatoes over the prepared baking sheet in one layer and roast until tender and starting to turn golden on the edges, 35 to 40 minutes.

While the potatoes are roasting, in a medium saucepan, combine the carrots, ¾ cup water, and ½ teaspoon of the salt. Bring to a boil over medium-high heat, stir, and quickly decrease the heat to medium-low. Partially cover and steam the carrots until tender, about 15 minutes. Drain the carrots in a colander and let them sit until they have dried, about 20 minutes.

Transfer the carrots to a blender, add the red wine vinegar and 1 tablespoon of the olive oil, and puree until smooth, adding a little water if necessary. Taste, add more vinegar to brighten the puree, if necessary, and season with salt and white pepper. Set aside.

Heat a large sauté pan over medium heat. Add the remaining 2 tablespoons olive oil, the mustard seeds, red pepper flakes, sugar, and remaining ½ teaspoon salt. Simmer, stirring frequently to prevent the spices from burning, until the mustard seeds start to pop, about 2 minutes. Quickly add the cabbage and sauté, stirring often, until completely wilted, about 3 minutes. Add the stock and the roasted potatoes and gently toss to combine. Cover and cook until most of the liquid has evaporated, about 4 minutes. Season with salt and white pepper to taste.

To serve, slather the carrot puree over four plates, scoop a mound of the sautéed cabbage and potatoes on top, and generously sprinkle with ginger-habanero vinegar. Garnish with the parsley leaves and serve.

"Wubit" by Mulatu Astatke & Black Jesus Experience from *Cradle of Humanity*

mushroom rice–stuffed cabbage

sauce piquant · onion-thyme cream

makes 4 servings

The mushroom rice in this recipe is inspired by djon-djon, a classic Haitian rice dish made with a rare black mushroom found in the mountainous region of northern Haiti. I serve the rolls with sauce piquant, a classic Creole sauce, and onion-thyme cream to tone down the heat and uplift the overall dish.

sauce piquant

2 tablespoons extra-virgin olive oil

¼ cup finely diced yellow onion

¼ cup finely diced red bell pepper

¼ cup finely diced celery

2 teaspoons minced garlic

¼ teaspoon minced fresh ginger

Pinch of ground cinnamon

¼ teaspoon cayenne pepper

½ teaspoon kosher salt, plus more as needed

¼ cup tomato paste

1 teaspoon molasses

1 tablespoon tamari

1 tablespoon apple cider vinegar

1 (28-ounce) can whole tomatoes, chopped, juices reserved

1 cup water

1 teaspoon minced fresh thyme

Freshly ground black pepper

mushroom rice

1½ cups short-grain brown rice, soaked in water plus 1 tablespoon vinegar overnight

½ cup sliced dried porcini mushrooms

2 cups boiling water

1 tablespoon extra-virgin olive oil

½ cup finely diced yellow onion

½ cup finely diced green bell pepper

½ cup finely diced celery

½ teaspoon kosher salt

8 ounces cremini mushrooms, stemmed and finely chopped

2¼ cups vegetable stock (page 230)

cabbage

2 tablespoons kosher salt

1 Savoy or green cabbage (about 2 pounds), core removed

Onion-Thyme Cream (page 231)

Make the sauce piquant: In a wide, large heavy pot over medium-high heat, warm the oil until shimmering. Add the onion, bell pepper, and celery and sauté until soft, 3 to 5 minutes. Add the garlic, ginger, cinnamon, cayenne, and the salt and cook until fragrant, about 3 minutes. Stir in the tomato paste, molasses, tamari, vinegar, tomatoes with their juices, and water. Raise the heat to high and bring to a boil. Quickly reduce the heat to medium-low and simmer, partially covered, for about 10 minutes. Stir in the thyme and season with salt and pepper to taste. Set aside.

Make the mushroom rice: Drain the rice and set aside. Put the porcini in a small heatproof bowl and pour the boiling water over them, making sure it covers the mushrooms (you may need to weight them down with a small plate). Let soak for 20 minutes. Drain through a fine-mesh sieve, reserving the soaking liquid, and chop the porcini finely.

Warm the olive oil in a medium saucepan over medium-high heat until shimmering. Add the onion, bell pepper, celery, and the salt and sauté until the vegetables soften, about 5 minutes. Stir in the cremini and reserved porcini mushrooms. Decrease the heat to medium-low and sauté until the mushrooms release their liquid and begin to brown, about 5 minutes.

Pour in the stock and mushroom liquid, add the rice, stir well, and bring to a boil over high heat. Reduce the heat to low, cover, and cook for 50 minutes, until most of the liquid has evaporated. Remove from the heat and steam with the cover on for 10 minutes.

Make the cabbage: In a large pot over high heat, bring 3 quarts water and the salt to a boil. Gently slide the cabbage into the water, cored side down. Boil until the outer leaves have softened, 5 to 7 minutes. Remove the outer leaves. Repeat until you have eight large leaves to stuff. On a clean work surface, trim enough of the rib from each leaf so that the leaves roll easily. Put ½ cup of the mushroom rice in the center of a leaf toward the bottom. Fold the sides of the leaf in, then roll the cabbage up into a package. Repeat with the remaining leaves. Bring the pot with the sauce piquant to a boil. Reduce the heat to low, place the rolls seam-side down in the pot, cover, and simmer for 20 minutes. To serve, spread a thin layer of sauce over four plates, arrange two cabbage rolls on each plate, and serve with a dollop of onion-thyme cream.

"Bourbon Street Jingling Jollies" by Duke Ellington from *New Orleans Suite*

pickled mustard greens

serrano chiles · peppercorns · raw cane sugar · apple cider vinegar

makes about 1 quart

Imagine my surprise when I saw pickled mustard greens in a dish at a Szechuan restaurant about a decade ago. I'm always looking for cultural, political, and culinary connections between Black and Chinese people (#AfroAsian #BBQBeansprouts), so I was happy to see the pickled greens, given how central mustard greens are to traditional African American cuisine. Incorporate these into your meals as you would other pickled and fermented vegetables.

1½ cups apple cider vinegar

½ cup unseasoned rice vinegar

2 tablespoons raw cane sugar

¼ teaspoon plus 1 tablespoon kosher salt

1 teaspoon whole black peppercorns

2 pounds mustard greens, stems thinly sliced and leaves coarsely chopped (keep stems and leaves separate)

2 serrano chiles, thinly sliced

In a medium sauté pan, combine the vinegars, sugar, ¼ teaspoon of the salt, and the peppercorns. Heat over low heat, stirring, until the sugar has completely dissolved, about 3 minutes. Remove from the heat and let cool while you prepare the mustard greens.

Meanwhile, in a large pot, bring 3 quarts water to a boil over high heat. Add the remaining 1 tablespoon salt and the mustard green stems and boil for 1 minute. Immediately remove the pot from the heat, add the mustard green leaves, and let sit for 1 minute. Drain in a colander and rinse with cool water.

Transfer the leaves and stems to a clean 1-quart canning jar. Add the chiles to the jar and pour the pickling liquid over everything. Let sit at room temperature for at least 2 hours, then seal the jar and refrigerate until ready to serve. The pickled mustard greens will keep in the refrigerator for up to 6 months.

"Contronatura" by Stereolab from *Dots and Loops*

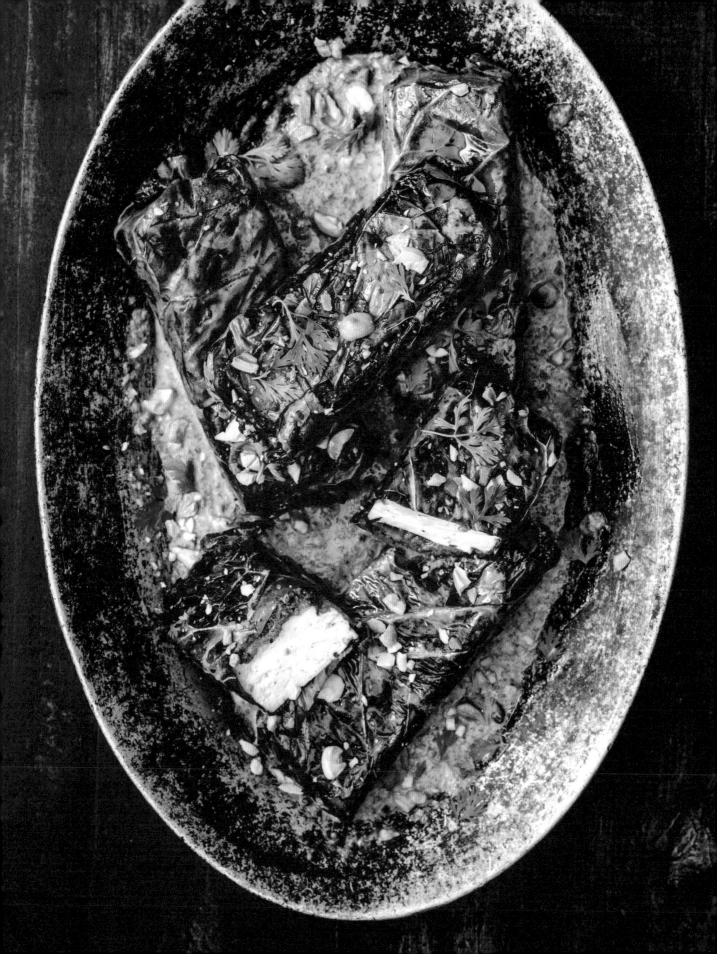

jerk tofu wrapped in collard leaves

cilantro sauce · cilantro leaves · crushed peanuts

makes 4 servings

The method of cooking fish in banana leaves inspired this recipe. Banana leaves play the dual role of imparting a floral, sweet, and grassy flavor to the fish as well as keeping it moist. In this recipe, I am more interested in highlighting the slightly bitter-earthy taste and the chewy texture of the collard leaves themselves, along with the tofu that has been soaked in a Jamaican-inspired marinade. Check the technique: After removing the fibrous stems from the collards, I blanch the leaves to soften them a bit. After that, I wrap the leaves around the marinated tofu, adding a sprinkle of crispy garlic before closing it up. Next, I sear the collard packets in a little peanut oil, then serve them over cilantro sauce with a garnish of cilantro leaves and crushed peanuts. If you are having any doubts about the awesomeness of this dish, I will share a quote from Kate Williams, the recipe tester for this book: "My tofu-hating husband loved this, so that's really saying something!" Use a quality extra-firm tofu like Nasoya. This dish is best eaten with a fork and knife.

2 (14- to 16-ounce) blocks extra-firm tofu, pressed (see page 144) and patted dry

2 cups Jerk Marinade (page 235)

1 tablespoon plus 2 teaspoons fine sea salt, plus more as needed

16 large collard leaves, tough part of the stem removed

1 cup arrowroot powder

Peanut oil, for frying

¼ cup Garlic Chips (page 232)

Cilantro Sauce (page 235)

Cilantro leaves, for garnish

Crushed peanuts, for garnish

Place one block of the tofu on a cutting board. Cut it in half horizontally, then cut vertically down the center to yield four pieces. Repeat with the second block of tofu.

Pour the marinade into a large baking dish, adding just enough water to ensure that it is runny, if necessary. Place the tofu in the marinade in one even layer. Cover and refrigerate for 8 hours or overnight, flipping the tofu every 30 minutes for the first 2 hours. Remove the tofu from the marinade, scrape off any excess, and transfer to a large plate. Strain the marinade through a fine-mesh sieve and set aside.

In a large pot, bring 2 quarts water to a boil over high heat. Add 1 tablespoon of the salt. Blanch the collard leaves, one at a time, for 30 seconds each, then lay them flat on clean kitchen towels to dry.

Combine the arrowroot and the remaining 2 teaspoons salt in a pie plate. Mix well. Coat each side of the tofu pieces with the arrowroot, shake off any excess arrowroot, and transfer them to a second large plate.

Lightly coat the bottom of a large cast-iron skillet with peanut oil and heat over medium-high heat until shimmering. Add half the tofu and fry until golden brown, 2 to 3 minutes. Gently flip each piece with a spatula and fry until golden brown on the second side. Lightly sprinkle both sides of the tofu with salt and transfer to a rack. Repeat to fry the remaining tofu. Wipe the skillet clean.

On a clean work surface, arrange two collard leaves lengthwise, overlapping each other by an inch or so, and place one piece of tofu in the center of the leaves. Smear 2 heaping tablespoons of the reserved marinade on top of the tofu, sprinkle a heaping teaspoon of garlic chips on top of the tofu, then fold the leaves around the tofu to create a packet. Repeat with the remaining collard leaves and tofu.

In the same skillet, warm 2 tablespoons peanut oil over medium-high heat, tilting the pan to coat it evenly with the oil. Place the packets in the skillet, folded-side up, and cook for about 1 minute. Gently flip each packet with a spatula, cover the skillet with a lid or some aluminum foil, and cook for about 5 minutes to warm through.

To serve, spread some cilantro sauce over four plates and place two of the tofu packets on each plate. Garnish with cilantro leaves and peanuts and serve.

"I Own the Night (feat. Saul Williams)" by Christian Scott aTunde Adjuah from *Ancestral Recall*

preparing tofu

I have a complicated relationship with tofu. On one hand, I have been critical of the "delete meat and add bland tofu" ethos prevalent in plant-based cooking throughout the 1980s and '90s, and I pushed people to think about using it sparingly as cooks do in East and Southwest Asia. On the other hand, I can get down with properly marinated tofu in stir-fried dishes, soups, and even on sandwiches. The best way to flavor your tofu is by letting it sit in a thin marinade. But before you do this, I suggest pressing the tofu. This procedure extracts excess water, makes the block more uniformly firm, and allows the tofu to absorb the marinade more easily. Just wrap the block of tofu in a clean kitchen towel (or paper towels), place it in a large bowl or a clean kitchen sink, and sit something heavy on top of it (like a 28-ounce can of tomatoes) for 20 minutes, turning the block over after 15 minutes. After that, you can cut the tofu into the desired shape (cubes, slabs, or slices) before marinating.

Make sure your marinade is runny enough to easily permeate the tofu. You can then place the tofu in a container, pour marinade over it, cover, and refrigerate for 8 hours or overnight. To really deepen the flavor of tofu, simmer it in marinade on the stovetop or bake it in the oven until the tofu absorbs most of the marinade.

gumbo des herbes with red beans and tempeh

yellow bell peppers · filé powder · thyme · sweet hot pepper vinegar

makes 6 to 8 servings

This gumbo is in honor of the late great chef, restaurateur, and activist Leah Chase. Serve it at your Mardi Gras party or whenever you have a surplus of greens that you need to use. One of the keys to nailing this dish is chopping the greens as finely as possible. Processing the greens in a food processor is a shortcut to speed along the process. If you want this recipe to really shine, make it a day before serving to allow the flavors to mingle overnight. I prefer eating this with Carolina Gold rice, but any white or brown rice will work fine.

8 ounces dried small red beans or kidney beans, picked through and soaked in water plus 3 tablespoons salt overnight (see page 48)

1 bay leaf

1 large white onion, cut in half

7 garlic cloves: 3 cut in half, 4 minced

1 dried red chile

2¼ teaspoons plus 1 tablespoon coarse sea salt, plus more as needed

½ pound collard greens, stemmed, leaves chopped into bite-size pieces

½ pound mustard greens, stemmed, leaves chopped into bite-size pieces

½ pound turnip greens, stemmed, leaves chopped into bite-size pieces

½ pound spinach, stemmed, leaves chopped into bite-size pieces

10 tablespoons extra-virgin olive oil

4 large yellow bell peppers, cut into ¼-inch dice

½ cup millet flour

2 large yellow onions, cut into ¼-inch dice

2 celery stalks, halved lengthwise and chopped

¼ teaspoon cayenne pepper

4 cups vegetable stock (page 230), plus more as needed

Sweet Hot Pepper Vinegar (page 234)

Safflower oil, for frying

2 (8-ounce) packages tempeh, sliced into bite-size pieces

Cooked rice, for serving

2 large scallions, thinly sliced, for serving

Filé powder, for serving

Fresh thyme, for serving

Drain the beans and put them in a medium saucepan. Add the bay leaf, 2 white onion halves, halved garlic cloves, dried chile, and enough water to cover them by 2 inches. Bring to a boil over medium heat. Skim off any foam, decrease the heat to medium-low, and simmer, partially covered, until just tender (the beans should not be mushy), 1 hour to 1½ hours. Add 1 teaspoon of the salt and cook for 10 minutes more. Drain the beans, reserving the cooking water. Discard the bay leaf, onion, garlic, and chile.

While the beans are cooking, bring a large, heavy-bottomed pot of water to a boil over high heat. Add 1 tablespoon of the salt and all the greens to the water. Bring back to a boil and cook until the greens are soft, about 5 minutes. Drain in a colander and let cool. Wipe out the pot.

While the greens are cooling, in the same pot, combine 2 tablespoons of the olive oil and the bell peppers. Sprinkle with ¼ teaspoon of the salt and sauté over medium-high heat until the peppers are just tender (be careful not to overcook them), 3 to 5 minutes. Using a slotted spoon, transfer the peppers to a bowl and set aside.

In the same pot, heat 6 tablespoons of the olive oil over medium-low heat. Whisk in the millet flour and cook, stirring often with a wooden spoon, until the mixture is caramel colored, about 20 minutes. Add the remaining 2 tablespoons olive oil, the yellow onions, and the celery and sauté until the vegetables are soft, about 10 minutes. Add the minced garlic, the remaining 1 teaspoon salt, and the cayenne and sauté until the garlic is fragrant, 3 to 5 minutes. Remove from the heat.

gumbo des herbes with red beans and tempeh, continued

In batches, transfer the cooled greens to a food processor and puree until finely chopped. (Alternatively, transfer the greens to a cutting board and chop them as finely as possible.) Transfer to the pot with the roux and vegetables. Stir in the stock, the beans, and 1 cup of the reserved bean cooking liquid. Bring to a boil; the mixture will be quite thick. Decrease the heat to low and simmer, partially covered, stirring occasionally to prevent the gumbo from sticking to the pot, until meltingly tender, about 45 minutes, adding more stock or reserved bean liquid as needed to loosen the gumbo and make it easier to stir. Remove from the heat and let the gumbo cool, then cover and refrigerate for 8 hours or overnight.

Before serving, warm the gumbo over medium heat, stirring to ensure it does not stick to the bottom of the pan. Aggressively season with sweet hot pepper vinegar to brighten up the gumbo and give it some kick.

While the gumbo is reheating, line a baking sheet with paper towels. Fill a heavy-bottomed pan with about 1 inch of safflower oil and heat the oil over medium-high heat. Working in batches, add the tempeh and cook until golden brown, about 2 minutes on each side. With a spider, transfer the tempeh to the prepared baking sheet and sprinkle with salt. Repeat to cook the remaining tempeh.

To serve, ladle the gumbo into bowls and top each with a heaping ½ cup of rice. Garnish with the sautéed bell peppers, tempeh, scallions, a pinch of filé powder, some thyme, and more sweet hot pepper vinegar. Serve.

"Gumbo" by Zion I from *The Take Over*

making roux

Roux—a combination of cooked fat and flour—is one of the cornerstones of classic New Orleans/Louisiana cooking. While mainly associated with gumbos, this mixture can be incorporated into sauces, soups, and stews to thicken them and add flavor. The standard technique for making one involves constantly whisking the two ingredients over low heat until the roux reaches your desired color—from light blond to dark chocolate. Obviously, the longer you cook it, the darker it gets. The keys to making an awesome roux are mindfulness and patience. If you stop stirring your roux, it can burn in a matter of seconds, and you will have to start from scratch. While all-purpose flour is most often used when making a traditional roux, I offer a gluten-free, millet flour-based roux in this book. Note: millet flour does not darken the way that all-purpose flour does, so time cooked, as suggested in the recipe, is the best cue.

slow-cooked collards

garlic · ginger · coconut palm sugar · apple cider vinegar

makes 4 to 6 servings

Nothing fancy here. Just a solid dish for when you need a flavorful side vegetable.

2 tablespoons
extra-virgin olive oil

2 cups finely diced
shallots (about 4 large
shallots)

2 teaspoons
minced garlic

2 teaspoons minced
fresh ginger

1 tablespoon coconut
palm sugar

½ teaspoon kosher salt,
plus more as needed

3 tablespoons
tomato paste

1 tablespoon Bragg
Liquid Aminos

2 medium bunches
collard greens (about
1 pound), ribs removed,
chopped finely

4 cups vegetable stock
(page 230)

3 tablespoons apple
cider vinegar, plus more
as needed

Warm the olive oil over medium-high heat in a heavy pot or Dutch oven until shimmering. Add the shallots and sauté, stirring often, until soft, 3 to 5 minutes. Add the garlic, ginger, sugar, and salt and cook until the garlic is fragrant, 1 to 2 minutes. Stir in the tomato paste and liquid aminos and cook, stirring often, until the mixture starts to thicken, 3 to 5 minutes. Add the collards and the stock and bring to a simmer.

Decrease the heat to low, cover, and cook, stirring occasionally, until the greens are meltingly tender, about 45 minutes to 1 hour. Pour in the vinegar, season with salt to taste, and serve, adding more vinegar if you'd like.

"Pynk" by Janelle Monáe from *Dirty Computer*

all-green everything salad with creamy sage dressing

kale · arugula · granny smith apples ·
candied pistachios

makes 4 to 6 servings

When conceiving this dish, I thought about how
pretty a monochromatic green salad would be on
a white plate. Well, this salad tastes as good as it
looks. It's the type of light-but-filling dish that I
often have for lunch to tide me over until dinner.
I also serve it alongside richer dishes to balance
them out. After tenderizing toothy kale by lightly
massaging it with lemon juice and salt, I toss the
kale and diced apples in a creamy, sweet, sage-
forward dressing so that every bite is fragrant and
lively. The candied pistachios balance the bitter
arugula and add texture.

dressing

2 tablespoons
unseasoned rice
vinegar

2 tablespoons fresh
lemon juice

1/4 cup silken tofu

2 tablespoons raw
cane sugar

1 teaspoon
minced garlic

2 teaspoons minced
fresh sage

6 tablespoons olive oil

Kosher salt

Freshly ground
white pepper

salad

6 cups bite-size
lacinato kale that has
been trimmed of the
tough stems

1/2 lemon

Kosher salt

3 large Granny Smith
apples, peeled,
cored, and diced

2 teaspoons
safflower oil

1/2 cup raw pistachios

2 tablespoons raw
cane sugar

2 cups bite-size arugula
that has been trimmed
of the tough stems

Make the dressing: In a blender, combine the vinegar, lemon juice, tofu, sugar, garlic, and sage. With
the blender running, slowly pour in the olive oil until
creamy. Season with salt and pepper to taste.

Make the salad: Put the kale in a large bowl. Lightly
spray with lemon juice and sprinkle with salt,
then massage the kale until it just starts to wilt,
about 2 minutes. Dump the apples into the bowl,
add just enough dressing to lightly coat, and toss
everything. Set aside.

Line a baking sheet with parchment paper.

Warm a cast-iron skillet over medium-high heat.
Add the oil and heat until shimmering. Lower the
heat to medium, add the pistachios and sugar,
and stir constantly until the sugar has melted and
the pistachios are fragrant and starting to brown,
about 1 1/2 minutes. Transfer the nuts to the baking
sheet and immediately spread them apart using
two forks. Set aside to cool for 15 minutes.

Add the arugula to the bowl with the kale and
apples, add more dressing, and toss to lightly coat.
Top with the candied pistachios, season with salt
and pepper to taste, then serve with the remaining
dressing on the side in case people want to drizzle
on more.

"Fool Forever" by Thao & The Get Down Stay Down from
A Man Alive

sweet parsley vinaigrette

flat-leaf parsley

makes ½ cup

I created this flavor-packed dressing for my Roasted Sweet Plantains, Pecan, and Millet Salad (page 150), but it soon became my go-to salad dressing for a few months. It also brings sautéed, roasted, and grilled vegetables to life.

2 tablespoons fresh lemon juice

2 tablespoons red wine vinegar

¼ cup minced flat-leaf parsley

¼ teaspoon Dijon mustard

2 teaspoons dark agave nectar

½ cup extra-virgin olive oil

Kosher salt

Freshly ground black pepper

In a bowl, whisk together the lemon juice, vinegar, parsley, mustard, and agave nectar. While whisking, slowly pour in the olive oil and whisk until emulsified. Season with salt and pepper to taste.

"Tasty (feat. Seneca B)" by Omaure from *Square One*

roasted sweet plantains, pecan, and millet salad

sweet parsley vinaigrette

makes 4 to 6 servings

This is a delicious and substantial salad that fuses ingredients from different parts of the African Diaspora. Millet, a staple food crop for a number of countries in sub-Saharan Africa, provides a mild, slightly nutty base on which to build a flavorful dish. Plantains, commonly eaten throughout Africa as well as in the Caribbean, Central America, and South America, are baked to yield crunchy-creamy chunks that add heartiness. Pecans, a staple in African American cooking, bring more complexity and texture. The flavorful parsley-based dressing adds freshness and zest.

2 large, ripe yellow plantains

1 tablespoon extra-virgin olive oil

¾ teaspoon kosher salt, divided

1 cup pearl millet, soaked in water plus 1 tablespoon vinegar overnight

2 cups water

½ cup chopped pecans, toasted

2 tablespoons minced parsley

Sweet Parsley Vinaigrette (page 149)

Freshly ground black pepper

¼ cup parsley leaves

Make the salad: Preheat the oven to 350°F. Line a baking sheet with parchment paper.

Slice off the ends of each plantain, score the peel in four even strips, lengthwise, and remove the strips. Cut the plantain into quarters, lengthwise, and slice them into bite-size pieces. In a bowl, toss the plantains with the olive oil and ¼ teaspoon salt. Spread in an even layer on the baking sheet and roast, stirring a few times to ensure even roasting, until starting to turn golden brown, about 30 minutes.

While the plantains are roasting, drain the millet. In a medium saucepan over medium-high heat, toast the millet, occasionally shaking the pan to ensure even cooking, until the millet smells nutty, about 3 minutes. Add the water and ½ teaspoon salt, raise the heat to high, and bring to a boil. Immediately decrease the heat to low, cover, and simmer until most of the liquid has been absorbed, about 15 minutes. Remove from the heat, transfer to a fine-mesh sieve, and rinse under cold water to stop the cooking. Set aside to thoroughly drain for 5 minutes, then transfer to a bowl.

Add the pecans, minced parsley, baked plantains, and half of the vinaigrette to the millet and toss to combine. Taste and add additional vinaigrette if needed. Season with salt and pepper to taste. Transfer to a serving bowl and sprinkle with parsley leaves.

"Manteca" by Quincy Jones from *You've Got It Bad Girl*

baked fonio and kale balls

chimichurri

makes 4 to 6 servings

I first learned about fonio, one of Africa's oldest grains, when Senegalese chef Pierre Thiam started touting its benefits a few years ago. According to Chef Thiam, some varieties of fonio are drought-resistant and can play an important role in addressing hunger in sub-Saharan Africa (similar to millet). In this recipe, I form the fonio—along with potato, alliums, and spices—into balls that are then baked and served with chimichurri, a green sauce packed with fresh herbs, garlic, olive oil, and vinegar.

chimichurri

6 tablespoons red wine vinegar

2 tablespoons unseasoned rice vinegar

1 cup finely diced red onion

2 teaspoons minced garlic

¾ cup olive oil

½ cup minced fresh cilantro

2 tablespoons minced fresh flat-leaf parsley

Pinch of cayenne pepper

Kosher salt

Freshly ground black pepper

fonio balls

1 large russet potato (about 1 pound), washed and scrubbed

1 teaspoon plus 1 tablespoon peanut oil

½ cup fonio

¼ teaspoon kosher salt

1 cup finely diced yellow onions

1 teaspoon minced garlic

1 tablespoon tomato paste

1 tablespoon Bragg Liquid Aminos

1 tablespoon yellow miso

2 cups stemmed chopped kale

Make the chimichurri: In a medium bowl, combine the vinegars, onion, and garlic and set aside for 30 minutes. Stir in the olive oil, cilantro, parsley, and cayenne pepper. Season with salt and pepper to taste. Set aside to allow the flavors to marry.

Make the balls: Preheat the oven to 400°F. With a fork, pierce the potato all over, then wrap in aluminum foil. Bake until tender, 50 to 60 minutes. Set aside to cool. When the potato is cool enough to handle, peel it, transfer to a bowl, and thoroughly mash with a fork. Set aside.

While the potato is baking, warm 1 teaspoon of the oil in a small saucepan over medium heat until shimmering. Add the fonio and stir until well coated with oil. Add 1 cup water and the salt and stir to combine. Raise the heat to high, bring to a boil, then quickly turn the heat to low. Simmer for 2 minutes. Remove from the heat and set aside to steam for 10 minutes.

In a small skillet, warm the remaining 1 tablespoon oil until shimmering. Add the onions and sauté, stirring often, until soft, about 5 minutes. Add the garlic and cook until it smells fragrant, 2 to 3 minutes. Stir in the tomato paste, liquid aminos, and miso and cook until well combined, about 3 minutes. Stir in the kale and cook, stirring frequently, until just wilted, 3 to 5 minutes. Transfer the mixture to a blender and puree until smooth. Pour the mixture into a food processor. Add the potato and fonio and process until the mixture is smooth.

With clean hands, form the mixture into golf ball-size balls. Transfer to a glass baking dish, using parchment paper to separate the layers. Refrigerate for 2 hours or up to 2 days before baking.

To bake, preheat the oven to 300°F and line a baking sheet with parchment paper. Spread the balls on the baking sheet and bake for 30 minutes, until slightly firm on the outside.

Serve the balls in a pool of chimichurri on small plates.

"Le Bien, Le Mal (feat. MC Solaar)" by Guru from *Guru's Jazzmatazz, Vol. 1*

charred lemon and spinach sauce

garlic · olive oil · umami powder

makes about 1 cup

This sauce is inspired by both pesto and pistou. I created it specifically for Grilled Broccoli Rabe (page 98), but you can mix it into soups and stews or eat it with pasta. It's also delicious as a spread for sandwiches—just omit the water to yield a thicker consistency.

1 large lemon	2 tablespoons water
2 cups baby spinach leaves	¼ cup Umami Powder (page 239)
½ teaspoon minced garlic	¼ teaspoon kosher salt, plus more as needed
¼ cup extra-virgin olive oil	Freshly ground black pepper

Using a Microplane, grate ½ teaspoon of the zest from the lemon and set aside. Cut the lemon in half crosswise.

Heat a cast-iron skillet over high heat. Place the lemon halves in the skillet, cut-side down, and cook until they are charred, about 3 minutes. Set aside.

In a blender or food processor, combine the spinach, garlic, lemon zest, olive oil, water, umami powder, salt, and the juice of one charred lemon half (reserve the other half for another use). Process until smooth. Transfer to a small bowl, taste, and season with salt and pepper. Use immediately.

"Africa Speaks (feat. Buika)" by Santana from *Africa Speaks*

green rice

kale · spinach · onion · green bell pepper

makes 4 to 6 servings

This simple and flavorful rice gets its color from spinach and kale.

1 cup tightly packed stemmed spinach leaves

1 cup tightly packed stemmed kale leaves

1½ cups vegetable stock (page 230)

2 tablespoons Cashew Cream (page 231)

1 teaspoon kosher salt

1 cup long-grain white rice, soaked in water plus 1 tablespoon vinegar overnight

1 tablespoon extra-virgin olive oil

½ cup finely diced yellow onion

½ cup finely diced green bell pepper

½ teaspoon minced garlic

In a blender, combine the spinach, kale, stock, cashew cream, and salt and puree until smooth. Set aside.

Drain the rice. Rinse it thoroughly and set aside.

In a medium saucepan over medium heat, warm the oil until shimmering. Add the onion and bell pepper and sauté until soft, about 5 minutes. Add the garlic and cook, stirring often, until fragrant, 2 to 3 minutes. Add the rice and cook until it starts smelling nutty, 2 to 3 minutes. Raise the heat to high, pour in the contents of the blender, and bring to a boil. Immediately reduce the heat to low, cover, and simmer until the rice is tender and most of the liquid has evaporated, 15 to 20 minutes.

Remove from the heat and set aside to steam for 10 minutes. Immediately before serving, fluff the rice with a fork.

"Nautilus" by Bob James from *One*

spinach salad with blackened chickpeas

roasted yellow bell peppers · creamy herb dressing · lemon zest · dill fronds

makes 4 servings

While I typically call for from-scratch chickpeas, I'm fine with using canned ones in this recipe. Once they are roasted and tossed in blackened seasoning, they make a great snack or addition to leafy salads such as this one.

creamy herb dressing

¾ cup silken tofu

2 tablespoons minced shallots

1 tablespoon minced fresh dill

1 tablespoon fresh parsley

¼ teaspoon Dijon mustard

Kosher salt

Freshly ground white pepper

spinach salad

1 (15.5-ounce) can chickpeas

2 large yellow bell peppers

1 tablespoon plus 1 teaspoon safflower oil

½ teaspoon kosher salt, plus more as needed

2 teaspoons Blackened Seasoning (page 239)

¾ pound spinach, torn into bite-size pieces

½ lemon

Freshly ground white pepper

1 tablespoon finely grated lemon zest

Dill fronds, for garnish

Make the dressing: In a blender, combine the tofu, shallots, dill, parsley, and mustard. Puree until creamy, then season with salt and pepper to taste. Set aside.

Make the salad: Drain the chickpeas in a colander, thoroughly rinse them in cold water, and set them aside to dry for 1 hour.

While the chickpeas are drying, roast the bell peppers using one of the methods on page 22. Seed and thinly slice them, then set aside.

Once the chickpeas have thoroughly dried, preheat the oven to 350°F. Line a rimmed baking sheet with parchment paper.

Transfer the dried chickpeas to a large bowl, add 1 tablespoon of the oil and ½ teaspoon of salt, and toss well to combine with clean hands. Spread the chickpeas in one even layer on the baking sheet. Bake, shaking the pan every 15 minutes to ensure even cooking, until golden brown and starting to turn crispy, about 45 minutes.

Immediately transfer the chickpeas to the bowl just used, drizzle the remaining 1 teaspoon oil over them, and sprinkle with the blackened seasoning. Toss well to combine, transfer back to the baking sheet, and set aside to cool for 15 minutes.

Place the spinach and bell peppers in a salad bowl. Lightly squeeze with the lemon juice, lightly sprinkle with salt, and toss to combine with clean hands. Stir the dressing a few times and lightly dress the vegetables. Add the chickpeas, season with pepper, and lightly drizzle with the dressing. Garnish with lemon zest and dill fronds.

"New Jack Bounce (Interlude)" by Christian Scott aTunde Adjuah from *Diaspora*

spinach and kale grit cakes

creamy creole sauce · thyme

makes 4 to 6 servings

This is a fun way to incorporate dark leafy greens into your meal. For a low-fat version, they can be cooked on a lightly greased baking sheet at 325°F until crisp, about 15 minutes on each side.

creamy creole sauce

3 tablespoons extra-virgin olive oil

3 tablespoons millet flour

1 cup 1/4-inch diced yellow onions

1/2 cup finely chopped celery

1/2 cup 1/4-inch diced green bell pepper

1 teaspoon minced garlic

1 teaspoon Creole Seasoning (page 239)

1/4 teaspoon kosher salt, plus more as needed

3 tablespoons tomato paste

1 tablespoon Bragg Liquid Aminos

1 cup vegetable stock (page 230)

1/3 cup Cashew Cream (page 231)

grit cakes

3 cups unflavored almond milk

1 cup vegetable stock (page 230)

1 cup stone-ground corn grits, soaked in water overnight and drained

1 tablespoon extra-virgin olive oil, plus more for frying

1 cup cleaned and chopped leek, white part only (about 1 medium)

1/2 teaspoon kosher salt

2 teaspoons minced garlic

3/4 cup stemmed and chopped lacinato kale greens

3/4 cup chopped baby spinach

1/3 cup thyme sprigs, for garnish

Make the sauce: In a medium saucepan over medium-low heat, warm 2 tablespoons of the oil until shimmering. Slowly whisk in the millet flour. Cook, stirring constantly, for about 15 minutes. Stir in the remaining 1 tablespoon oil, the onions, celery, and bell pepper and cook, stirring frequently, until the vegetables soften, about 5 minutes. Stir in the garlic, creole seasoning, salt, tomato paste, and liquid aminos. Cook, stirring constantly, for 2 minutes. Stir in the vegetable stock and cashew cream and bring to a simmer. Simmer the sauce, stirring occasionally, until starting to thicken, about 20 minutes. Season with salt to taste. Remove from heat and set aside.

Make the grit cakes: In a medium saucepan, combine the almond milk and stock and bring to a simmer over medium heat. While whisking constantly, slowly pour in the grits. Continue to whisk until no lumps remain. Bring to a simmer, still whisking, then reduce the heat to low. Simmer the grits, stirring every 2 to 3 minutes to prevent sticking, until tender and very thick, 30 to 45 minutes.

Meanwhile, warm the olive oil in a small skillet over medium heat. When the oil is shimmering, add the leek and salt. Cook, stirring, until well-browned, 10 to 15 minutes. Add the garlic and sauté until fragrant, 2 to 3 minutes. Remove from the heat and set aside.

Combine the kale greens, spinach, and 6 tablespoons water in a blender. Puree until very smooth, scraping down the sides as necessary, 1 to 2 minutes. Set aside.

Once the grits are done, scrape in the spinach and kale green mixture and the leek mixture and stir well. Continue to simmer on low heat, stirring frequently, until most of the additional liquid has been absorbed and the grits are once again very thick, 10 to 15 minutes.

Pour the grits into a 9-inch square baking dish and spread them out with a rubber spatula. Refrigerate and allow the grits to rest until firm, about 3 hours or up to overnight.

When you're ready to finish the cakes, preheat the oven to 250°F.

Flip the grits out onto a cutting board and slice into 16 two-inch squares.

In a large nonstick skillet, warm a scant tablespoon of olive oil over medium-high heat. When the oil is hot, pan-fry the cakes in batches until golden brown and crisp, 2 to 3 minutes per side. Transfer the cooked cakes to a baking sheet and keep them warm in the oven until all of the cakes are cooked.

Before serving, warm the sauce. Spread sauce on individual plates, top with a few grit cakes, pour sauce over the grit cakes, then garnish with thyme.

"Portrait of Wellman Braud" by Duke Ellington from *New Orleans Suite*

fungi

marinated trumpet mushrooms

molasses · tamari · chipotle · paprika

makes 2 servings

I refuse to call this "mushroom bacon." Bacon is bacon. These are tasty, thinly sliced trumpet mushrooms that have been tossed in a spicy sauce, then dehydrated in the oven. Let it be what it is: delicious!

2 tablespoons safflower oil

2 tablespoons raw cane sugar

1 teaspoon molasses

1 tablespoon chopped canned chipotle chile

1 teaspoon smoked paprika

¼ cup tamari

8 ounces trumpet mushrooms, cut lengthwise into ⅛-inch-thick slices

Preheat the oven to 225°F. Line a baking sheet with parchment paper.

In a large bowl, whisk together the safflower oil, sugar, molasses, chipotle, paprika, tamari, and ¼ cup water. Add the mushrooms and toss to coat well.

Spread the mushrooms on the prepared baking sheet and bake for 2 hours. Remove from the oven, transfer to a cooling rack, and let cool completely.

"All I Blow Is Loud" by Juicy J from *Stay Trippy*

choosing, storing, and cleaning mushrooms

If possible, choose loose mushrooms over prepackaged. This allows you to examine each one before buying. Your mushrooms should look healthy, without discoloration, so put them back if they are slimy. You also want them to smell fresh and earthy, so avoid sour-smelling mushrooms at all costs. I store them in the refrigerator inside a breathable container like an open plastic bag or a lidded container that is only partially covered. Be sure to use mushrooms within a few days because they go bad quickly.

In order to avoid waterlogging your mushrooms, gently wipe them with a damp paper towel when cleaning. I know this is a tedious process, but it is worth it to maintain the integrity of your mushrooms. If you are in a rush, you can quickly rinse them in cold water and immediately pat them dry with paper towels.

cornmeal-fried oyster mushroom po'boy

memphis coleslaw · creole rémoulade

makes 4 sandwiches

My plant-based journey has not been linear. Many people stop eating animal products and never look back. Not me. I started experimenting with veganism late in high school. I had periods in college where I was a strict vegan and other times when I wasn't (trust me, it was extremely challenging being a vegan while studying abroad in France in 1997). Nowadays, I have a plant-centered diet, but I tend to avoid labeling myself. I am driven by a desire to see justice for all living beings. I also know that there is a growing body of medical research that connects eating a plant-based diet with a lower risk of heart disease and other preventable diet-related illnesses, so I am also about that plant-based life for myself, my wife, and my girls. That being said, this po'boy takes me back to the early days of living in New Orleans when I was all about fish po'boys. Change is good.

3 tablespoons ground flaxseeds

3 tablespoons plus 1½ cups water, plus more as needed

1 cup white rice flour

½ cup arrowroot powder

½ cup stone-ground yellow cornmeal

2 teaspoons kosher salt, plus more as needed

2 teaspoons freshly ground black pepper

Safflower oil, for frying

1 pound oyster mushrooms, tough ends removed, torn into generous bite-size pieces

2 (15-inch) loaves soft-crusted French or Italian bread

Creole Rémoulade, for dressing (page 237)

2 cups Memphis Coleslaw (page 135)

Freshly ground white pepper

Crystal hot sauce

In a medium bowl, whisk together the flaxseeds and 3 tablespoons of the water with a fork to combine.

Add the rice flour, arrowroot powder, cornmeal, salt, and black pepper to the flax mixture and stir to combine. Stir in the remaining 1½ cups water and mix well.

Fill a Dutch oven or wok with safflower oil to a depth of about 2 inches and heat the oil to 350°F over medium-high heat. Heat the oven to 200°F. Line a platter with paper towels.

When the oil is hot, in three or four batches, dip the mushrooms in the batter and toss to coat them well. Carefully transfer them to the hot oil and fry, until crisp and golden brown, 4 to 5 minutes. (If needed, gently agitate them with a slotted spoon to break apart any mushrooms that begin to stick together.) Use a slotted spoon or a spatula to transfer the mushrooms to the platter, season lightly with salt, then place in the warm oven. Repeat with the remaining mushrooms, adding more water to the batter, as needed, if it becomes too thick to coat.

While the mushrooms are frying, halve the bread horizontally, then crosswise, and lightly toast it.

Spread the cut sides of the bread generously with rémoulade (I'm talking about a messy slather) and top the bottom halves evenly with the coleslaw. Add a generous handful of the mushrooms, sprinkle with pepper and douse with hot sauce. Cover with the top halves of the bread, and enjoy.

"No Indictment (feat. King Keon)" by SOL Development from *The Sol of Black Folk*

grilled maitake mushrooms

garlic oil · salt · pepper

makes 4 servings

In order to make sure I have my needs met at summer cookouts, I often bring maitake mushrooms (also known as hen of the woods) to throw on the grill. They don't require a lot of attention. In fact, I will often huddle them away from the main flame so they can cook slowly until crisp on the outside. If using an electric grill, just set it to low and cook the mushrooms until they are browned and crisp. Grilling them over charcoals can be a little trickier. You just don't want them too close to the flame or they will burn quickly. Once they're done, I add them to the plate along with whatever folks are eating at cookouts these days. My favorite way to have them, though, is atop slow-cooked grits. Plain and simple.

2 pounds maitake mushrooms, halved through the stem

Kosher salt

Freshly ground black pepper

½ cup Garlic Oil (page 232)

Heat a gas grill to low and lightly oil the grill grates.

Generously season the mushroom halves with salt and pepper, then drizzle each half with about 2 tablespoons of garlic oil.

Place over the grill, cover, and cook, turning after 5 minutes, until browned and crisp, about 10 minutes.

"Strange Piano" by Quasimoto from *The Further Adventures of Lord Quas*

millet roux mushroom gumbo

scallions · thyme · filé powder

makes 6 to 8 servings

Believe me, I'm not above using store-bought vegetable stock, or a quality vegan bouillon cube, for that matter, when I'm in a pinch. But nothing compares to the clean, fresh, full-bodied flavor of homemade stock. If you cut corners and use the premade stuff in this dish, folks probably won't know. But trust me, you will be glad you put in the effort to make your own.

If you aren't familiar with classic Louisiana cooking, roux, a combination of equal parts flour and fat, is the foundation of a tasty gumbo. In addition to adding bold flavor to gumbos, roux serves as a thickener. Typically, roux calls for all-purpose flour (cooking it over low heat removes the flour's raw taste), but I had been working on a gluten-free roux for months, and I finally struck gold. I find that millet flour not only works well as a substitute for wheat flour, but gives the roux a nutty flavor that further emboldens the taste of the overall dish. To be clear, there is no getting around the time-consuming nature of roux preparation. This one requires over an hour of stirring, so grab a bottle of wine, recruit a few friends to help (take turns every 15 minutes), and do dat. Millet flour does not turn as dark (chocolate) as roux made with wheat flour. You will know your millet-based roux is ready when it is the color of a roasted chickpea.

This gumbo (see photo on page 169) makes six to eight full servings, but if it is served as a part of a larger spread, it can easily feed more. Enjoy it along with white or Green Rice (page 155).

3 tablespoons plus ½ cup extra-virgin olive oil, plus more for frying

8 ounces shiitake mushrooms, stemmed, caps sliced ¼ inch thick

8 ounces cremini mushrooms, sliced ¼ inch thick

Fine sea salt

1 pound portobello mushrooms, sliced ½ inch thick

¾ cup millet flour

½ cup ¼-inch-diced yellow onion

½ cup ¼-inch-diced celery

½ cup ¼-inch-diced green bell pepper

2 garlic cloves, minced

6 cups vegetable stock (page 230), at room temperature

2 tablespoons tamari

2 bay leaves

Pinch of cayenne pepper

6 tablespoons fresh thyme

Freshly ground white pepper

Cooked rice, for serving

½ cup chopped scallions, plus more for garnish

Filé powder, for garnish

In a large cast-iron skillet, heat 1 tablespoon of the olive oil over medium heat. Add the shiitakes, cover, and cook, stirring occasionally, until fork-tender, 5 to 7 minutes. Transfer the mushrooms to a bowl and set aside.

In the same skillet, heat 2 tablespoons of the olive oil over high heat. Add the cremini mushrooms in one layer and cook, without stirring, until most of the liquid released by the mushrooms has evaporated and the mushrooms have started to brown on the bottom, 2 to 3 minutes. Turn each mushroom with a fork and cook for an additional minute or two, until browned on the second side. Transfer to the bowl with the shiitakes, sprinkle with salt, and stir to evenly coat.

Coat the skillet with olive oil and heat over high heat. Working in batches, add as many of the portobellos as will fit without crowding the pan and cook until golden brown on the bottom, about 2 minutes. Turn each mushroom with a spatula and cook for a minute or two more, until browned on the second side. Transfer the mushrooms to a paper towel–lined plate and sprinkle with salt on both sides. Repeat with the remaining portobellos, adding more oil between batches as necessary.

millet roux mushroom gumbo, continued

Add ½ cup of oil to the skillet and warm over medium-high heat until shimmering. While whisking, slowly add the flour, a little at a time, and whisk until mixed well. Cook, stirring frequently with a wooden spoon, until the mixture is slowly bubbling, then decrease the heat to low. Cook the roux, stirring frequently to prevent burning, until it turns the color of a roasted chickpea and has a nutty aroma, about 1¼ hours. Add the onion, celery, and bell pepper, stir until well incorporated, and cook, stirring occasionally, until the vegetables are starting to soften, about 5 minutes. Add the garlic and cook for 3 minutes more.

Remove the skillet from the heat. Transfer the contents of the skillet to a heavy-bottomed pot or a Dutch oven. Quickly whisk in the stock and set the pot over high heat. Cook, whisking, until the mixture comes to a boil. Add the tamari, bay leaves, cayenne, and 1 teaspoon salt. Decrease the heat to medium-low and simmer for about 45 minutes.

Add the shiitake and cremini mushrooms to the gumbo and simmer, stirring occasionally, for 5 minutes.

Stir 3 tablespoons of the thyme into the gumbo and simmer for 3 minutes more. Season with salt and white pepper to taste. Remove and discard the bay leaves.

To serve, ladle the gumbo into shallow bowls over rice and top with a few slices of the seared portobello. Garnish with the remaining 3 tablespoons thyme, the scallions, and a sprinkle of filé powder and serve.

"Fantastic Freaks at the Dixie" by Fantastic Freaks from *Wild Style Original Soundtrack*

tubers

potatoes

smashed fried potatoes 172

mashed potatoes and cauliflower 174

millet, red lentil, and potato cakes 175

brown stew with root vegetables 178

sweet potatoes and yams

roasted okinawan sweet potato wedges 180

candied yams 182

sweet potato, russet potato, and
tempeh hash 183

ash-roasted sweet potatoes 185

sunchokes

barbecue sunchoke chips 186

creamy grits with sunchoke puree
and tomato gravy 188

rigatoni with sunchoke-tomato sauce 190

sunchoke cream 191

taro

taro fire fries with green herb aioli 195

boiled taro 196

mini taro stacks 197

taro root cakes with shoyu-chili
dipping sauce 198

smashed fried potatoes

caramelized onion rings · sweet corn relish ·
spicy spring pea sauce

makes 4 to 6 servings

Heel up, wheel up, bring it back, come rewind.

(Sound of a DJ rapidly spinning a record backward)

My Smashed Potatoes, Peas, and Corn with Chile-Garlic Oil from *Afro-Vegan* got so much love, I had to remix it. That recipe was a deconstructed version of irio, a staple of the Kikuyu people consisting of pureed white potatoes with green peas and sweet corn mixed in. In *Afro-Vegan*, I smashed steamed potatoes and baked them before covering them with a lightly sautéed mixture of fresh green peas and corn. In this version, I steam new potatoes, smash them, then pan-fry them in peanut oil until crisp. I serve them topped with sweet corn relish and caramelized onion rings alongside a bowl of flavor-packed pureed peas for folks to spoon on like they would ketchup. The day I made these for my family, my eldest daughter said it was the best dish I'd ever made.

16 small new potatoes
(a little larger than a
walnut)

½ cup peanut oil

2 large yellow onions,
cut into ½-inch-
thick slices

Kosher salt

Sweet Corn Relish
(page 34), for serving

Freshly ground
black pepper

Spicy Spring Pea Sauce
(page 30), for serving

Fit a large pot with a steamer insert or a colander and fill with 2 inches of water. Put the potatoes in the steamer, cover, and cook over medium heat until fork-tender, about 45 minutes, adding more water to the pot as necessary. Remove the potatoes from the steamer and let cool for 5 minutes.

While the potatoes are steaming, warm ¼ cup of the oil in a large skillet over medium heat until shimmering. Reduce the heat to low and add the onion slices, keeping them intact. Cook, gently stirring for even cooking, until just starting to caramelize, about 30 minutes. Season with salt and set aside.

On a clean work surface, gently press each potato with the palm of your hand to flatten it to about ½ inch thick. Set aside.

Line a baking sheet with paper towels. In a large skillet, warm the remaining ¼ cup peanut oil over medium-high heat. Add half of the potatoes in a single layer and cook until crispy and browning, about 5 minutes. Salt the potatoes, gently flip them, and fry for 4 to 5 minutes more. Salt the second side and transfer to the prepared baking sheet. Repeat with the remaining potatoes.

To serve, arrange the potatoes on a serving platter, top with the onions and sweet corn relish, and season with pepper. Put the pea sauce in a medium bowl and serve it alongside the potatoes.

"Scenario (Remix)" by A Tribe Called Quest from *The Love Movement*

mashed potatoes and cauliflower

olive oil · almond dukkah

makes 4 to 6 servings

I really enjoy pureed cauliflower as its own thing, but I'm not feeling it as a replacement for mashed potatoes. My brain has a hard time enjoying it when presented that way. I do, however, get down with potatoes mashed with cauliflower. For the longest time I stayed away from that combination, but I changed my mind when my sister-in-law Danfeng served it at a family meal. I appreciate the fact that the cauliflower makes it a lower-carb dish than potatoes alone, but I really like the light-ness and flavor of the two vegetables together. After a few tests of this recipe, I decided that making the mashed potatoes and then folding in Creamy Cauliflower played better than cooking the cauliflower with the potatoes.

1 tablespoon kosher salt, plus more as needed

1½ pounds Yukon gold potatoes (about 5 large), peeled and thinly sliced

2 tablespoons extra-virgin olive oil, plus more for drizzling

¼ cup oat milk, warmed

Creamy Cauliflower (page 102)

Freshly ground black pepper

Almond Dukkah (page 240)

In a large pot, bring 1 gallon water to a boil over high heat. Add the salt and the potatoes to the boiling water and cook for 15 to 20 minutes, until soft. Drain the potatoes in a colander and set aside to dry a little.

Return the potatoes to the pot and set it over low heat. Using a fork or potato masher, mash the potatoes. Mix in the olive oil and oat milk until well combined. Fold in the creamy cauliflower. Season with salt and pepper to taste. Transfer to a serving dish, garnish with dukkah, drizzle with olive oil, and serve.

"The Festival (feat. Little Dragon)" by Mac Miller from *GO:OD AM*

millet, red lentil, and potato cakes

spicy green sauce · butter lettuce · benne seeds

makes 4 servings

In August 2017, Mitchell Davis, chief strategy officer of the James Beard Foundation, asked me to help curate the menu (along with chefs Dan Barber and Mary Sue Milliken) for the Bill & Melinda Gates Foundation Global Goals Awards ceremony. The awards recognize outstanding activists and campaign groups who have made a demonstrable positive impact and who inspire others to accelerate progress toward the United Nations' Sustainable Development Goals (there are seventeen of them). Our menu and accompanying narrative were crafted with an eye toward Sustainable Development Goal #2: to end hunger, achieve food security, improve nutrition, and promote sustainable agriculture. I created an entrée using millet—a crop that could play an important role tackling hunger in exploited/developing countries in sub-Saharan Africa because of its high nutritional value and ability to grow with very little water. The meal was fantastic, and my dish was a big hit. That November, the *New York Times* published my millet cake recipe in an article on Black vegans. The next month, *New York Times* food editor Sam Sifton included it on his Best Recipes of 2017 list. To really make this dish pop, you should eat it with something acidic, like Pikliz (page 134) or Pickled Mustard Greens (page 140).

1 russet potato, scrubbed

2 tablespoons ground flaxseeds

½ cup millet, rinsed

2 teaspoons fine sea salt, plus more as needed

½ cup red lentils, picked through (see page 48) and rinsed

2 tablespoons peanut oil or safflower oil

¾ cup finely chopped yellow onion

2 large garlic cloves, minced

1¾ teaspoons Berbere Spice Blend (page 238)

2 tablespoons millet flour

1½ cups panko bread crumbs, pan-toasted in 1 tablespoon peanut or olive oil

4 ounces butter lettuce (1 medium head), leaves separated

Smoky-Spicy Green Sauce (page 236), for dressing the lettuce and serving

Toasted benne seeds or brown sesame seeds, for garnish

Pikliz (page 134), for serving

Preheat the oven to 400°F.

With a fork, pierce the potato all over, then wrap it in aluminum foil. Bake until tender, 50 to 60 minutes. Set aside to cool. When the potato is cool enough to handle, peel it, transfer the flesh to a bowl, and thoroughly mash with a fork. Transfer ½ cup of the mashed potato to a medium bowl and set aside (reserve the rest for another use).

While the potato is cooking, in a small bowl, whisk together the flaxseeds and 6 tablespoons water with a fork. Cover and refrigerate for 15 minutes, until thickened.

In a small saucepan, toast the millet over medium heat, shaking the pan often to ensure even cooking, until the millet smells fragrant, 3 to 5 minutes. Add 1 cup water and ½ teaspoon of the salt, raise the heat to high, and bring the water to a boil. Immediately decrease the heat to low, cover, and cook until the water has evaporated, 18 to 20 minutes. Remove from the heat and set aside, covered, to steam until ready to use.

While the millet is cooking, in a small saucepan, combine the lentils and 1½ cups water. Bring to a boil over high heat, decrease the heat to low, skim off any foam, cover, and simmer until just tender, 5 to 7 minutes. The lentils should be soft but not falling apart, with a little bite remaining. Stir in a generous pinch of salt. Set aside, uncovered, to cool.

In a medium skillet, warm the peanut oil over medium-high heat until shimmering. Add the onion and sauté, stirring often, until soft, 5 to 7 minutes. Add the garlic and sauté until it starts to smell fragrant, 3 to 4 minutes. Stir in the berbere spice blend and ½ teaspoon of the salt and cook, stirring, until the onion and garlic are thoroughly coated with the spices, about 2 minutes.

Transfer the onion mixture to the bowl with the mashed potato. With a wooden spoon, stir in the millet, lentils, millet flour, and the flax mixture until thoroughly combined. Season with salt.

With clean hands, form the mixture into 9 cakes, using about 5 heaping tablespoons of the mixture per cake. Transfer to a glass baking dish, using parchment paper to separate the layers. Cover and refrigerate the cakes for 2 hours or up to 2 days before broiling.

Position an oven rack 5 to 6 inches from the broiler heat element and preheat the broiler. Line a baking sheet with parchment paper.

Put the toasted panko in a shallow dish and season with the remaining 1 teaspoon salt. Gently place each cake in the panko, coating both sides and shaking off any excess crumbs. Set the breaded cakes on the prepared baking sheet.

Broil the cakes until the panko is starting to brown, 2 to 3 minutes. Remove the baking sheet from the oven, gently flip each cake with a spatula, and broil for 2 to 3 minutes more, until starting to brown on the second side.

In a bowl, gently toss the lettuce with enough spicy green sauce to lightly coat.

To serve, stack the lettuce on a large platter and sprinkle generously with benne seeds. Arrange the cakes on the platter and serve family-style, with small bowls of spicy green sauce and pikliz alongside.

"Party Isn't Over/Campfire/Bimmer" by Tyler, The Creator (feat. Laetitia Sadier, Frank Ocean)

brown stew with root vegetables

kidney beans · guinness stout

makes 6 to 8 servings

Inspired by Jamaican brown stew, aka brown stew chicken, a classic dish popular throughout the Caribbean, this slightly sweet, savory, and spicy stew is a great way to showcase root vegetables. The original dish is "brown" from cooking chicken in fat and then simmering it in a mixture of brown sugar, aromatics, and spices, which yields a pecan-colored, rich, and delicious broth. Once, when vacationing with my parents in Fort Walton Beach, Florida, we stopped by a Caribbean restaurant and ordered a vegetarian brown stew—a rich gravy with lots of sautéed onions and bell peppers that tasted great with rice and peas (and plantains). I wanted to ask the chef about her recipe, but she had left for the day. In my re-creation of that memorable dish, I caramelize onions and add a smattering of coconut palm sugar and a smidgen of molasses, but a lot of the sweetness in this stew comes from roasting diced root vegetables, which deepens their flavor. I also add—and you're gonna love this—Guinness stout, which gives the stew a robust, chocolaty flavor. I add kidney beans for protein, but you should have this with Farro and Kidney Beans with Burnt Scallions (page 64) or your own take on rice and peas, because why not.

1 cup dried kidney beans, soaked in water plus 1 tablespoon kosher salt overnight

2 bay leaves

1 large white onion: half left intact, half diced

5 garlic cloves: 3 cut in half, 2 minced

1 dried red chile

3 (2-inch) pieces fresh ginger

2 teaspoons kosher salt, plus more as needed

2 cups $\frac{1}{2}$-inch diced peeled parsnips

2 cups $\frac{1}{2}$-inch diced peeled turnip

2 cups $\frac{1}{2}$-inch diced peeled russet potato

2 cups peeled and $\frac{1}{2}$-inch diced carrots

5 tablespoons extra-virgin olive oil

1 teaspoon ground allspice

1 teaspoon smoked paprika

$\frac{1}{8}$ teaspoon cayenne pepper

2 teaspoons Bragg Liquid Aminos

2 tablespoons tomato paste

1 cup Guinness stout

3 cups vegetable stock (page 230)

1 habanero chile, stem intact

Freshly ground white pepper

$\frac{1}{2}$ cup minced fresh cilantro

Preheat the oven to 450°F. Line 2 baking sheets with parchment paper.

Drain the beans and put them in a medium saucepan. Add the bay leaves, the intact onion half, garlic halves, chile, and ginger, and add water to cover by 2 inches. Bring to a boil over medium heat. Skim off any foam, decrease the heat to medium-low, and simmer, partially covered, until the beans are starting to turn tender, about 40 minutes, adding more water as needed to keep the beans covered. When the beans are just tender, add 1 teaspoon of the salt and cook for 10 minutes more. Drain the beans. Remove and discard the bay leaves, onion, garlic, chile, and ginger.

Meanwhile, in a large bowl, combine the parsnips, turnip, potato, carrots, 3 tablespoons of the olive oil, and $\frac{1}{2}$ teaspoon of the salt and toss to coat. Spread the vegetables in one even layer on the prepared baking sheets and roast until the vegetables are tender and caramelized on the edges, stirring every 10 minutes for even browning, 30 to 40 minutes.

While the beans are cooking and the vegetables are roasting, in a large pot, combine the remaining 2 tablespoons olive oil and the diced onion and cook over medium heat until soft, about 10 minutes. Add the allspice, smoked paprika, cayenne, minced garlic, and remaining ½ teaspoon salt and stir to combine. Cook, stirring occasionally, until the garlic smells fragrant, 2 to 3 minutes. Stir in the liquid aminos and tomato paste and cook, stirring often, until the tomato paste starts to stick to the bottom of the pan, about 5 minutes.

Once the beans and the roasted vegetables are ready, add them to the pot with the onion and spices. Stir in the Guinness stout and stock. Add the habanero and simmer, partially covered, for 35 minutes, stirring occasionally, removing the habanero after 10 minutes of simmering.

Taste and season with salt and white pepper. Garnish with the cilantro and serve.

"Fever" by Junior Byles from *Curly Locks*

roasted okinawan
sweet potato wedges

coconut milk · shredded coconut · cinnamon

makes 4 to 6 servings

Once in Oahu, Hawaii, I stopped by a supermarket to pick up some light snacks to take to the Hanauma Bay Nature Reserve. In the deli, I spotted some beautiful purple potatoes bathed in coconut milk. They were delicious and went well with the fresh fruits, carrots, nuts, hummus, and crackers. After that, I started to notice Okinawan sweet potatoes everywhere on the island—farmers' markets, grocery stores, restaurants. This simple and delicious recipe is inspired by that beachside snack. It can work at any meal or as an appetizer or snack.

2 tablespoons plus ¼ teaspoon kosher salt

3 pounds Okinawan sweet potatoes, peeled and cut into wedges

2 tablespoons coconut oil

1 (13.5-ounce) can unsweetened coconut milk

3 tablespoons coconut palm sugar

¼ cup finely shredded unsweetened coconut

Ground cinnamon, for serving

In a large pot over high heat, bring 3 quarts water to a boil. Add 2 tablespoons of the salt. Gently slide in the sweet potatoes, cover, remove from the heat, and set aside for 1 hour. Drain the sweet potatoes in a colander and set aside for 30 minutes to dry.

Preheat the oven to 400°F. Line a baking sheet with parchment paper.

In a large bowl, combine the sweet potatoes, coconut oil, and the remaining ¼ teaspoon salt and gently toss to coat. Gently transfer the sweet potatoes to the prepared baking sheet and spread in an even layer. Roast until tender, about 50 minutes, turning the wedges a few times to ensure even cooking.

While the sweet potatoes are roasting, combine the coconut milk and sugar in a small saucepan over medium heat. Bring to a gentle simmer and cook, stirring constantly to prevent the mixture from boiling, until the liquid has reduced by roughly half, about 30 minutes.

To serve, place the sweet potato wedges in a serving dish and pour the coconut milk over them. Sprinkle with the shredded coconut and cinnamon and serve.

"Over the Rainbow" by Israel Kamakawiwo'ole from *Alone in IZ World*

candied yams

cinnamon · molasses · maple syrup

makes 6 to 8 servings

If you don't like sweet dishes, you might want to skip this recipe. There is no getting around the flavorful syrup that is the hallmark of candied yams. This recipe is my nod to the classic side dish that is ubiquitous on holiday tables throughout the South. Traditional versions rely heavily on lots of butter and white and brown sugar. This syrup takes a lighter-handed approach, combining a tad of vegan butter with cane sugar, molasses, and maple syrup for sweetness plus orange and lemon juices and lemon zest to brighten it. Garnet yams, which have a soft, sweet, pumpkinlike flavor, are the perfect tuber to set this dish off.

2 tablespoons plus
½ teaspoon kosher salt,
plus more as needed

2½ pounds Garnet
yams, peeled and
cut into ½-inch-thick
rounds

2 tablespoons olive oil

2 tablespoons
vegan butter

¼ cup raw cane sugar

2 tablespoons molasses

2 tablespoons pure
maple syrup

¼ cup fresh
orange juice

1 tablespoon fresh
lemon juice

¼ teaspoon grated
lemon zest

2 tablespoons Cashew
Cream (page 231)

1 (2-inch) cinnamon
stick

½ teaspoon ground
cinnamon

In a large pot over high heat, bring 3 quarts water to a boil. Add 2 tablespoons of the salt. Gently slide in the yams, cover, remove from the heat, and set aside for 1 hour. Drain the yams in a colander and set aside for 30 minutes to dry.

Preheat the oven to 425°F. Line a baking sheet with parchment paper.

In a large bowl, gently toss the yams with the olive oil. Spread them on the prepared baking sheet in a single layer and roast for 20 minutes, turning them over after 10 minutes for even cooking. Remove from the oven and lower the oven temperature to 350°F.

While the yams are roasting, combine the butter, sugar, molasses, maple syrup, orange juice, lemon juice, lemon zest, 2 tablespoons water, cashew cream, and the remaining ½ teaspoon salt in a saucepan over medium heat. Simmer, stirring often, until hot to the touch and the sugar has dissolved, about 5 minutes. Set side.

Place the cinnamon stick at the bottom of a 2-quart baking dish and layer the roasted yams in it. Pour the molasses mixture over the yams. Bake, covered with aluminum foil, for 30 minutes total, thoroughly basting the sweet potatoes with the liquid in the baking dish every 10 minutes. Remove the foil, sprinkle with the ground cinnamon, and bake, uncovered, until the yams are tender and the sauce has reduced and thickened, about 20 minutes.

"Candy" by Cameo from *Word Up!*

sweet potato, russet potato, and tempeh hash

lemon juice

makes 4 servings

This is a fairly easy one-skillet dish that can be eaten at any meal. My inspiration is traditional breakfast hashes. I fry cubes of tempeh for protein, and use sweet potatoes and russet potatoes for diverse colors and flavors. Feel free to add other vegetables that you might have at home when sautéing the onions for an even more robust dish.

1 (8-ounce) package tempeh, cut into ½-inch cubes

½ cup tamari

¼ cup unseasoned rice vinegar

1 tablespoon coconut palm sugar

1 teaspoon minced garlic

6 tablespoons peanut oil, plus more for frying

1 medium sweet potato (about ¾ pound), peeled and cut into ½-inch dice

1 medium russet potato (about ¾ pound), peeled and cut into ½-inch dice

2 cups diced yellow onions

Kosher salt

Freshly ground black pepper

1 lemon, halved

Prepare a steamer basket in a large pot and fill with 2 inches of water. Put the tempeh in the steamer basket, bring the water to a boil over high heat, and reduce the heat to medium-low. Cover and steam for 15 minutes.

While the tempeh is steaming, make the marinade by combining the tamari, vinegar, ¼ cup water, sugar, garlic, and 4 tablespoons of the peanut oil in a blender and pureeing until smooth. Pour the marinade into a bowl, add the tempeh, and set aside for 1 hour, tossing the tempeh every 15 minutes for even marinating. The tempeh can marinate for up to 24 hours covered and refrigerated.

While the tempeh is marinating, pour the sweet potato and russet potato into the steamer basket just used. Fill the pot with 2 inches of water, cover, and bring to a boil. Reduce the heat to medium-low and steam for 15 minutes.

Drain the tempeh, reserving the marinade for another use.

Line a plate with paper towels and set aside. In a large cast-iron skillet, pour enough peanut oil to reach ¼ inch up the sides of the pan. Over medium-high heat, warm the oil until shimmering. Add the tempeh and fry, stirring to ensure all sides are browned, about 8 minutes. With a slotted spatula, transfer the tempeh to the plate and set aside.

Add the remaining 2 tablespoons oil to the pan just used and warm over medium-high heat until shimmering. Add the onions and cook, stirring occasionally, until soft, about 5 minutes. Add the sweet potato and russet potato and cook, stirring occasionally, until the vegetables are lightly brown and crisp, 10 to 15 minutes. Stir in the tempeh and season with salt and pepper to taste. Give a generous squeeze of lemon, and serve from the skillet.

"Ego Trippin' (Original 12" Version)" by Ultramagnetic MC's from *Critical Beatdown*

ash-roasted sweet potatoes

toasted pecan meal · flaky sea salt ·
spicy tamarind sauce

makes 4 servings

Now, I know you're thinking, "Why go through the trouble of roasting sweet potatoes in ash when I can cook them in the oven?" I get it–lighting up coals just to have them burn to ash so you can cook food is a lot of effort. But guess what? You can feed two birds with one scone (wink, wink) by grilling something over charcoal (like the Whole Charcoal-Roasted Kohlrabi on page 89) and then cooking sweet potatoes in the residual ash. After her first bite of these luscious sweet potatoes, my wife described their flavor as "primal"–explaining that she imagined our long-ago ancestors enjoying a similar sweet-smoky essence back when they chiefly cooked over open fires. Making a recipe like this is an extreme form of home cooking, and it puts our convenience-obsessed food culture in perspective. You can wrap the sweet potatoes in aluminum foil and bake them at 425°F until they are soft, 45 minutes to 1 hour, if you prefer. But if you want the rich, complexly flavored sweet potatoes shown here, you have to earn them.

Make the tamarind sauce: In a small bowl, combine the boiling water and tamarind pulp. Set aside to soak for 20 minutes.

Strain the tamarind mixture into a small saucepan and discard the solids. Bring the liquid to a simmer over medium heat. Stir in the dates, sugar, cayenne, ginger, and salt and simmer, stirring, until all the spices have dissolved. Carefully transfer to a blender and puree until smooth.

Check the consistency of the sauce; if it is thick, like ketchup, transfer it to a bowl for serving. If it is on the thinner side, return it to the saucepan and simmer until it thickens up, 3 to 4 minutes, then transfer it to a serving bowl.

Make the sweet potatoes: Using lump charcoal, light a fire in a grill and let the coals burn down to embers.

Burrow the sweet potatoes in the embers and cook, using tongs to rotate them a quarter turn every 10 minutes or so, until they are fork-tender, 45 minutes to 1 hour. With the tongs, transfer the sweet potatoes to a plate and set aside to cool.

In a food processor, pulse the pecans until finely ground, about 1 minute. Scrape into a small bowl and set aside until ready to serve.

To serve, cut each sweet potato in half lengthwise and sprinkle with ¼ cup of the pecan meal and a few pinches of flaky salt. Serve the sweet potatoes with the bowl of tamarind sauce alongside.

"Young Black Men and Prison" by Angela Davis from *The Prison Industrial Complex*

spicy tamarind sauce

1 cup boiling water

2 heaping tablespoons tamarind pulp

¼ cup pitted Medjool dates

2 tablespoons coconut palm sugar

¾ teaspoon cayenne pepper

½ teaspoon minced fresh ginger

½ teaspoon fine sea salt

sweet potatoes

4 medium sweet potatoes, scrubbed and pierced all over with a fork

1 cup pecan halves, toasted

Flaky sea salt, for finishing

barbecue sunchoke chips

peanut oil · bbq seasoning · sea salt

makes 4 servings

If you've never eaten sunchokes—also known as Jerusalem artichokes, earth apples, and sunroot—don't be intimidated. Think of them as a cooler cousin of potatoes. While many conventional supermarkets carry them these days, you are most likely to find them at specialty grocery stores and farmers' markets when they are in season from fall through spring (they reach peak flavor in winter). If you like barbecue potato chips, you'll love these barbecue sunchoke chips, which are a great introduction to this edible tuber. The peanut oil in which they are fried is a perfect complement to the slightly nutty and savory profile of sunchokes, and the barbecue seasoning is 100!

I like to eat these with an ice-cold beer while binge-watching episodes of *Sanford and Son*. Sometimes I just repeat the "Lamont Goes African" episode from season 2, where he reinvents himself by adopting a Congolese name (Kalunda, because Lamont is a "slave name"), wearing a dashiki, and making Fred get rid of all the pork in the house because "the human body was not designed to digest pork." That whole episode is filled with gems.

Fill a large bowl halfway with cold water and mix in the lemon juice and salt.

With a mandoline or a sharp chef's knife, cut the sunchokes into paper-thin slices, as long and thinly as possible, sliding them into the cold water as you slice them. Drain them in a colander and rinse them well, then dry them between two clean kitchen towels.

Pour the BBQ seasoning into a large paper bag, add a pinch of salt, and set aside. Line two large baking sheets with paper towels.

Fill a deep, heavy pot with peanut oil to a depth of 3 inches and heat the oil over high heat to 370°F. Working in batches, carefully drop a large handful of the sunchokes into the hot oil, stir them a few times with a fork to prevent them from sticking together, and cook until golden, 2 to 3 minutes. Using a spider, transfer them to the prepared baking sheets to drain. Repeat to fry the remaining sunchokes.

When all the sunchoke chips are fried, quickly pour them into the bag with the seasoning. Fold the bag over a few times, then shake vigorously to coat the chips in the seasoning. Pour the chips into a bowl and serve. They should last a few days sealed in a bag, but I doubt they make it past one sitting.

"40 Acres and My Props" by Showbiz & A.G. from *Runaway Slave*

1 teaspoon fresh lemon juice

1 teaspoon fine sea salt, plus more as needed

1 pound large sunchokes, scrubbed

2 tablespoons BBQ Seasoning (page 240)

Peanut oil, for frying

creamy grits with sunchoke puree and tomato gravy

ayocote negro beans · scallions · habanero hot sauce

makes 4 to 6 servings

The idea of combining beans with grits came during a meal at Kin Khao, a fantastic Thai restaurant in San Francisco. One of the starters was nam tok beans, a combination of ayocote negro beans with lime, chile, rice powder, light soy sauce, shallots, scallions, mint, and cilantro. The mix of flavors was impeccable, and the plump, meaty texture of the beans stood out. I immediately thought, "I have to use these in a recipe," and I later came up with the idea of adding them to a New Orleans–inspired tomato gravy to pour over grits. Now, you might be thinking, "Beans and grits? That's an odd combination!" I thought the same thing, but I was reassured by the heirloom bean whisperer Steve Sando, owner of Rancho Gordo, who reminded me that beans and corn are natural together.

I had been meditating on creative ways to use sunchokes for a minute. Having mostly eaten them deep-fried, as a garnish, I was pleasantly surprised at how tasty they are prepared as a mash (similar to mashed potatoes). I thought folding a sunchoke puree into creamy grits would be a good look. Sunchokes, or Jerusalem artichokes, are complex-flavored tubers; they are slightly sweet and nutty, with an earthy flavor profile that adds depth and a little smokiness to grits. For those not accustomed to the unique flavor of sunchokes, you may want to start out with ¼ cup of the puree. If you love it, use ½ cup.

If you can't find ayocote negro beans (also known as black runner beans) in your area, hit up Rancho Gordo and order a few bags (get some Royal Corona beans for the Big Beans, Buns, and Broccoli Rabe recipe on page 95, while you're at it). Make sure you soak the grits in stock overnight to reconstitute them and shorten their cooking time. If possible, make the sunchoke puree ahead of time to keep things moving once you start this recipe.

grits

¾ cup yellow stone-ground grits

3 cups vegetable stock (page 230)

tomato gravy

⅓ cup dried black runner beans, soaked overnight in water plus 1 tablespoon kosher salt

1 bay leaf

1 large yellow onion: half diced, half left intact

5 garlic cloves: 3 cut in half, 2 minced

1 dried red chile

1 teaspoon kosher salt, plus more as needed

¼ cup peanut oil

2 tablespoons millet flour

1 tablespoon sun-dried tomato paste

1 (15-ounce) can diced tomatoes, with their juices

2 cups vegetable stock (page 230)

2 tablespoons Cashew Cream (page 231)

Freshly ground black pepper

sunchoke puree

1½ pounds sunchokes, gently peeled

1 teaspoon coarse sea salt

2 tablespoons peanut oil

to finish

1 teaspoon coarse sea salt, plus more as needed

1 cup vegetable stock (page 230)

Freshly ground white pepper

Habanero hot sauce

½ cup chopped scallions

Place the grits in a large bowl, add the stock, and set aside to soak overnight.

Make the tomato gravy: Drain and rinse the beans. Put them in a medium saucepan and add enough water to cover them by 2 inches. Add the bay leaf, onion half, halved garlic cloves, and dried chile. Bring the water to a boil over high heat. Skim off any foam and decrease the heat to medium-low. Partially cover and simmer until just tender, 45 minutes to 1 hour (the cooking time will greatly depend on the freshness of the beans). Once the beans are just tender, add the salt and simmer for 10 more minutes. Drain the beans. Remove the bay leaf, onion, garlic, and chile and discard them.

In the same saucepan, warm the oil over medium heat until shimmering. Add the diced onion and garlic and cook until soft, about 5 minutes. Stir in the millet flour and cook, whisking continuously, until the flour starts to darken a bit, about 10 minutes. Whisk in the tomato paste. Stir in the tomatoes and their juices and the stock. Carefully transfer the mixture to a blender, puree until smooth, then return it to the pot. Decrease the heat to low and add the reserved beans to the sauce. Simmer for about 30 minutes. Add the cashew cream and simmer for 5 more minutes. Taste and season with salt and black pepper.

Make the sunchoke puree: While the tomato gravy is cooking, in a medium saucepan, bring 4 cups water to a boil over high heat. Decrease the heat to medium-low, add the sunchokes and salt, and simmer until fork-tender, 15 to 20 minutes. Combine the sunchokes and their cooking water with the peanut oil in a blender and blend until creamy. Use a silicone spatula to scrape the puree into a small bowl and set aside.

Finish the grits: Skim any hulls or chaff that has risen to the top of the soaking liquid, then pour the grits and their soaking liquid into a medium saucepan. Add the salt and bring to a boil over high heat, whisking vigorously until no lumps remain. Decrease the heat to low. Simmer, whisking occasionally to prevent the grits from sticking, until the grits have absorbed most of the liquid and are beginning to thicken, 2 to 5 minutes. Add the stock and simmer for 10 minutes, whisking occasionally, until most of the liquid has been absorbed.

Keep the heat on low, whisking frequently, until the grits are soft and fluffy, about 30 minutes.

Stir ¼ to ½ cup of the sunchoke puree into the grits and season with salt and white pepper to taste. The grits should be slightly firm and creamy. Add water to thin them, if necessary.

To serve, ladle equal portions of the grits into shallow soup bowls. Top each serving with tomato gravy. Garnish with a few dashes of hot sauce, the scallions, and a few turns of white pepper, then serve.

"Do I Need You" by Ann Peebles from *I Can't Stand the Rain*

soaking grits

I always soak my grits in liquid overnight. Doing this hydrates the kernels, which reduces the cooking time and yields creamier grits. You can cook the grits in their soaking liquid, so measure out the amount that you would cook them in before soaking.

rigatoni with sunchoke-tomato sauce

basil · umami powder

makes 4 to 6 servings

I dedicate this recipe (see photo on page 193) to my baby girl, Zenzi, who would be happy if all she could eat was bread, crackers, and (you guessed it) pasta. This easy, delicious weeknight recipe is one of her favorites. The first time I made it, she asked why I used rigatoni instead of penne, her favorite at the time. I told her the big, hollow shape of rigatoni is perfect for tucking more sauce into each bite. She agreed. I like serving this with Broccolini, which I blanch and toss in olive oil. Usually, I encourage Zenzi to eat her veggies before she has her pasta, for obvious reasons.

2 tablespoons
extra-virgin olive oil

1 cup finely chopped
white onion

4 garlic cloves, minced

½ teaspoon coarse
sea salt, plus more
as needed

2 tablespoons
tomato paste

1½ cups canned
crushed tomatoes,
with their juices

¾ cup water

1 cup Sunchoke Cream
(opposite page)

Freshly ground
white pepper

1 pound rigatoni

Umami Powder
(page 239), for serving

¼ cup torn fresh
basil leaves

Red pepper flakes,
for serving (optional)

In a medium saucepan, warm the olive oil over medium-high heat until shimmering. Add the onion and sauté until it starts to brown, 6 to 8 minutes. Add the garlic and salt and cook until the garlic is browning and smells fragrant. Stir in the tomato paste and mix well. Pour in the canned tomatoes with their juices and the water and mix well. Decrease the heat to low, cover, and simmer, stirring occasionally to prevent the sauce from sticking to the bottom of the pan, for 15 minutes. Pour in the sunchoke cream, stir well, and simmer for a few minutes to warm through. Season with salt and white pepper to taste. Remove from the heat and set aside.

Bring a large pot of water to a boil over high heat. Generously salt the water, then gently drop in the pasta. Cook, stirring occasionally, until al dente, 10 to 12 minutes. Drain the pasta and toss it with the sauce in a large bowl.

To serve, divide the pasta and sauce among individual serving bowls, generously dust with umami powder, and garnish with the basil. Finish with a few turns of white pepper (and red pepper flakes, if you'd like), then serve.

"Insieme" by Vhelade from *AfroSarda*

sunchoke cream

millet flour · vegetable stock · cashews

makes about 1 cup

The soft, sweet nuttiness of sunchokes adds a lot of flavor to dishes, and I frequently fold this sunchoke cream into soups and stews, much in the way one would use heavy cream. I also finish dishes with it when they need a cooling component—something creamy to pull all the ingredients together (see my Citrus and Garlic-Herb Braised Fennel on page 51).

2 tablespoons extra-virgin olive oil

4 ounces sunchokes, peeled and finely chopped

¼ cup diced yellow onion

1 tablespoon millet flour

1 cup vegetable stock (page 230)

1 tablespoon white wine

½ teaspoon coarse sea salt, plus more as needed

¼ cup cashews, soaked in water overnight and drained

Freshly ground white pepper

In a medium saucepan, warm the olive oil over medium heat. Add the sunchokes and sauté until they just start to soften, about 1 minute. Add the onion and sauté until soft, 3 to 5 minutes, being careful not to let it brown. Tip in the flour and mix well. Add the stock, wine, and salt. Decrease the heat to medium-low and simmer, stirring often, until the sunchokes are fully tender, about 10 minutes.

Drain the sunchoke mixture in a colander set over a bowl, reserving the cooking liquid. Transfer the sunchoke mixture to a blender and add the cashews. Puree, adding the reserved cooking liquid a little bit at a time until the sunchoke puree easily pours from the blender (you will likely need between ¼ cup and ½ cup of the liquid). Season with salt and white pepper and serve.

"Cold Coffee and Cocaine" by Prince from *Piano & a Microphone 1983*

taro fire fries with green herb aioli

pili pili sauce · fresno chiles · cayenne · parsley

makes 4 to 6 servings

Back in 2014, I was a guest speaker at the thirtieth Veg Food Fest in Toronto, and I had a ball! I gave a talk to hundreds of people about the contemporary food justice movement in the United States, followed by a cooking demonstration and book signing of *Afro-Vegan*. To all my fans in The 6ix and throughout Canada, much respect! For real. Y'all showed me so much love that weekend and continue to send good vibes and support from afar (shout-out to NeedleGroove in Montreal). Anyway, some of the organizers took me out on the town that night, and we hit up a few bars for drinks and bites. This is when I was introduced to a vegan version of poutine, a Canadian dish of French fries topped with cheese curds and brown gravy. Can't say I was sold on poutine (no offense, friends), but it did inspire this recipe. I like the concept: crisp French fries with a mélange of mouth-watering toppings. So I play off that structure here using batons of taro (instead of potatoes) topped with spicy pili pili sauce, Fresno chiles, a dusting of cayenne, and creamy herb-infused aioli to calm down all that heat. Sh***************t. This is pro-level snack food. Trust me, you will need a stack of serviettes to wipe all the remnants of that yummy sauce from your mouth and fingers when you're done!

green herb aioli

1 cup vegan mayonnaise

¼ cup minced fresh parsley

1 tablespoon minced garlic

1 teaspoon fresh lemon juice

1 teaspoon minced fresh thyme

⅛ teaspoon fine sea salt

fries

¼ cup extra-virgin olive oil

½ teaspoon fine sea salt

2 pounds fresh taro root, peeled and cut into ½-inch-thick fries

Pili Pili Sauce (page 236)

2 Fresno chiles, thinly sliced

2 tablespoons minced fresh parsley, plus ⅓ cup loosely packed whole leaves

Cayenne pepper (optional)

Make the aioli: In a food processor, combine all the ingredients for the aioli and puree until the mixture is green. Transfer to a squeeze bottle and set aside.

Make the fries: Position a rack in the upper third of the oven and preheat the oven to 425°F. Line a baking sheet with parchment paper.

In a large bowl, combine the olive oil and salt and mix well with a fork to combine. Set aside.

Spread the fries in a single layer on the prepared baking sheet and bake for 15 minutes, turning them every 5 minutes to ensure even cooking. Remove the fries from the oven and gently pour them into the bowl with the oil and salt. Toss to coat evenly, return them to the baking sheet, and bake for 10 to 15 minutes more, until the fries are browning and crisp.

To serve, transfer the fries to a large plate and generously sprinkle with pili pili sauce. Generously squirt the aioli over the top. Top with the Fresno chiles and parsley. If you really want to take this dish to the next level of heat, sprinkle the fries with some cayenne. Serve immediately.

"Unstoppable (feat. Santigold & Lil Wayne)" by Drake from *So Far Gone*

boiled taro

salt · cinnamon ·
vanilla–coconut palm sugar syrup

makes 4 servings

Sometimes we just have boiled taro around the
house to snack on. I add a cinnamon stick to the
water to infuse the taro with its distinctive flavor
and make a simple syrup of coconut palm sugar
for dipping.

1 cup coconut
palm sugar

1 vanilla bean, split
lengthwise and seeds
scraped out

1 tablespoon
kosher salt

1 (2-inch) cinnamon
stick

4 apple-size taro roots,
scrubbed

In a small saucepan, combine the sugar, vanilla
bean pod and seeds, and ½ cup water. Bring to
a simmer over medium-high heat, stirring until the
sugar has completely dissolved, about 3 minutes.
Set the syrup aside.

In a medium saucepan, bring 2 quarts water to a
boil over high heat. Add the salt, cinnamon stick,
and taro. Lower the heat to medium and simmer
until the taro is fork-tender, about 30 minutes.
Drain and set aside to cool. Once the taro is cool
enough to handle, peel it and cut it into chunks.

Serve the taro in a bowl, drizzled with the simple
syrup, along with a bowl of the simple syrup.

"Hard Times" by Baby Huey & The Baby Sitters from *The Baby
Huey Story: The Living Legend*

mini taro stacks

thai red curry · herbed bread crumbs

makes 4 to 6 servings

I have a special reverence for taro. Whenever my family goes on vacation, we try to incorporate some activities that allow us to connect with local people, learn about the history of that area, and experience indigenous culture. My wife and I spent a day on a taro farm in Kauai, Hawaii, during our honeymoon, and we respectfully incorporate it into our meals at home. This is an experimental dish that I created after having taro in a curry. Since we mostly use premade curry pastes at home, I suggest you do the same.

1 tablespoon kosher salt, plus more as needed

7 apple-size taro roots (about 2 pounds), scrubbed

1 (14-ounce) can unsweetened coconut milk

1½ teaspoons Thai red curry paste

1 cup vegetable stock (page 230)

1 (1-inch) piece fresh ginger, peeled and thinly sliced

2 tablespoons Bragg Liquid Aminos

2 tablespoons fresh lime juice

1 tablespoon coconut palm sugar

2 cups torn bread (from a day-old baguette)

2 tablespoons chopped fresh cilantro

2 tablespoons chopped fresh flat-leaf parsley

2 tablespoons chopped fresh Thai basil (sub Genovese basil if you can't find Thai)

1 teaspoon minced garlic

1 tablespoon coconut oil, plus more as needed

In a large pot, bring 4 quarts water to a boil over high heat. Add the salt and the taro. Boil, partially covered, until the taro are fork-tender, about 25 minutes. Drain the taro in a colander and let cool for 15 minutes. Peel the taro roots and cut them into ¼-inch-thick rounds. Set aside.

Meanwhile, in a medium saucepan, whisk together ¼ cup of the coconut milk and the curry paste and set the pan over medium heat. Stir in the remaining coconut milk, the stock, ginger, liquid aminos, lime juice, and sugar. Simmer, stirring often and being careful not to let the mixture boil, until the sauce starts to thicken, about 10 minutes. Using a slotted spoon, remove the ginger and set the sauce aside.

In a food processor, combine the bread, cilantro, parsley, basil, and garlic. Process until broken down into coarse crumbs.

In a large skillet, warm the coconut oil over medium heat. Add the bread crumbs and cook, stirring frequently, until golden brown, 5 to 7 minutes. Transfer to a bowl and season with salt. Set aside.

Preheat the oven to 375°F. Line a baking sheet with paper towels and lightly grease a standard muffin tin with coconut oil.

Coat the bottom of a small skillet with coconut oil and warm the oil over medium-high heat. Fry the taro, in batches, until brown and crisp, about 2 minutes per side. Transfer to the prepared baking sheet and season with salt.

Stack the taro slices in the prepared muffin tin until they reach the top of each hole, stacking the rounds from largest to smallest, starting from the bottom of each cup.

Pour enough curry sauce over the stacks to reach the top layer. Keep the remaining sauce warm over low heat.

Bake the taro stacks until the sauce is bubbling and lightly caramelized, about 25 minutes.

To serve, pour the remaining curry sauce into a rimmed serving plate or wide, shallow bowl. Use a small spatula to remove the taro stacks from the muffin tin and place them on top of the sauce. Sprinkle generously with the bread crumbs. Serve hot.

"Here Comes the Floods" by JoshuaGabriel from *21st Century Blues*

taro root cakes with shoyu-chili dipping sauce

porcini powder · shiitake mushrooms ·
cured black olives · scallion

makes about 12 cakes

I like small-plate meals: leisurely dining with a group of folks and ordering a diversity of things. In fact, some of my most memorable meals involve tapas at Spanish bars, small bites at Japanese izakayas, and dim sum at Chinese restaurants. If you've never had dim sum, it is a traditional meal of steamed, fried, and baked small-bite portions of foods like dumplings, various meats and seafood, noodles, and buns. Hands down, my favorite dim sum dish is turnip or radish cakes (the meat-free version), a dish traditionally made of Chinese turnips, rice flour, sausage, and dried shrimp. The cakes are steamed and then fried. Several years back, at an all-vegetarian dim sum restaurant in San Francisco, I was amped to get turnip cakes, but they weren't on the menu. Instead, they offered taro cakes, which are similar to turnip cakes but a little denser. They are primarily composed of taro and rice flour, and are steamed and fried like turnip cakes. This is my take on them. I add diced shiitake mushrooms and cured black olives to deepen the flavor. After cutting the cake in half widthwise, I suggest cutting each cake into 2-inch squares. Feel free to vary the size of the cakes to suit your needs.

1 tablespoon plus
½ teaspoon kosher salt

1¼ pounds taro roots,
peeled and diced

2 tablespoons peanut
oil, plus more as
needed

½ cup finely diced
yellow onion

8 ounces shiitake
mushrooms, stemmed
and finely chopped

1 tablespoon Umami
Powder (page 239)

½ cup finely chopped
pitted oil-cured
black olives

2 tablespoons thinly
sliced scallion

1 teaspoon
minced garlic

1¾ cups rice flour

¼ cup arrowroot
powder

1 tablespoon shoyu

Shoyu-Chili Dipping
Sauce (page 235)

In a large pot, bring 3 quarts water to a boil over high heat. Add 1 tablespoon of the salt and the taro. Boil, partially covered, until the taro is fork-tender, about 25 minutes. Drain the taro in a colander and let cool for 15 minutes. Transfer the taro to a medium bowl and mash with a fork until relatively smooth.

Meanwhile, in a large skillet or a wok, warm the peanut oil over medium heat until shimmering. Add the onion and cook, stirring often, until it is soft and translucent, about 5 minutes. Add the shiitake mushrooms and porcini powder and sauté until the shiitakes have released their liquid and are soft, about 5 minutes. Add the olives, scallion, and garlic and cook until the garlic smells fragrant, about 2 minutes. Set aside.

In a large bowl, combine the rice flour, arrowroot, and remaining ½ teaspoon salt. While whisking, slowly pour in 1¼ cups water and the shoyu and whisk until the batter is smooth, adding more water by the tablespoon if needed. With a wooden spoon, mix in the mashed taro and the onion-mushroom mixture until well blended. Set aside to rest for 30 minutes.

Generously oil an 8-inch cake pan. Stir the batter, then scrape it into the prepared pan.

Place a steamer basket or a colander in a large stockpot and fill the pot with enough water to reach the top edge of the steamer. Place the pan with the batter in the steamer, cover the pot, and set the pot over high heat. Steam until the batter is set, about 30 minutes.

Unmold the taro cake onto a clean cutting board and let cool until firm enough to slice cleanly, about 15 minutes. Cut the taro cake in half widthwise, then cut each half into 2-inch squares.

Coat a large skillet with peanut oil and heat over medium-high heat until shimmering. Working in batches, add the taro cakes and fry until golden brown and crisp, about 2 minutes per side.

Transfer to a platter and serve the hot, crisp cakes with the dipping sauce on the side.

"The Sacred Bird" by Blitz the Ambassador from *The Burial of Kojo (Original Motion Picture Soundtrack)*

roots

oven-roasted baby beets

lemon · yogurt · cumin seeds · olive oil

makes 4 servings

This simple and fun beet salad was inspired by a dish in Melissa Clark's *Dinner in an Instant*. She has always been one of my favorite cookbook authors, and her recipes are always on point.

1 pound mixed baby beets (about 12), scrubbed and stem end trimmed

1 lemon

¾ cup nondairy yogurt

1 teaspoon agave nectar

1 teaspoon cumin seeds, toasted

Extra-virgin olive oil

Flaky sea salt

Preheat the oven to 400°F.

Place the beets in a roasting pan and add ¼ cup water. Cover the pan tightly with aluminum foil and roast until the beets are tender, about 40 minutes. Set aside to cool for about 5 minutes.

With a Microplane, grate the zest of the lemon and set it aside. Cut the lemon in half. In a small bowl, stir together the yogurt and agave nectar, then squeeze in enough lemon juice to thin the yogurt so it easily pours from a spoon.

On a clean work surface, using a clean towel, rub the beets to remove their skins. Thinly slice half the beets and cut the remaining beets in half.

Arrange the beets on a serving platter. Drizzle the yogurt over the beets. Garnish with the lemon zest, cumin seeds, a glut of olive oil, and flaky salt and serve.

"Sour Mango" by Gabriel Garzón-Montano from *Jardín*

baked beet green and kale crisps

olive oil · umami powder

makes 4 to 6 servings

Wait, wait, wait. Don't throw away those beet greens; you can sauté them like you would any number of dark leafy greens; puree them into a smoothie for a hit of calcium, iron, and vitamins A and C; or bake them with kale for a fun, nutritious snack. Because you never know how many leaves you will get with your beetroots, I pair them with kale to supplement (and add their vibrant green color). Combine however many beet leaves you have with enough kale to equal approximately 1 pound greens total. The easiest way to make these is letting them crisp in a dehydrator, but oven baking them works just as well.

1 pound beet greens and curly kale, ribs removed and torn into bite-size pieces

2 tablespoons extra-virgin olive oil

3 tablespoons Umami Powder (page 239)

Preheat the oven to 275°F and line two baking sheets with parchment paper.

Combine the greens and oil in a large bowl. Massage the greens until just starting to wilt, about 2 minutes. Sprinkle in the umami powder and toss to coat the leaves.

Divide the greens between the baking sheets and spread in one even layer. Bake for 30 minutes, turning the leaves over after 15 minutes to ensure even cooking.

Remove from the oven, set aside to cool for 5 minutes, and serve as a snack.

"Brokenfolks" from Georgia Anne Muldrow from *VWETO II*

lacto-fermented beets, tomatoes, and basil

walnuts · olive oil · flaky sea salt

makes 4 to 6 servings

I created this dish for a gathering in October 2018. There were beautiful tomatoes at the farmers' market, and beets were in full force. Lacto-fermenting the beets was a great way for me to enhance their flavor while maintaining their nutrient density. The intensely flavored beets, fresh fall tomatoes, and a touch of basil make this a vibrant salad. The beets will take at least one week to ferment, so I would get them going and buy tomatoes soon before serving this salad.

1 tablespoon
kosher salt

3 cups filtered water

1 pound small beets,
trimmed and scrubbed

1½ pounds heirloom
tomatoes of varying
shapes, sizes, and
colors, thinly sliced

¾ cup walnut halves,
toasted, skins removed
(page 210)

Extra-virgin olive oil,
for drizzling

2 tablespoons minced
fresh basil, plus ¼ cup
torn fresh basil leaves

Flaky sea salt and
freshly ground
black pepper

In a small saucepan, combine the salt and filtered water and heat over medium heat, stirring, until the salt has completely dissolved. Refrigerate the brine until completely cool.

Thinly slice the beets crosswise into rounds between ⅛ and ¼ inch thick. Stack the beets in a clean 1-gallon canning jar. Pour the cooled brine over the beets and place a plate on top. Place a 28-ounce can of tomatoes over the plate to ensure that the beets stay submerged. Cover the jar with cheesecloth and set it aside at room temperature to ferment for at least 1 week. Once the beets are fermented to your taste, cover the jar and refrigerate. The beets will keep in the refrigerator for up to 3 months.

To serve, arrange the beets and tomatoes on a serving platter. Drizzle with olive oil, sprinkle with the walnuts, garnish with the basil, and season with flaky salt and pepper.

"Is You Is or Is You Ain't My Baby? (Rae and Christian Remix)" by Dinah Washington from *Verve Remixed*

caraway-roasted beets and carrots

creamy citrus vinaigrette · pistachios · cilantro

makes 4 servings

This is a fun salad that I like serving in cups. The magic of this dish is digging all the way to the bottom of the glass and scooping up dressing as you drag all the other ingredients into your mouth.

roasted beets and carrots

1½ tablespoons extra-virgin olive oil

1 tablespoon white wine vinegar

2 teaspoons caraway seeds, toasted and ground

¼ teaspoon kosher salt

2½ cups ½-inch-diced red beets (about 1 pound)

2 cups ½-inch-diced golden beets (about 12 ounces)

1 cup ½-inch-diced orange carrots (about 8 ounces)

½ cup ½-inch-diced yellow carrots (about 4 ounces)

creamy citrus vinaigrette

⅓ cup silken tofu

2 tablespoons fresh navel orange juice

1 teaspoon finely grated lemon zest

2 tablespoons fresh lemon juice

2 tablespoons white wine vinegar

1 tablespoon dark agave nectar

1 teaspoon Dijon mustard

½ teaspoon minced garlic

¼ teaspoon kosher salt

3 tablespoons extra-virgin olive oil

Freshly ground white pepper

to finish

½ cup roasted salted pistachios, chopped

¼ cup packed coarsely chopped fresh cilantro, plus ½ cup loosely packed whole fresh cilantro leaves

Make the roasted beets and carrots: Preheat the oven to 375°F. Line two baking sheets with parchment paper.

In a large bowl, combine the olive oil, vinegar, caraway, and salt and mix well. Add the beets and carrots and toss well with clean hands to combine.

Pour the vegetables onto the prepared baking sheets, spread them into one layer, tightly cover the baking sheets with aluminum foil, and roast until just tender, about 45 minutes. Remove the foil and roast for 15 minutes more, stirring every 5 minutes. Remove from the oven and let cool.

Make the citrus vinaigrette: While the vegetables are roasting, in a blender, combine the tofu, orange juice, lemon zest, lemon juice, vinegar, agave, mustard, garlic, and salt. Blend until smooth. With the blender running, slowly pour in the olive oil through the hole in the lid and blend until emulsified. Season with white pepper and set aside until ready to serve.

To serve, arrange four wide-mouth jars on a work surface. Pour 2 tablespoons of the dressing into each of the jars and evenly divide the beets and carrots among them. Top each jar with 2 tablespoons of the pistachios and evenly divide the cilantro among the jars. Serve immediately or cover the jars and refrigerate until ready to serve.

"Food Fight (feat. stic.man)" by J. Bless and Seasunz from *Earth Amplified*

creamy carrot-coconut soup

ras el hanout · almond dukkah · parsley

makes 4 servings

I hope this recipe serves as a model for how easily you can convert farm-fresh ingredients into a simple, delicious pureed winter soup. The foundation is a mixture of sautéed aromatics, a blend of fragrant spices (store-bought ras el hanout is fine), a clean homemade stock, and something creamy. After that, it's simply a matter of choosing garnishes that will enhance the flavor, add freshness, and make a beautiful presentation.

2 tablespoons
extra-virgin olive oil

2 cups diced
yellow onions

1 teaspoon
minced garlic

1½ teaspoons ras
el hanout

1½ pounds carrots,
chopped

4 cups rich vegetable
stock (page 231)

¼ cup unsweetened
canned coconut milk

2 tablespoons fresh
lemon juice

¼ cup Almond Dukkah
(page 240), for garnish

2 tablespoons minced
fresh parsley, for
garnish

In a medium saucepan, warm the olive oil over medium heat until shimmering. Add the onions and sauté until just soft, about 5 minutes. Add the garlic and cook until fragrant, 2 to 3 minutes. Add the ras el hanout and stir to combine. Add the carrots and stock and bring to a simmer. Cook, partially covered, until the carrots are meltingly tender, about 30 minutes.

Working in batches, transfer the soup to a blender and puree, then return it to the pot (or puree it directly in the pot using an immersion blender). Stir in the coconut milk and lemon juice and simmer for a few minutes to combine. Thin the soup with water if necessary (the soup should easily pour from a spoon).

Ladle the soup into four bowls, top evenly with the dukkah and parsley, and serve.

"Hunter" by Björk from *Homogenic*

quick-pickled carrots, green beans, and grape tomatoes

butter lettuce cups · peanuts · cilantro

makes about 1 quart / 12 servings

I make refrigerator pickles often during the summer. Quick pickling is a fun way to preserve surplus vegetables from your garden or local farms, and it is a great way to use odds and ends from leftover vegetables after making a dish. Either way, the method in this recipe can be adapted using any number of fresh vegetables, so experiment to see what works for you. The combination of vegetables and Southeast Asian-inspired brine is a nod to one of my favorite dishes in Thai cuisine—green papaya salad. Instead of using papaya, however, I call for julienned carrots for a twist, and I suggest serving the pickled vegetables inside lettuce cups.

4 large orange carrots (about 1 pound), peeled and julienned

4 ounces green beans, trimmed

8 grape tomatoes, halved

3 Thai chiles, stemmed, seeded, and julienned

1 (3 by 5-inch) strip kombu

1 whole garlic clove, peeled

8 whole black peppercorns

1¾ cups unseasoned rice vinegar

1 cup distilled white vinegar

3 tablespoons fresh lemon juice

2 tablespoons fresh lime juice

1 tablespoon tamari

½ cup coconut palm sugar

1 tablespoons kosher salt, plus more for serving

24 butter lettuce leaves (from about 3 large heads)

½ cup chopped toasted peanuts

¼ cup chopped fresh cilantro

Pack the carrots, green beans, tomatoes, chiles, kombu, garlic, and peppercorns into a sterilized quart-size canning jar.

In a medium saucepan over medium-high heat, combine the vinegars, 2 tablespoons of the lemon juice, the lime juice, tamari, sugar, and salt and simmer until hot to the touch and the sugar and salt have dissolved. Remove from the heat to cool for 15 minutes. Pour into the canning jar and set aside to cool completely. Cover with a lid and refrigerate overnight to let the flavors develop, removing the kombu after 2 hours.

To serve, place the lettuce leaves in a large bowl and drizzle with the remaining 1 tablespoon lemon juice and a sprinkle of salt. Gently toss to coat the leaves.

Next, arrange one large lettuce leaf and one small lettuce leaf on a serving platter, overlapping the leaves slightly to form a cup. With tongs, lift enough vegetables from the brine to fill the cup and place in the center of the lettuce leaf cup. Repeat with the remaining lettuce and vegetables. Sprinkle with the peanuts and cilantro before serving.

"Mango Walk" by The Senior Allstars from DUB from *Jamdown: Darker Than Blue*

oven-roasted carrots with carrot top–walnut pesto

clementine juice · ginger · lemon zest · za'atar

makes 6 to 8 servings

While clementine juice plays brilliantly off of the earthy and sweet flavor of orange and red carrots, I felt like something was missing when solely basting them in juice. Carrot top pesto was my answer. For the longest time I avoided making carrot top pesto—for whatever reason, I felt like it was cliché. But it all made sense when I paired the pesto with these carrots. Its beautiful color, rich flavor, and chunky-sauciness took this from a pretty good side to a party-worthy standout. The ginger is subtle, but the za'atar adds 'nuff zing. If clementines aren't available, you can use navel oranges, though they aren't as sweet.

8 large carrots with tops (between 3 and 4½ ounces each)

¼ cup fresh clementine juice

½ cup plus 2 tablespoons extra-virgin olive oil

1 teaspoon minced fresh ginger

¼ teaspoon kosher salt, plus more as needed

3 tablespoons Umami Powder (page 239)

⅓ cup chopped toasted walnuts, skin removed (see sidebar)

2 teaspoons minced garlic

2 heaping tablespoons white miso paste

1 tablespoon lemon juice, plus more as needed

Freshly ground white pepper

1 heaping teaspoon lemon zest, for garnish

1 heaping tablespoon minced flat-leaf parsley, for garnish

Za'atar (page 240), for garnish

Preheat the oven to 400°F.

Separate the carrots and their green tops and chop the tops. Measure out 2 cups of the tops and set aside (reserve the rest for another use or discard them). Spread the carrots in a single layer in a large baking dish.

In a small bowl, combine the clementine juice, 2 tablespoons of the oil, the ginger, and salt and mix well with a fork to combine. Pour the mixture over the carrots and slather them well with clean hands. Cover the dish with aluminum foil and roast until the carrots are just starting to become tender, about 45 minutes. Remove the foil, gently turn the carrots with a fork to further coat them with the oil mixture, and return to the oven, uncovered, until fork-tender and browning, about 15 more minutes. Remove from the oven and let cool to room temperature.

Meanwhile, in a food processor, combine the carrot tops, umami powder, walnuts, garlic, miso, and lemon juice. Blend to combine. With the machine running, slowly pour in the remaining ½ cup olive oil through the feed tube and process until combined. Transfer the pesto to a small bowl and add enough water to loosen it up a bit (it should be thick but not pasty). Season with salt and white pepper to taste. Transfer to a small bowl for serving.

Transfer the carrots to a platter and sprinkle with the lemon zest, parsley, and za'atar. Serve with the bowl of pesto alongside.

"Higher" by 0h No from *Dr. No's Experiment*

removing skin from walnuts

I often call for removing the bitter outer skin of walnuts before adding them to dishes. Just toast them in a 350°F oven for 8 minutes, stirring halfway through. After letting the walnuts cool, transfer them to a sieve and stir them against the wire until the skins loosen and fall off.

barbecue carrots with slow-cooked white beans

pikliz · scallions · country bread

makes 4 servings

Even though this is a fall/winter dish, whenever I eat it, I can't help but ruminate on family cookouts when I was a kid. The luscious barbecue spice-infused beans bring back memories of swimming, wrestling with my cousins, and playing video games in between bites of potato salad, baked beans, and other family favorites. The finger-licking barbecue carrots in this dish are a standout on their own, but their interplay with the beans is outstanding. I suggest adding vinegary pikliz or Memphis Coleslaw (page 135) to brighten each bite, but you can add any number of pickled vegetables for this purpose. Serve this with a thick, toasted slice of country bread for mopping up the saucy elements of the dish and balancing the intensely-flavored carrots and beans.

8 (4-ounce) carrots, trimmed and peeled

3 tablespoons extra-virgin olive oil

5 tablespoons BBQ Seasoning (page 240)

1 cup great northern beans, picked over and soaked in water with 1 tablespoon salt overnight

1 (2-inch) piece kombu

1 large white onion, halved: half kept intact, half finely diced

5 garlic cloves: 3 kept whole, 2 minced

1 dried red chile

1¼ teaspoons kosher salt, plus more for seasoning

2 tablespoons tomato paste

1 cup chopped canned tomatoes, with their juices

1 tablespoon Bragg Liquid Aminos

1 (3-inch) rosemary sprig

1 bay leaf

Pikliz (page 134), for garnish

Thinly sliced scallions, for garnish

Freshly ground black pepper

Toasted country bread, for serving

Preheat the oven to 300°F. Line a rimmed baking sheet with parchment paper.

Spread the carrots out in an even layer on the prepared baking sheet. Rub with 2 tablespoons of the oil, followed by 4 tablespoons of the BBQ seasoning. Cover the baking sheet tightly with aluminum foil and bake until the carrots are super tender, about 2 hours.

While the carrots slow-roast, cook the beans: Drain the beans and pour them into a medium saucepan or Dutch oven. Cover them with 3 inches of water and bring to a boil over high heat. Lower the heat to medium and add the kombu, onion half, peeled garlic cloves, and chile. Partially cover and simmer until just tender, 1 to 1½ hours. When the beans are 10 minutes from being done, add 1 teaspoon of the salt and simmer for another 10 minutes. Drain the beans, reserving 3 cups of the cooking liquid. Remove the kombu, onion, garlic, and chile, and discard.

While the beans are cooking, warm the remaining 1 tablespoon olive oil in a medium skillet over medium-high heat until shimmering. Add the diced onion and sauté until soft, about 5 minutes. Add the minced garlic and ¼ teaspoon of the salt and cook until the garlic smells fragrant, 2 to 3 minutes. Add the tomato paste and remaining 1 tablespoon BBQ seasoning and cook, stirring often, until the paste begins to stick to the bottom of the pan, 1 to 2 minutes. Add the tomatoes and liquid aminos, bring to a simmer, and continue to cook, stirring often until the mixture is dark red and thick, about 5 minutes.

Return the drained beans to their pot and scrape in the contents of the skillet. Add the reserved cooking liquid, rosemary, and bay leaf and bring to a simmer over medium heat. Reduce the heat to low and simmer until the beans are very flavorful and the sauce has thickened, about 1 hour. Remove and discard the bay leaf.

Once the carrots have become super tender, remove them from the oven and increase the temperature to 450°F. Uncover the carrots and carefully flip each over. When the oven is hot, bake the carrots until sizzling and caramelized all over, flipping the carrots and rotating the baking sheet as needed, 7 to 10 minutes.

To serve, ladle the beans into four bowls. Top each bowl with two carrots, and garnish with pikliz and scallions. Season with salt and pepper to taste and pass the toasted country bread.

"Atari" by Hiatus Kaiyote from *Choose Your Weapon*

grated parsnip and carrot salad

ginger vinaigrette · parsley

makes 4 to 6 servings

My last semester of college, I studied in Angers, a small town in western France, and I would often travel to Paris to visit friends and enjoy the city on weekends and breaks. As a plant-based baller on a budget, I discovered that the ubiquitous carottes râpées—grated carrot salad—was a lifesaver in such an expensive city. Those salads were cheap, vegan, and really tasty, plus they helped me value the simplicity of raw vegetables dressed with a little bit of salt, fat, and acid. Here I toss grated carrots and parsnips with a simple ginger vinaigrette. Feel free to experiment with other root vegetables, and if you have fresh-out-of-the-ground organic vegetables, try this salad simply coated in a few glugs of olive oil, fresh lemon juice, and good-quality salt so the brilliance of the vegetables can shine through.

⅓ pound parsnips, peeled and coarsely grated

⅔ pound carrots, peeled and coarsely grated

2 tablespoons minced parsley

¼ cup unseasoned rice vinegar

2 teaspoons minced fresh ginger

1 teaspoon light agave nectar

¼ cup olive oil

Kosher salt

Freshly ground white pepper

Combine the parsnips, carrots, and parsley in a large bowl and set aside. In a blender, combine the rice vinegar, ginger, and agave. Pulse a few times to combine, then, with the blender running, slowly pour in the oil through the hole in the lid and blend until emulsified. Season to taste with salt and pepper. Pour enough dressing over the vegetables to lightly dress. Toss. Transfer to a serving bowl and serve.

"Ma colère" by Françoiz Breut from *Françoiz Breut*

dressing salads

Monifa Dayo, my talented chef friend, gave me the best advice for making flavorful salads, which I will share with you: Before coating the leaves with dressing, lightly spray them with fresh lemon juice, sprinkle with salt, and toss to coat. This technique helps amplify the flavors of the dressing once it's added. If using a dressing that has been refrigerated, make sure to bring it to room temperature before tossing. Also, be sure to add just a little dressing at a time so the salad is lightly coated but not drowning in it.

lentil soup

parsnips · sweet potatoes · carrots

makes 6 to 8 servings

This is the type of simple, hearty, and warming soup that I cook throughout the winter. I made a version of it for my wife when we started dating in 2007. That one was an empty-the-refrigerator soup using carrots and parsnips that I had gotten from the market that week. My inspiration was dal, an Indian spice-filled lentil soup. I remember that evening like yesterday. It was a rainy night in San Francisco, and I thought killing a simple soup would be more impressive than cooking something fancy. We ate it with sourdough bread and drank red wine. That evening was a turning point in our relationship. Now, I can't guarantee that you'll get busy if you make this for some cutie, but I promise y'all will be full and happy.

3 tablespoons olive oil

1 cup diced
yellow onion

¾ cup peeled and finely
diced parsnips

¾ cup peeled and finely
diced sweet potatoes

¾ cup peeled and finely
diced carrots

2 teaspoons kosher
salt, plus more to taste

2 cups dried lentils

2 cups canned diced
tomatoes

8 cups rich vegetable
stock (page 231)

3 tablespoons fresh
lemon juice, plus more
to taste

¼ cup coconut oil

6 garlic cloves, minced

1 to 2 dried red chiles

1 tablespoon
cumin seeds

1 teaspoon
sweet paprika

Freshly ground
black pepper

In a large pot over medium-low heat, warm the olive oil until shimmering. Add the onion, parsnips, sweet potatoes, carrots, and salt and cook, stirring often, until the vegetables are soft, 8 to 10 minutes. Stir in the lentils, tomatoes, and stock. Bring to a boil, reduce the heat, then simmer over low heat until the lentils are tender, about 45 minutes. Stir in the lemon juice.

When the lentils are almost finished, melt the coconut oil in a small skillet over medium heat. Add the garlic and chiles and cook, stirring frequently, until aromatic, 1 to 2 minutes. Add the cumin seeds and cook for 30 seconds. Stir in the paprika, let it sizzle, then immediately scrape the mixture into the hot lentil soup. Stir well, then season to taste with salt, pepper, and additional lemon juice. Serve.

"Spit Game" by Nappy Nina from *The Tree Act*

roasted parsnips with onion-mustard sauce

caramelized onions · mustard seeds · thyme · crushed peanuts

makes 4 servings

Inspired by the Senegalese poulet yassa–a dish of chicken and caramelized onion with lemony mustard sauce–this recipe pairs mildly sweet, earthy, and nutty parsnips with a juicy and flavorful marinade of peanut oil, black pepper, onions, mustard seeds, garlic, habanero, and Dijon mustard. The parsnips are then topped with seasoned caramelized onions and garnished with peanuts and thyme, adding to the layers and levels of deliciousness. This is a richly flavored side dish that should be served alongside a neutral starch such as rice or mashed potatoes to balance its intensity.

1 tablespoon plus 1 teaspoon kosher salt

2 pounds parsnips, peeled

½ cup fresh lemon juice

¼ cup plus 2 tablespoons peanut oil

Freshly ground black pepper

2 large Vidalia or yellow onions, sliced into ½-inch rings

1 teaspoon yellow mustard seeds

1 teaspoon minced garlic

⅛ teaspoon minced habanero chile, or to taste

1 tablespoon Dijon mustard

¼ cup crushed peanuts

1 tablespoon fresh thyme leaves

In a large pot, bring 3 quarts water to a boil over high heat. Add 1 tablespoon of the salt and the parsnips to the water and cook until starting to soften, 4 to 5 minutes. Drain the parsnips and set aside to cool slightly.

In a large bowl or baking dish, combine the lemon juice, 6 tablespoons water, ¼ cup of the peanut oil, the remaining 1 teaspoon salt, and a few turns of pepper. Mix well with a fork to combine. Once the parsnips are cool enough to handle, cut them in half lengthwise and add them to the bowl with the marinade. Add the onions and toss well to ensure that all the vegetables are coated. Cover and refrigerate for at least 2 hours or up to overnight, tossing the vegetables every 30 minutes or so for the first 2 hours.

In a large sauté pan, warm the remaining 2 tablespoons peanut oil over medium-low heat. Remove the onions from the marinade and add them to the pan. Sauté, stirring frequently, until deep golden brown and soft, 30 to 45 minutes. Add the mustard seeds, garlic, and habanero and sauté, stirring well, until the garlic smells fragrant, 3 to 4 minutes. Scrape the vegetables into a bowl.

Preheat the oven to 450°F. Line a large rimmed baking sheet with parchment paper.

Remove the parsnips from the marinade and place them cut-side up on the prepared baking sheet (reserve the marinade in the bowl). Roast the parsnips, gently stirring every 10 minutes, until fork-tender and starting to brown, about 30 minutes.

In a blender, combine ½ cup of the onion mixture, the reserved marinade, and the mustard and blend until creamy. Pour the contents of the blender into a small pan and simmer over medium heat, stirring often, until the sauce starts to thicken, 3 to 5 minutes.

To serve, spread the onion-mustard sauce over a serving plate and place the parsnips over the sauce, cut-side up. Garnish with the remaining onion-mustard sauce, onions, the peanuts, and thyme and serve family-style.

"Takuta (feat. Babatunde Olatunji)" by Youssou N'Dour from *History*

root vegetable kakiage tempura with tamari-kombu dipping sauce

shichimi togarashi · black sesame seeds

makes 8 servings

Kakiage is a type of tempura in which vegetables are cut into a julienne—long, thin strips—before dipping into a batter and deep frying. When my wife was obsessed with making tempura for three months, kakiage was our favorite. In this recipe I call for parsnips, carrots, and burdock, but any hardy root vegetable would work. Be sure to revisit my tips for making tempura on page 18 to ensure that you nail this recipe. The tamari-kombu dipping sauce provides a range of flavors that enhance the taste of the kakiage: umami from the kombu; sweet from the coconut palm sugar and mirin; savory from the tamari; nutty from the sesame oil; spicy from the ginger; and bitter-peppery from the daikon. Give folks the option of adding a final layer of zest by serving shichimi togarashi—a common Japanese spice mixture found at Asian markets and some conventional supermarkets—mixed with black sesame seeds to sprinkle onto the kakiage.

tamari-kombu dipping sauce

1 (3 by 5-inch) strip kombu

½ teaspoon coconut palm sugar

½ cup tamari or soy sauce

½ cup mirin

1 teaspoon toasted sesame oil

½ teaspoon fresh ginger juice (see sidebar, page 54)

¾ cup coarsely grated peeled daikon radish

root vegetable kakiage tempura

4 to 6 cups sunflower oil, for frying

2¼ cups cake flour

5 tablespoons arrowroot powder

2 teaspoons baking powder

1 teaspoon fine sea salt

¼ teaspoon ground black pepper

2 cups chilled club soda

1 cup thinly sliced white onion

¾ pound parsnips, peeled and julienned

¾ pound carrots, peeled and julienned

¾ pound burdock, peeled and julienned

¼ cup shichimi togarashi, for serving

1 tablespoon black sesame seeds, for serving

¼ cup minced scallions, for serving

Make the dipping sauce: In a small saucepan over medium-high heat, combine the kombu, sugar, and 1 cup water. Bring to a boil. Immediately remove from the heat. Stir in the tamari, mirin, sesame oil, and ginger juice, and set aside to cool for 15 minutes. Stir in the daikon immediately before serving.

Make the kakiage: Cut three 4 by 4-inch squares of parchment paper and set aside.

Pour enough oil into a cast-iron skillet to measure at least 1 inch deep. Place over medium-high heat and bring the temperature of the oil up to 375°F. Heat the oven to 200°F.

Prepare an ice bath in a large bowl.

While the oil is heating, whisk the flour, arrowroot, baking powder, salt, and pepper in a second large bowl.

Add the club soda and 4 ice cubes to the flour mixture and gently stir with a spoon until the batter just comes together, being careful not to overmix (it is fine if there are a few lumps). Place the bowl with the batter into the large bowl with the ice bath to keep the batter cold.

Add the onion and root vegetables to the batter and mix gently to coat.

Working in batches, grab a handful of vegetables, pile them on a piece of parchment paper, then gently slide the paper with the vegetables on it into the oil (remove the parchment paper with tongs after it detaches from the kakiage). Deep-fry the kakiage for 1 minute or so, then gently turn over with a spatula. Cook for another minute, until crisp and golden. Using a wire skimmer or slotted spoon, transfer the kakiage to a paper towel-lined plate to drain. Place the plate in the warm oven. Repeat, in batches, with the remaining vegetables and keep them warm in the oven.

Combine the shichimi togarashi and the sesame seeds in a small bowl, then pour into a pile on a large serving platter. Pile the scallions onto the platter, and place the dipping sauce onto the platter.

Transfer the kakiage to the platter and serve.

"Guerrilla" by Leon Fanourakis from *Chimaira*

how to julienne vegetables

This recipe calls for matchstick-size vegetables, also known as julienne. To julienne, simply peel your root vegetables and cut them into 3-inch lengths, trimming each side to lie flat on the work surface (yielding a rectangular shape). Next, cut the vegetable rectangle lengthwise into $\frac{1}{8}$-inch-thick slices and stack the slices. Then slice crosswise the vegetable stacks widthwise into matchsticks lengths.

turnip green soup

roasted turnips · shallots · thyme

makes 4 to 6 servings

This recipe is an update of a favorite recipe from my book *Vegan Soul Kitchen*. This soup is very nurturing and, dare I say, healing. During winter months, if I'm feeling a cold creeping on, I make this soup and take it easy, and typically bounce back. I don't get caught up in monitoring nutrients and micronutrients, but turnips are rich in fiber, vitamins K, A, C, E, and B, and minerals like manganese, potassium, and copper. Turnips also aid in digestion and have a number of immune-boosting benefits. I call for young (or baby) turnips since they are tender, mild, and slightly sweet. If you can't find them, four large ones that have been peeled will suffice (you might need to buy the greens separately since bigger turnips are often sold pre-trimmed). While roasting tenderizes and draws out the natural sweetness of baby turnips, it also mellows the bitterness of larger ones. In the end, the combination of tender vegetables and a complex and flavorful broth makes this a satisfying soup.

2 bunches young/baby turnips with greens (about 2 pounds)

3 shallots, cut into ¼-inch rounds

2 tablespoons extra-virgin olive oil

½ teaspoon kosher salt, plus more as needed

1 tablespoon minced garlic

6 cups rich vegetable stock (page 231)

2 thyme sprigs

Freshly ground white pepper

Apple cider or other vinegar

Preheat the oven to 400°F. Line a baking sheet with parchment paper.

Separate the turnips and the turnip greens; set the greens aside. Cut the turnips into ½-inch pieces and transfer to a medium bowl. Add the shallots, 1 tablespoon of the olive oil, and ¼ teaspoon of the salt and toss to combine. Spread the turnips and shallots over the prepared baking sheet and roast for 1 hour, stirring every 15 minutes to ensure even cooking.

While the turnips are roasting, trim the tough stems from the greens and discard. Chop the greens into bite-size pieces, rinse well, and drain.

In a large saucepan, combine the remaining 1 tablespoon olive oil and the garlic and sauté over medium heat until the garlic is fragrant, 2 to 3 minutes. Add the greens and remaining ¼ teaspoon salt. Sauté the greens, stirring occasionally, until tender, about 5 minutes.

Add the stock to the saucepan and set aside.

When the turnips are finished roasting, transfer them to the saucepan. Bring to a boil, then decrease the heat to maintain a simmer and cook, partially covered, for 20 minutes, adding the thyme in the last 2 minutes. Season with salt and white pepper to taste.

To serve, ladle the soup into warm bowls and drizzle with vinegar to your liking.

"Focus" by H.E.R. from *H.E.R.*

quick-sautéed turnip stems

garlic · lemon · salt

makes about 1 cup

This is probably the simplest dish in this book.
I hope that it inspires you to thinly slice stems
from turnips, collards, mustards, and other dark
leafy greens and quickly sauté them in fat. They
can be eaten as a side, used as a garnish, or
folded into soups, stews, or other dishes for more
texture. I add lemon to brighten them up, but I
encourage you to experiment with different acids.

2 teaspoons
extra-virgin olive oil

1/2 teaspoon
minced garlic

2 cups thinly sliced
turnip stems

1/8 teaspoon kosher salt,
plus more as needed

1/2 large lemon

In a large skillet, combine the olive oil and garlic
and cook over medium heat until the garlic just
starts smelling fragrant, 2 to 3 minutes. Add the
turnip stems and salt and cook, stirring often,
until tender, about 3 minutes. Season with salt
to taste. Give the turnip stems a big squeeze of
lemon. Incorporate them into another dish or
transfer to a bowl before serving.

"Don't Try to Use Me" by Horace Andy from *Wicked Dem a Burn:
The Best of Horace Andy*

sautéed turnip greens with penne

crispy garlic · garlic oil · umami powder

makes 4 to 6 servings

I was one of those people who rolled my eyes when parents talked about having to "sneak" vegetables into their kids' meals. Because my elder daughter, Mila, has such a voracious appetite for vegetables, I assumed that those parents were doing it all wrong. If *those parents* had just introduced their kids to a variety of vegetables early on, their kids would love veggies, too. Or so I thought. Well, life comes at you fast. My younger daughter, Zenzi, is the polar opposite of our big girl. When she was younger, we had to practically force her to eat anything, let alone vegetables. She's gotten more adventuresome over the years, but I'm always thinking of fun ways to creep veggies into her food. Since Zenzi loves pasta in any form, I was confident she would devour this dish—and she did. The technique is inspired by the homie Adam Mansbach's broccoli rabe and orecchiette.

2½ pounds turnip greens, washed

1 tablespoon kosher salt, plus more as needed

6 tablespoons extra-virgin olive oil

3 large garlic cloves, thinly sliced

¾ pound spinach or whole-wheat penne rigate

Red pepper flakes, for garnish (optional)

½ cup Umami Powder (page 239)

Freshly ground white pepper

Remove the tough stems from the turnip leaves. Next, stack four or five leaves, roll them into a tight cylinder lengthwise, and slice crosswise into thin ribbons. Repeat with the remaining leaves.

Bring a large pot of water to a boil and add the salt. Add the turnip greens, bring the water back to a rolling boil, and blanch the greens for 1 minute. Using a spider, lift the greens from the water, transfer them to a colander, and set aside to cool, reserving the water in the pot. Once the greens have cooled, roughly chop them and set aside.

Warm a large Dutch oven over medium-low heat. Add the oil and heat until shimmering. Scrape in the garlic, spreading it in one even layer with a fork. Sauté, without disturbing, until the garlic is just starting to turn golden, 3 to 4 minutes. Strain the oil into a small heatproof bowl and transfer the garlic to a small bowl. Add 4 tablespoons of garlic oil and the reserved greens to the Dutch oven and cook, stirring often, until the greens are well-coated with oil, about 3 minutes. Set aside.

Bring the just-used water to a boil. Add the pasta and cook, following the instructions on the package, until al dente. Drain the pasta, reserving 1 cup of water. Add the pasta and reserved water to the Dutch oven with the greens and cook over high heat until the liquid is almost evaporated, 3 to 4 minutes. Mix well and season with salt to taste.

To serve, divide the pasta evenly among plates and sprinkle with the crispy garlic, red pepper flakes, and umami powder. Drizzle with garlic oil and finish with freshly ground white pepper.

"RST (feat. DOOM & Mach-Hommy)" by Your Old Droog from *It Wasn't Even Close*

brown sugar–glazed turnips

raw cane sugar · molasses · mustard powder · orange juice

makes 4 servings

If you could hear the oohs and ahhs when I bring this side dish to holiday parties. In their raw form, magenta-colored red scarlet turnips are vibrant and beautiful, but they gorgeously glow up when cooked in this sweet glaze. While white turnips mostly have a mildly sweet-peppery flavor, they often have a bitter edge. Scarlet turnips are slightly sweeter, and this vibrant glaze (a combination of raw cane sugar and molasses) plays off of them perfectly. Don't worry, if you can't locate red scarlet turnips, white will work just fine. Either way, these Brown Sugar–Glazed Turnips will be a standout.

½ cup raw cane sugar

¼ cup fresh orange juice

1 tablespoon molasses

1 teaspoon mustard powder

¼ teaspoon kosher salt, plus more as needed

2 pounds small red scarlet turnips, quartered

1 lemon, halved

Freshly ground white pepper

2 tablespoons chopped fresh parsley

In a large skillet, combine the sugar, orange juice, 2 tablespoons water, the molasses, mustard powder, and salt. Cook over medium-high heat, stirring, until all the sugar and the mustard powder have dissolved. Add the turnips, decrease the heat to low, cover, and cook, shaking the pan occasionally, until the turnips are just tender, 10 to 15 minutes.

Remove the lid, raise the heat to medium, and cook, shaking the pan occasionally, until the turnips are glazed and turning golden, about 10 minutes. Remove from the heat.

Squeeze the lemon over the turnips and season with salt and pepper. Transfer to a serving bowl and top with the parsley. Serve.

"Glowed Up (feat. Anderson .Paak)" by Kaytranada from *99.9%*

cupboard

stocks and broths

bouquet garni   230

vegetable stock   230

corn stock   230

mushroom stock   230

rich vegetable stock   231

creams

cashew cream   231

coconut cream   231

onion-thyme cream   231

flavored oils

pili pili oil   232

garlic oil (and garlic chips)   232

lemon oil   232

> charred lemon oil
> charred lemon–thyme oil

thai basil oil   233

scallion oil   233

charred habanero oil   233

vinegars

ginger-habanero vinegar   234

sweet hot pepper vinegar   234

sauces, spreads, and marinades

jalapeño pepper jelly   234

cilantro sauce   235

> creamy cilantro sauce

persillade   235

jerk marinade   235

shoyu-chili dipping sauce   235

smoky-spicy green sauce   236

pili pili sauce   236

creole rémoulade   237

roasted red pepper sauce   237

seasonings

plantain powder   238

berbere spice blend   238

blackened seasoning   239

creole seasoning   239

garam masala   239

umami powder   239

xinjiang spice mix   240

za'atar   240

bbq seasoning   240

almond dukkah   240

bouquet garni

Bouquet garni is a bundle of herbs tied together with kitchen twine and used to flavor stock, soups, and stews.

1 bay leaf

2 thyme sprigs

2 rosemary sprigs

4 parsley sprigs

1 teaspoon whole black peppercorns (optional)

Place a 4-inch square of cotton cheesecloth on a work surface. Stack the bay leaf, herbs, and pepper-corns (if using) on top, gather the cheesecloth to enclose them, and tie a length of unwaxed cotton twine around the bundle to keep everything together, knotting the twine securely.

vegetable stock

makes about 8 cups

1 tablespoon olive oil

1 large onion, unpeeled, thinly sliced

3 celery stalks, thinly sliced

1 large carrot, coarsely grated

8 ounces any mushrooms and their stems

¼ head green cabbage (about 8 ounces), thinly sliced

1 head garlic, broken apart, unpeeled cloves smashed with the flat side of a knife

1 bouquet garni

In a large pot, warm the olive oil over medium-high heat. Add the onion, celery, carrot, mushrooms, cabbage, and garlic and cook until softened, 5 to 7 minutes. Add 10 cups water, raise the heat to high, and bring the water to a boil. Decrease the heat to medium-low, add the bouquet garni, and simmer, partially covered, for about 2 hours. Strain the stock through a fine-mesh sieve, pressing down on the solids to extract as much liquid as possible. Use immediately, or let cool and store in airtight containers in the refrigerator for up to 3 days or in the freezer for up to 6 months.

corn stock

makes about 8 cups

7 ears fresh corn, husked and kernels removed

1 yellow onion, quartered

1 celery stalk, thinly sliced

1 garlic clove, smashed

1 tablespoon whole white peppercorns

1 bay leaf

1 teaspoon kosher salt

1 bouquet garni

In a large pot, combine all the ingredients except the bouquet garni. Add 10 cups water and bring to a boil over high heat. Decrease the heat to medium-low, add the bouquet garni, and simmer, partially covered, for about 1 hour. Strain through a fine-mesh sieve, pressing down on the solids to extract as much liquid as possible. Use immediately, or let cool and store in airtight containers in the refrigerator for up to 3 days or in the freezer for up to 6 months.

mushroom stock

makes about 8 cups

1 carrot, chopped

1 yellow onion, quartered

2 garlic cloves, unpeeled, smashed

8 ounces shiitake mushrooms

8 ounces white mushrooms, sliced

1 bay leaf

1 teaspoon kosher salt

1 teaspoon whole black peppercorns

1 bouquet garni

In a large pot, combine all the ingredients except the bouquet garni. Add 10 cups water and bring to a boil over high heat. Decrease the heat to medium-low, add the bouquet garni, and simmer, partially covered, for about 1 hour. Strain through a fine-mesh sieve, pressing down on the solids to extract as much liquid as possible. Use immediately, or let cool and store in airtight containers in the refrigerator for up to 3 days or in the freezer for up to 6 months.

rich vegetable stock

makes about 8 cups

1 large onion, unpeeled, quartered

2 large carrots, cut into chunks

1 large parsnip, peeled and cut into chunks

3 tablespoons olive oil

1 head garlic, broken

apart, unpeeled cloves smashed with the flat side of a knife

8 ounces any mushrooms and their stems

1 teaspoon kosher salt

1 bouquet garni (opposite page)

Preheat the oven to 450°F. Line a baking sheet with parchment paper.

In a large bowl, combine the onion, carrots, parsnip, and olive oil and toss to coat the vegetables. Transfer to the prepared baking sheet and roast until just tender, about 30 minutes, stirring every 10 minutes to ensure even cooking.

Transfer the roasted vegetables to a large pot and add the garlic, mushrooms, salt, and 10 cups water. Bring to a boil over high heat. Decrease the heat to medium-low, add the bouquet garni, and simmer, partially covered, for about 1 hour. Strain through a fine-mesh sieve, pressing down on the solids to extract as much liquid as possible. Use immediately, or let cool and store in airtight containers in the refrigerator for up to 3 days or in the freezer for up to 6 months.

cashew cream

makes about 1 cup

1 cup raw cashews, soaked in water overnight and drained well

Combine the cashews and ½ cup water in a blender and blend until smooth and creamy. Use immediately or store in an airtight container in the refrigerator for up to 4 days.

coconut cream

makes about ½ cup

1 (13.5-ounce) can unsweetened coconut milk, unopened

Refrigerate the unopened can of coconut milk for 6 hours or up to overnight.

Open the can. Using a spoon, skim the solidified white cream from the top, being careful not to dip into the coconut water below it. Transfer the cream to a medium bowl and reserve the coconut water in the can. Using a large whisk, whip the cream, slowly adding the coconut water, until it is silky enough to just pour off a spoon. Reserve the remaining coconut water for another use.

onion-thyme cream

makes about ½ cup

1 tablespoon safflower oil

¼ cup minced onion

Kosher salt

6 tablespoons raw cashew, soaked in water overnight and drained

2 tablespoons water

1 tablespoon fresh lemon juice

1 teaspoon finely grated lemon zest

½ teaspoon minced thyme

1 green onion, thinly sliced

In a small saucepan over medium heat, warm the oil until shimmering. Add the onion and a pinch of salt and sauté until translucent, being careful not to brown, 3 to 5 minutes. Transfer the mixture to a blender. Add the cashews, water, lemon juice, lemon zest, and thyme and puree until smooth. Season with salt to taste and fold in the green onion. Use immediately or store in an airtight container in the refrigerator for up to 3 days, or freeze for up to 2 weeks.

pili pili oil

makes about 1 cup

2 teaspoons
smoked paprika

2 (2-inch) thyme sprigs

2 (2-inch) rosemary
sprigs

9 small fresh bird's-eye
or Thai chiles

1 cup olive oil

In a small saucepan, combine all the ingredients and heat over low heat, stirring occasionally, until the olive oil starts to sizzle and the paprika has completely dissolved. Immediately remove from the heat and set aside to cool.

Transfer all the ingredients to a small jar or bottle, seal, and refrigerate for a few days before using. Store in the refrigerator for up to 2 weeks.

garlic oil (and garlic chips)

makes ¾ cup oil and ½ cup chips

¾ cup olive oil

16 large garlic cloves,
thinly sliced

In a medium skillet, warm the olive oil over low heat. Add the garlic and cook, stirring occasionally, until crispy and golden brown, 8 to 10 minutes. Strain the oil through fine-mesh sieve into a bowl, reserving the garlic chips. Use immediately or store in separate airtight containers in the refrigerator for up to 1 week.

lemon oil

makes about 1 cup

1 large lemon

1 garlic clove, smashed

½ teaspoon kosher salt

1 cup olive oil

Using a Microplane, grate 1 tablespoon of the zest from the lemon into a heatproof bowl. Thinly slice the lemon and add it to the bowl as well. Add the garlic and salt and set aside.

In a small skillet, warm the olive oil over medium-high heat until it just starts to smoke. Immediately remove the pan from the heat and pour the oil into the bowl. Let the oil cool to room temperature. Use immediately or store in an airtight container in the refrigerator for up to 1 week.

charred lemon oil

Zest the lemon as directed, but cut it in half instead of slicing it. Heat a large cast-iron skillet over high heat. Place the lemon halves in the skillet, cut-side down, and cook until they are charred, 2 to 3 minutes. Give them a squeeze over the bowl with the zest, then add them to the bowl (no need to cut them into slices) and proceed as directed above.

charred lemon–thyme oil

Char the lemon as directed above, and add a sprig of thyme to the bowl before pouring in the oil.

thai basil oil

makes about 1 cup

If Thai basil is not available, use whatever kind you have available. This method can be used to make oil flavored by other soft fresh herbs such as parsley, cilantro, tarragon, and the like as well. If the flavor of your herb oil is too intense for a dish, simply dilute it with more oil before using.

½ cup packed fresh Thai basil

1 cup olive oil

In a blender, combine the basil and olive oil and puree. Pour into a small saucepan and bring to a simmer over medium heat. As soon as the oil starts to bubble, remove it from the heat. Set aside to cool, then strain through a fine-mesh strainer. Store the basil oil in an airtight container in the refrigerator for up to 1 week.

scallion oil

makes about ½ cup

8 scallions, washed, dried well, and cut on an angle into thin slices

½ cup peanut oil

Put the scallions in a small heatproof bowl and set aside. In a small skillet, warm the peanut oil over medium-high heat until it just starts to smoke. Immediately remove the pan from the heat and pour the oil over the scallions. Let cool to room temperature. Use immediately or store in an airtight container in the refrigerator for up to 1 week.

charred habanero oil

makes 1 cup

For a milder oil, leave the chile intact and let it sit in the oil. For a hotter one, blend it. Use two chiles if you really like it hot.

1 or 2 habanero chiles

1 cup safflower oil

Preheat the broiler to high.

Place the habanero on a baking sheet and broil, turning to ensure even cooking, until well charred, 3 to 5 minutes. Let cool.

For milder oil, in a small bowl, combine the whole habanero, stem still attached, and the safflower oil and let sit for at least 1 day before using.

For hotter oil, stem and seed the habanero, then transfer it to a blender. Add the safflower oil and puree until smooth, then strain through a fine-mesh strainer, discarding the solids.

Store the habanero oil in an airtight container in the refrigerator for up to 1 week.

ginger-habanero vinegar

makes about 1 cup

3 habanero chiles, stemmed and seeded

½ cup unseasoned rice vinegar

½ cup distilled white vinegar

1½ teaspoons minced fresh ginger

1 teaspoon raw cane sugar

Pinch of kosher salt

Place the chiles in a heatproof bowl. In a small saucepan, combine the vinegars, ginger, sugar, and salt and bring to a boil over high heat. Immediately pour the vinegar mixture over the chiles and let cool completely. Transfer to a jar, seal, and store at room temperature for up to 1 year.

sweet hot pepper vinegar

makes 1 cup

2 serrano chiles

1 cup apple cider vinegar

2 teaspoons coconut palm sugar

1½ teaspoons kosher salt

Place the chiles in a clean 1-pint jar.

In a small saucepan, combine the vinegar, sugar, and salt and bring to a simmer over medium-high heat, stirring, until the sugar has dissolved and the liquid is hot to the touch. Immediately pour the vinegar over the chiles. Seal the jar and store in the refrigerator for up to 1 year.

jalapeño pepper jelly

makes about 3 cups (three ½-pint jars)

½ cup coarsely chopped seeded jalapeños (about 3 medium)

½ cup coarsely chopped green bell pepper

3 cups organic cane sugar

½ cup apple cider vinegar

1 (3-ounce) package liquid pectin

Sterilize three ½-pint jars and their lids or similarly sized lidded storage containers (see page 35).

In a food processor, combine the jalapeños and the bell pepper and process, scraping down the sides as needed, until the peppers are very finely chopped, 15 to 20 seconds. (They will let off quite a bit of liquid; this is okay.)

Transfer the contents of the food processor to a 4-quart stainless-steel or enameled Dutch oven. Add the sugar and vinegar and bring to a rolling boil over medium-high heat, stirring continuously. Boil, still stirring, for 3 minutes, then squeeze in the pectin. Return the mixture to a rolling boil, stirring continuously, and cook for 1 minute. Immediately remove from the heat and let rest until the foam has settled, about 1 minute. Skim off and discard any remaining foam.

Spoon the jelly into the sterilized jars and let cool for 1 hour. Seal the jars and refrigerate until chilled before using. The jelly will keep in the refrigerator for up to 3 months and up to 2 years if processed in a hot water bath and kept in a cool, dry place.

cilantro sauce

makes about 1 cup

2 garlic cloves, minced

3 tablespoons extra-virgin olive oil

¼ teaspoon ground coriander

¼ teaspoon coarse sea salt, plus more as needed

1 cup tightly packed fresh cilantro leaves

2 tablespoons fresh lemon juice

½ jalapeño

In a small skillet, combine the garlic, olive oil, coriander, and salt. Bring to a simmer over medium heat and cook just until the garlic is fragrant, about 1½ minutes. Remove from the heat and let cool.

Transfer the oil mixture to a blender. Add the cilantro, lemon juice, jalapeño, and ¼ cup water and blend until smooth. If necessary, season with additional salt to taste. Use immediately or store in an airtight container in the refrigerator for up to 1 week.

creamy cilantro sauce

Blend in ¼ cup cashew cream (page 231) to make the sauce creamy and add enough water so that it pours easily from a spoon.

persillade

makes ¾ cup

2 tablespoons olive oil

1 tablespoon minced garlic

½ cup finely chopped fresh flat-leaf parsley

In a small skillet, combine the olive oil and garlic and heat over medium-low heat, stirring often to prevent the garlic from burning, until the garlic just starts to turn golden, about 3 minutes. Quickly scrape the contents of the skillet into a mortar or small bowl, add the parsley, and stir well to combine. Use immediately or store in an airtight container in the refrigerator for up to 2 weeks.

jerk marinade

makes 2 cups

1 cup chopped yellow onion

3 scallions, thinly sliced

1 tablespoon minced fresh ginger

1 tablespoon minced garlic

2 tablespoons muscovado sugar

1 tablespoon ground allspice

1 teaspoon freshly grated nutmeg

1 tablespoon freshly ground black pepper

Pinch of cayenne pepper

2 Scotch bonnet or habanero chiles, stemmed, seeded, and minced

2 tablespoons fresh lime juice

2 tablespoons apple cider vinegar

6 tablespoons shoyu

¼ cup coconut oil

2 tablespoons minced fresh thyme

Fine sea salt

Combine all the ingredients except the salt in a food processor, add ¼ cup water, and puree until well combined. Season with salt to taste. Store in an airtight container in the refrigerator until ready to use, up to 1 week.

shoyu-chili dipping sauce

makes about 1 cup

6 tablespoons shoyu

¼ cup unseasoned rice vinegar

2 tablespoons water

1 teaspoon sesame oil

2 red chilies, thinly sliced

½ teaspoon minced ginger

Combine all the ingredients in a bowl and set aside for 30 minutes before using. Use immediately or store in an airtight container in the refrigerator for up to 1 week.

smoky-spicy green sauce

makes about 1 cup

This recipe is courtesy of Nesanet Abegaze, owner of Azla Vegan, an Ethiopian restaurant in Los Angeles.

4 green bell peppers

1 large jalapeño

½ cup boiling water

2 tablespoons extra-virgin olive oil

1 teaspoon minced fresh ginger

1 teaspoon minced garlic

½ teaspoon coarse sea salt, plus more as needed

¼ cup minced cilantro

1 teaspoon bourbon

Freshly ground white pepper

Roast the bell peppers and jalapeño using one of the methods on page 22 and seed them. Set aside.

Put the date in a small bowl and pour the boiling water over it. Let soak for 10 minutes.

In a medium skillet, combine the olive oil, ginger, garlic, and salt and sauté over medium heat until the garlic starts to smell fragrant, about 3 minutes.

Transfer the mixture to a blender. Drain the date and add it to the blender. Add the bell peppers, jalapeño, cilantro, and bourbon and puree until smooth. Season with salt and white pepper to taste. Use immediately or store in an airtight container in the refrigerator for up to 1 week.

pili pili sauce

makes about 1 cup

1 tablespoon peanut oil

¼ cup finely diced white onion

2 teaspoons finely grated orange zest

1 teaspoon minced garlic

1½ teaspoons paprika

½ teaspoon coarse sea salt

2 to 6 bird's-eye chiles, seeded

¾ cup red wine vinegar

2 tablespoons fresh lemon juice

1 teaspoon bourbon

1 teaspoon pure maple syrup

½ teaspoon unsulfured molasses

1 teaspoon minced fresh basil

½ teaspoon freshly ground white pepper

In a small saucepan, warm the oil over medium-low heat until shimmering. Add the onion and sauté until soft, 5 to 7 minutes. Add the orange zest, garlic, paprika, and salt and sauté until the garlic is fragrant, 2 to 3 minutes.

Transfer the mixture to a blender. Add the chiles, vinegar, lemon juice, bourbon, maple syrup, and molasses and puree until smooth.

Pour the mixture back into the saucepan. Partially cover and simmer over low heat, stirring occasionally, until the mixture starts to reduce, about 45 minutes. Stir in the basil and white pepper and simmer for 2 minutes more. Use immediately or store in a tightly sealed jar in the refrigerator for up to 1 week.

creole rémoulade

makes about 1½ cups

¾ cup vegan
mayonnaise

¼ cup Creole-style
mustard or other
whole-grain mustard

2 tablespoons fresh
lemon juice

1½ tablespoons drained
capers, finely chopped

1½ tablespoons finely
chopped gherkins

¼ teaspoon
cayenne pepper

Kosher salt and freshly
ground black pepper

In a medium bowl, whisk together the mayonnaise, mustard, lemon juice, capers, gherkins, and
cayenne. Season to taste with salt and pepper.
Transfer to an airtight container and refrigerate until
ready to use. The rémoulade will keep for 4 days in
the refrigerator.

roasted red pepper sauce

makes about 2½ cups

3 large red bell peppers

3 tablespoons peanut oil

1 large yellow onion,
diced

¼ teaspoon kosher salt,
plus more as needed

1 large garlic clove,
minced

½ teaspoon minced
seeded habanero

1 cup vegetable stock
(page 230)

Roast the bell peppers using one of the methods
on page 22, then seed them. Set aside.

In a large saucepan, warm the peanut oil over
medium heat until shimmering. Add the onion and
the salt, decrease the heat to medium-low, and
sauté until deep golden brown, about 15 minutes.
Add the garlic and habanero and sauté until the
garlic is fragrant, 2 to 3 minutes.

Scrape the contents of the pan into a blender, add
the roasted bell peppers and the stock, and puree
until smooth. Pour the puree back into the pan
and simmer over low heat until the sauce starts
to thicken, about 10 minutes.

Season with salt to taste. Use immediately or store
in an airtight container in the refrigerator for up to
1 week.

plantain powder

makes about ½ cup

I'll admit that most of the time, I just buy savory plantain chips at the store and pulverize them in a spice grinder to make plantain powder. If you want to make them from scratch, here's how.

1 green plantain (about 4 ounces)

1 tablespoon peanut oil

Fine sea salt

Preheat an oven to 350°F. Line a baking sheet with parchment paper.

Cut the ends off the plantain, then score the peel lengthwise in four even strips, being careful not to cut into the flesh of the fruit. Gently remove the skin. If the skin is difficult to peel, soak the whole plantain in just-boiled water for 3 to 4 minutes, then try again.

With a mandoline or a very sharp knife, cut the plantain into paper-thin rounds and transfer to a medium bowl. Pour in the peanut oil and gently toss with clean hands to coat the plantains.

Spread the plantain slices on the prepared baking sheet in an even layer and sprinkle with salt. Bake until the slices are crisp and starting to turn golden, about 20 minutes, turning them over with a fork after 10 minutes. Set aside to cool.

Transfer the chips to a spice grinder or a mortar and pulverize into a fine powder. Store in an airtight container in the refrigerator for up to 1 week.

berbere spice blend

makes about ½ cup

6 cardamom pods

3 tablespoons smoked paprika

1 tablespoon coarse sea salt

1 teaspoon cumin seeds, toasted

1 teaspoon fenugreek seeds, toasted

1 teaspoon allspice berries, toasted

1 teaspoon red pepper flakes

1 teaspoon dried thyme

2 whole cloves

1 dried chipotle chile, stemmed and broken into pieces

1 teaspoon whole black peppercorns

½ teaspoon coriander seeds, toasted

½ teaspoon ground ginger

½ teaspoon cayenne pepper

In a medium cast-iron skillet, toast the cardamom pods over medium-low heat, shaking the pan occasionally to prevent burning, until fragrant, 2 to 3 minutes. Transfer the pods to a small plate and set aside to cool. Once cooled, crack open the pods with your fingers and transfer the seeds within to a mortar or spice grinder (discard the pods). Add the remaining ingredients and grind into a fine powder. Transfer to a jar and seal tightly. Store at room temperature for up to 1 month.

blackened seasoning

makes about ½ cup

2 tablespoons paprika

1 tablespoon cumin seeds, toasted

2 teaspoons coriander seeds, toasted

2 teaspoons whole black peppercorns

1½ teaspoons coarse sea salt

1½ teaspoons garlic powder

1 teaspoon whole white peppercorns

1 teaspoon onion powder

1 teaspoon dried thyme

½ teaspoon cayenne pepper, or to taste

Combine all the ingredients in a mortar or spice grinder and grind into a fine powder. Transfer to a jar and seal tightly. Store in an airtight container at room temperature for up to 2 weeks.

garam masala

makes about ¼ cup

1 tablespoon cumin seeds, toasted

1½ teaspoons coriander seeds, toasted

1½ teaspoons ground cardamom

1½ teaspoons freshly ground black pepper

1 teaspoon ground cinnamon

½ teaspoon ground cloves

½ teaspoon freshly grated nutmeg

Combine all the ingredients in a mortar or spice grinder and grind into a fine powder. Transfer to a jar and seal tightly. Store in an airtight container at room temperature for up to 2 weeks.

creole seasoning

makes about ¼ cup

1 tablespoon garlic powder

1 tablespoon paprika

2 teaspoons coarse sea salt

2 teaspoons freshly ground black pepper

2 teaspoons onion powder

2 teaspoons chili powder

2 teaspoons red pepper flakes

1 teaspoon dried thyme

1 teaspoon dried oregano

½ teaspoon cayenne pepper

Combine all the ingredients in a mortar or spice grinder and grind into a fine powder. Store in an airtight container at room temperature for up to 6 months.

umami powder

makes about 1 cup

¾ ounce dried porcini mushrooms

¾ cup raw cashews

3 tablespoons nutritional yeast

2 tablespoons pine nuts

1 teaspoon fine sea salt

Grind the dried porcinis in a spice grinder and transfer to a food processor. Add the cashews, nutritional yeast, pine nuts, and salt and pulse until broken down into a fine meal. Store in an airtight container at room temperature for up to 2 weeks.

xinjiang spice mix

makes about ¼ cup

1 dried bird's-eye chile

1 star anise pod

2 tablespoons cumin seeds, toasted and ground

1 tablespoon whole black peppercorns

1 teaspoon Szechuan peppercorns

1 teaspoon garlic powder

1 teaspoon onion powder

½ teaspoon ground ginger

½ teaspoon ground cardamom

½ teaspoon coarse sea salt

Combine all the ingredients in a mortar or spice grinder and grind into a fine powder. Store in an airtight container at room temperature for up to 6 months.

za'atar

makes about ⅓ cup

3 heaping tablespoons dried thyme

2 heaping tablespoons dried oregano

Scant 1 tablespoon ground sumac

1 teaspoon cumin seeds, toasted

1 heaping tablespoon sesame seeds, toasted

Freshly ground black pepper

Combine the thyme, oregano, sumac, and cumin in a mortar or spice grinder and grind into a fine powder. Add the sesame seeds and a few grinds of pepper and stir well to combine. Transfer to a jar and seal tightly. Store at room temperature for up to 6 months.

bbq seasoning

makes about ½ cup

1 teaspoon whole white peppercorns

2 tablespoons sweet paprika

2 tablespoons smoked paprika

1 tablespoon raw cane sugar

2 teaspoons fine sea salt

1 teaspoon onion powder

1 teaspoon garlic powder

1 teaspoon ground cumin

1 teaspoon chili powder

Pinch of cayenne pepper

In a mortar, grind the peppercorns finely using the pestle. Add the remaining ingredients and grind into a uniform powder.

Warm a large skillet over medium heat, pour in the spice mixture, and toast, shaking the pan frequently, until the mixture starts to smell fragrant, about 1 minute. Transfer to a bowl and let cool. Store in an airtight container at room temperature for up to 2 weeks.

almond dukkah

makes about ½ cup

7 tablespoons finely chopped almonds, toasted

2 tablespoons black sesame seeds, toasted

½ teaspoon coarse sea salt

2 teaspoons coriander seeds, toasted

2 teaspoons cumin seeds, toasted

Put the almonds, sesame seeds, and salt in a small bowl. Combine the coriander and cumin seeds in a mortar and pound with the pestle until smashed but not finely ground. Add to the bowl with the almonds and mix well. Store in an airtight container in the refrigerator for up to 2 weeks.

acknowledgments

This book could not have come to life without the support of my family. Thank you Jidan for giving me space to work on this project, taking the girls most weekends and holidays, and generally being a supportive friend, wife, and mother. I'm the luckiest man in the world to have you as my partner. Thank you, Mila and Zenzi, for inspiring this book. Becoming your Baba is the best thing that ever happened to me, and I love you more than anything.

Mom and Dad, thank you for your unwavering love and support. I hope that I make you very proud.

Mama Wong and Baba Koon, thank you for the innumerable ways that you support me and our family. I am honored to be your son-in-law.

Danielle Svetcov, thank you for being my super agent, confidant, occasional therapist, and fan. Big thanks to the whole team at Levine Greenberg Rostan for your support.

The team at The Lavin Agency, many thanks for making sure that I can spread the gospel around the globe.

My MoAD family, I am eternally grateful for your genuine support: Linda Harrison (always with us in spirit), Elizabeth Gessel, Mark Sabb, Paul Plale, James G. Leventhal, and the rest of the staff and board.

Thank you to Heidi Swanson, Erin Scott, Latham Thomas, Kalalea, and Nicole Taylor for support, advice, and friendship over the years.

Kate Williams, this book could not have happened without your hard work and brilliance. You are, forks down, the most bad-ass recipe tester out in these streets. I'm indebted to you for the expertise and enthusiasm that you brought to this book.

Thank you to Polly Webb and Amanda Yee for enthusiasm, support, and vital feedback on this project.

Thank you to "Money" Mike Molina, Stephen Satterfield, and Tunde Wey for your help and guidance on my introduction.

Leda Scheintaub, thank you for always having my back and testing recipes for me in a pinch.

Monifa Dayo, thank you for recipe development, food consulting, and food styling.

Adam Mansbach, thank you for enthusiastically supporting me in taking my game to the next level—from last minute editing to introducing me to the right people.

Torrance Rodgers, thank you for letting me borrow your precious vinyl.

Weyland Southon and Alicia Yang, thank you for introducing me to my wife!

Gregory Johnson, thank you for frequent check-ins, top-notch editing, and brilliant advice.

Ietef aka DJ Cavem, thank you for inspiring me to "Keep it 100."

Michael Orange, thank you for supporting my movement since day one.

Thank you to my YMCA bootcamp family, with a special shout-out to Al Smith Fernandez and David Derryck.

Aaron Wehner, publisher of Ten Speed Press, thank you for believing in me, trusting my vision, and giving me a platform.

Kelly Snowden, my brilliant editor at Ten Speed Press, working with you has been such a joy and a pleasure. Thank you for your patience, vision, sense of humor, and ability to bring the best out of me.

Betsy Stromberg, senior art director at Ten Speed, thank you for genuinely investing in the beauty of this book. I had fun hanging out on set!

Kim Keller, production editor at Ten Speed, thank you for your attention to detail, kindness, and genuine enthusiasm for making this a successful project.

Thank you to Ten Speed Press publicist David Hawk, Ten Speed Press marketing manager Windy Dorresteyn, and Ten Speed Press production manager Serena Sigona.

Thank you to the copyeditor Ivy McFadden and proofreader Amy Kovalski.

To Ed Anderson (photographer), Lillian Kang (food stylist), and Veronica Laramie (assistant food stylist) and Monifa Dayo: you are the reason this book is so gorgeous! Thank you for being fun, hard working, and brilliant at your craft.

Thank you to all the unnamed people who are important in my work and life.

about the author

Bryant Terry is a James Beard Award-winning chef, educator, and author, renowned for his activism to create a healthy, just, and sustainable food systems. He is in his fifth year as chef-in-residence at the Museum of the African Diaspora (MoAD) in San Francisco, where he creates public programming that celebrates the intersection of food, farming, health, activism, art, culture, and the African Diaspora. In regard to his work, Bryant's mentor Alice Waters says, "Bryant Terry knows that good food should be an everyday right and not a privilege." *San Francisco Magazine* included Bryant among "Eleven Smartest People in the Bay Area Food Scene," and *Fast Company* named him one of "Nine People Who Are Changing the Future of Food."

Afro-Vegan, Bryant's fourth book, was published by Ten Speed Press April 2014. Two months later, Amazon named it one of the best cookbooks of the year, and it was included on several year-end best cookbooks lists. Bryant is also the author of the critically acclaimed *Vegan Soul Kitchen: Fresh, Healthy, and Creative African-American Cuisine,* which was named one of the best vegetarian/vegan cookbooks of the last twenty-five years by *Cooking Light Magazine.* He coauthored *Grub* in 2006 (with Anna Lappe), which the *New York Times* called "ingenious."

Bryant currently serves on the advisory board for From Mothers to Mothers, an undergraduate student project based at UC Berkeley that focuses on Postpartum Justice. Bryant and the group hosted their first summit at MoAD in the Spring of 2019, and they are currently working with Bay Area restaurants to create and highlight postpartum recipes on their menus for nursing mothers. Bryant also served as the humanities advisor on and wrote the forward for the *Between Meals* cookbook project, which shares the recipes and stories of newly-arrived refugee and immigrant women.

Bryant's work has been featured in the *New York Times, Food and Wine, Gourmet, Sunset, O: The Oprah Magazine, Essence, Yoga Journal,* and *Vegetarian Times* among many other publications. As an exclusive speaker signed with the Lavin Agency, Bryant presents frequently around the country as a keynote speaker at community events, conferences, corporations, and colleges including Brown, Columbia, NYU, Smith, Stanford, and Yale.

In 2013 he was the face of a Scion/Toyota ad campaign shot by Doug Prey. That same year he worked with Barry Jenkins on Olivari Olive Oil's "The Little Things Are Everything" campaign. Bryant has made hundreds of national television and radio appearances, including being a guest on *The Martha Stewart Show, Emeril Green, All Things Considered, Morning Edition,* and *The Splendid Table.*

In 2002 Bryant founded b-healthy (Build Healthy Eating and Lifestyles to Help Youth), a multiyear initiative in New York City designed to empower youth to be more active in working toward a more sustainable food system.

Bryant graduated from the Chef's Training Program at the Natural Gourmet Institute for Health and Culinary Arts in New York City. He holds a M.A. in History from NYU and a B.A. with honors in English from Xavier University of Louisiana. He lives in Oakland, California, with his wife and their two daughters.

To learn more about Bryant, visit his website at www.bryant-terry.com and follow him on instagram: @bryantterry

index

Published in the United States by Ten Speed Press,
an imprint of Random House, a division of Penguin
Random House LLC, New York.
www.tenspeed.com

Ten Speed Press and the Ten Speed Press colophon
are registered trademarks of Penguin Random
House LLC.

Library of Congress Cataloging-in-Publication Data
Names: Terry, Bryant, 1974- author.
Title: Vegetable kingdom : cooking the world of plant-
    based recipes (a vegan cookbook) / Bryant Terry.
Description: Emeryville : Ten Speed Press, 2020. |
    Includes bibliographical references and index. |
    Summary: More than 100 beautifully simple recipes
    that teach you the basics of a great vegan meal
    centered on real food, not powders or meat
    substitutes.
Identifiers: LCCN 2019034347 | ISBN 9780399581045
    (hardcover) | ISBN9780399581052 (epub)
Subjects: LCSH: Vegetarian cooking. | Cooking (Natural
    foods) | LCGFT: Cookbooks.
    Classification: LCC TX837 .T4344 2020 | DDC
    641.5/636–dc23
LC record available at https://lccn.loc.gov/2019034347

Hardcover ISBN: 978-0-399-58104-5
eBook ISBN: 978-0-399-58105-2

Printed in China

Food styling by Lillian Kang
Prop styling by Ethel Brennan and Ed Anderson
Design by Betsy Stromberg

10 9 8 7 6 5 4 3

First Edition

"With *Vegetable Kingdom*, Bryant Terry positions great cooking exactly where it belongs: smack dab in the midst of our lives. Here is the kind of cooking in context—among kids and friends, ancestors and communities—that has the power to bring us profound meaning and pure pleasure. Bryant understands that our kitchens are where sustenance, and substance, simmer. With an inspired soundtrack and a loving spirit, he reminds us that the familiar, exotic, and delicious kingdom of vegetables offers all the richness we could ever want."

CAL PETERNELL, chef and author of *Twelve Recipes; A Recipe for Cooking*; and *Almonds, Anchovies, and Pancetta*

"I absolutely love *Vegetable Kingdom*, which is an inventive, mouth-watering feast of many kinds, and at the same time sensual, musical, intellectual, and cultural. What Bryant Terry has done most beautifully is to root African Diasporic and Asian cuisines in their proper soil of family and community. This book feels like home in the deepest sense—full of brilliant colors, sounds, smells, and flavors—and it is our great fortune to be invited in."

JAMEL BRINKLEY, National Book Award finalist and author of *A Lucky Man*

"Contemporary, inviting, flavorful—but most of all, this is an ode to the beauty of vegetables. Bryant's approach to cooking is one of pure joy and his recipes are a triumph that reflect this in the truest sense."

NIK SHARMA, author of *Season*